Paul Bergne (1937–2007) was a researcher of the history and politics of Central Asia at St Antony's College, Oxford. In 2001 he was the personal representative of the UK Prime Minister in Afghanistan. Before that he served for nearly forty years as a British diplomat and his last overseas posting was as ambassador to Uzbekistan and Tajikistan. He travelled widely in the South Caucasus and Central Asian republics of the former Soviet Union, and in Afghanistan.

'Bergne conveys the material and story with clarity and insight. His book is a valuable addition to the scholarship in English about the complex but important twentieth-century history of the region.'
— Bijan Omrani, *Asian Affairs*

THE BIRTH OF
TAJIKISTAN

National Identity and the Origins of the Republic

PAUL BERGNE

I.B. TAURIS
LONDON · NEW YORK

For Suzanne

New paperback edition published in 2018
by I.B.Tauris & Co. Ltd
London • New York
www.ibtauris.com

First published in hardback in 2007 by I.B.Tauris & Co. Ltd

Cover photo: Young Pioneers at the celebration of the 15th anniversary of the October
Revolution. Stalinabad, Tajikistan, 1932. Photo taken by Hans Adler.
Original cover design: Toby Macklin.

ISBN: 978 1 78831 271 4
eISBN: 978 1 78672 951 4
ePDF: 978 0 85771 091 8

A full CIP record for this book is available from the British Library
A full CIP record is available from the Library of Congress

Library of Congress Catalog Card Number: available

Printed and bound by CPI Group (UK) Ltd, Croydon, CR0 4YY

CONTENTS

ABBREVIATIONS

AO	Autonomous Oblast'
APPO	Agitation and Propaganda
BNSR	Bukharan People's Soviet Republic
CPSU	Communist Party of the Soviet Union
EKOSA	Economic Committee for Central Asia
GARF	State Archive of the Russian Federation
GBAO	Gornyi Badakhshan Autonomous Oblast'
Gosbank	State Bank
GPU	Chief Political Directorate
IKKI	Executive Committee of the Communist International
Ispolkom	Executive Committee (of Soviet)
KGB	Committee of State Security
Komsomol	Communist Union of Youth
KPSS	Communist Party of the Soviet Union
KUTV	Communist University of the Toilers of the East
Likbez	Anti-Illiteracy Campaign
MKK VKP(b)	
MVD	Ministry of Internal Affairs
Narkom	People's Commissar
Narkomfin	People's Commissariat for Finance
Narkompros	People's Commissariat for Education
NKVD	People's Commissariat for Internal Affairs
Obkom	Oblast' Committee (of the Party)
OGPU	United State Political Directorate

OKRIK	Okrug Executive Committee
Orgotdel	Organisation Department
Proverkom	Auditing Committee
Raikom	Raion Committee (of the Party)
Revkom	Revolutionary Committee
RIK	Raion Executive Committee
RKKA	Red Army
RKP(b)	Russian Communist Party (Bolsheviks)
RSDRP	Russian Socialist Democratic Workers' Party
RSFSR	Russian Soviet Federative Socialist Republic
RTsKhDNI	Russian Centre for the Preservation of Documents of Recent History
RVS	Revolutionary War Soviet
SDLK	Latvian Social Democratic Party
Selsovet	Village Council
Sredazburo	Central Asia Office (of CPSU Central Committee)
Sredazselkhozsnab	Central Asian Agricultural Supply Agency
TaASSR	Tajik Autonomous Soviet Socialist Republic
Tajikinpros	Tajik Information Service
TaSSR	Tajik Soviet Socialist Republic
TASSR	Turkestan Autonomous Soviet Socialist Republic
TsIK	Central Executive Committee
TsK	Central Committee
TsKK	Central Control Commission
Turksholk	Turkestan Silk Agency
Upolnarkomtorg	Plenipotentiary People's Commissar for Trade
Uzavtopromtorg	Uzbek Motor Industry Trading Agency
Uzbekbirlyashu	United Uzbek Agency
UzSSR	Uzbek Soviet Socialist Republic
VChK	All-Union Extraordinary Committee
VKP (b)	All Union Communist Party (Bolsheviks)
Voenkhoz	War Committee for the Economy
Voenvod	War Committee for the Water Supply
VRK	
VSNKh	Supreme Soviet of People's Economy
VTsK NTA	All Union Central Committee for the New Turkic (and Tajik) Alphabet

TRANSLITERATION

The correct English rendering of names originally written in other alphabets is cause for constant scholarly dispute. Central Asian names present particular problems in that they have been written in various alphabets, including Arabic, Russian and Latin, all of which, at one time or another, have claimed to be definitive. For example, three "correct" ways can be claimed for writing the word Tajik (Tojik, Tadzhik). Chapter 8 on the debate over the choice of Latin alphabet for the Tajik language gives some idea of the problems raised and the passions they aroused. I have no wish to arouse passions, and renounce any claim to authority in this thorny subject. In the text, I have contented myself with giving the closest English phonetic equivalent to all proper names mentioned, while trying to achieve a consistent spelling for each name throughout. In the notes, when the references are to Russian-language sources, I have given a transcription from the original Russian letters, adding the English phonetic equivalent in brackets. I have also used transliterations from the Russian spelling for Soviet and Party institutions.

I have used the Russian terminology for the names of administrative districts and regions (e.g. volost', oblast') rather than attempting to translate these terms for which there is often no exact English equivalent. A guide to the administrative terms used in Central Asia throughout the period covered by this study can be found under Note 9 to Chapter 2. With regard to the huge number of Soviet and Party institutions, many of which became known by their Russian abbreviations (e.g. Sredazburo, Komsomol, Ispolkom etc), in the text I have mostly described them in English translation with the Russian abbreviation in brackets afterwards.

As for the party itself, in the text I have not tried to keep pace with its various changing titles during the period in question. I have simply called it the "Communist Party", "Party" or CP. For an account of its successive titles, the reader can consult Note 3 for Chapter 5.

ACKNOWLEDGEMENTS

This book was made possible through the generosity of the Leverhulme Trust, which kindly funded this project. My thanks are also due to Professor Robert Service of St Antony's College for guidance on how to navigate the Moscow archives and to Professor Kiril Andersen, the head of the Russian Centre for the Preservation of Documents of Recent History for facilitating my access to the Centre's archives. Sergei Vladimirovich Mironenko, director of the State Archive of the Russian Federation, also gave me good advice on where to look for useful records on Central Asia. In Oxford, Dr Sergei Andreev was extremely generous with advice and the loan of documents from his collection. Dolat Khudanazarov, former presidential candidate of Tajikistan, kindly lent me his own research materials on Shohtimur as well as supplying otherwise unknowable details from this period of Tajik history. Of all the scholarly works I consulted, special recognition is due to that of Lutz Rzehak, formerly of the Humboldt University in Berlin, on whose outstanding book (*Vom Persischen zum Tadschikischen*, Reichert, Wiesbaden, 2001) I have drawn heavily. By good fortune, an old friend, Susan McQuail, turned out to be the daughter of the architect Hans Adler who from 1931 to 1932 was charged by the Soviet government with designing the first modern buildings in the new Tajik capital, Dushanbe (then Stalinabad). Thanks to her generosity, I was able to use one of Adler's unique collection of photographs for the book's cover. Finally, my thanks to Dr Laura Newby of St Hilda's College, Oxford for scholarly advice and guidance, and to Zina Rohan for help over style.

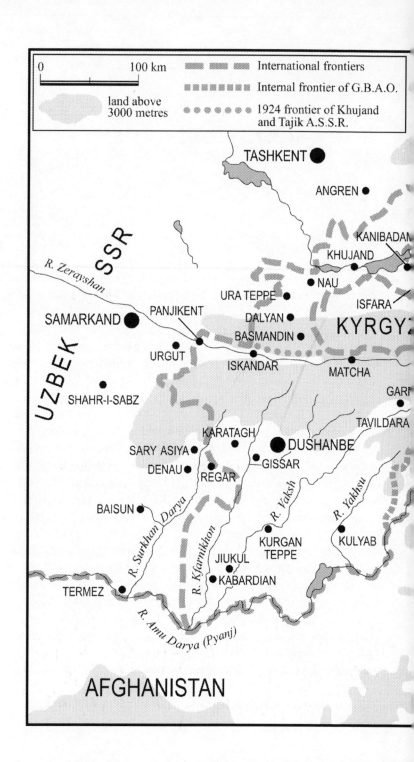

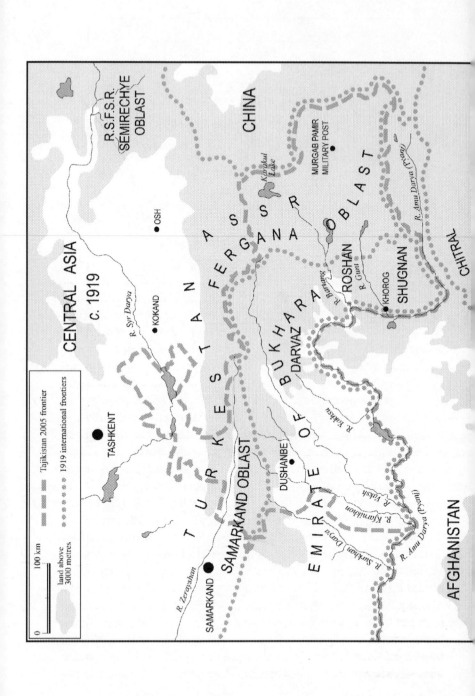

CENTRAL ASIA
c. 1919

- - - Tajikistan 2005 frontier
∙∙∙∙∙ 1919 international frontiers

land above
3000 metres

0   100 km

R.S.F.S.R.
SEMIRECHYE
OBLAST

CHINA

●OSH

R. Syr Darya

●KOKAND

T U R K E S T A N

TASHKENT

F E R G A N A

Karakul
Lake

MURGAB PAMIR
MILITARY POST ●

O B L A S T

R. Amu Darya (Panj)

SAMARKAND OBLAST

R. Zerayshan

SAMARKAND

DUSHANBE ●

DARVAZ

BUKHARA

R. Bartang
ROSHAN
R. Gunt
KHOROG
SHUGNAN

CHITRAL

E M I R A T E   O F

R. Vaksh

R. Surkhan Darya

R. Kjavukhon

R. Yaksh

R. Amu Darya (Pyani)

AFGHANISTAN

INTRODUCTION

On the 16th October 1929, the Third All-Tajik Congress of Soviets in Dushanbe publicly announced that Tajikistan had been promoted to the status of a Soviet Socialist Republic in its own right. Until that day, the country had been a mere Autonomous Republic within the Soviet Socialist Republic of Uzbekistan. The wife of Abdurahim Khojibaev, later to become chairman of the Council of People's Commissars of the Tajik SSR, was standing in the crowd beneath the tribune on that day. She recalled the fervour and "elan" of the assembled crowd who, in her words, repeatedly interrupted the announcement with applause and shouts of "hurrah", while many embraced one another. As she put it, "all evinced an astonishing enthusiasm".[1]

Knowing what we now know about the stage-management of "spontaneous" Soviet celebrations, Western readers will naturally be inclined to treat such an enthusiastic account with a certain scepticism. Khojibaev was a leading Bolshevik, although he, like so many of the Soviet Union's original Bolsheviks, was shot by Stalin in the 1930s. His daughter and biographer, Baroat Khojibaeva, who recorded her mother's reminiscence, was herself raised very much in the Soviet tradition. Nonetheless, the student of the period is justified in concluding that, behind the propaganda, there was also genuine emotion. This might not have been strong amongst ordinary Tajiks of the 1920s, many of whom supported the anti-Soviet Basmachi uprising, or were primarily concerned with staying alive. But at least it might have figured amongst what Marxist literature describes as "intellectuals" and "party workers". The West has long been inclined to dismiss the status of "Union Republic" in the USSR as a bogus form of independence, a Russian bear-hug from which none had any genuine right to extricate themselves. At a distance of seventy years, however, it may be admitted that the qualified autonomy implicit in "Union Republic" status was no less real than what was being offered to many of the colonial empires to which the Soviets saw their own solution as being vastly superior.

My purpose is to explore how Tajikistan, which had not existed as an ethnically defined political unit before the Bolshevik revolution, became in 1924 an autonomous republic within the Uzbek SSR, and in 1929 achieved union republic status. This political trajectory was paralleled by a profound shift in the way the Tajiks saw themselves. The early twentieth century had seen the non-national, Islamic and tribal ethos and identities of pre-Soviet Central Asia being eroded by pan-Turkic nationalism which had no room for the Tajiks or their Persian language, which was regarded as the remnant of a feudal and reactionary time. This book seeks to trace the Tajiks' journey to the national identity they developed in the 1920s when their aspirations received recognition in the creation of a state. This was a national formation which, whatever the limitations and uncertainties, its Tajik inhabitants came to regard as the first political expression of their national identity since the end of the Samanid empire in AD 999. It was then that the last "Iranian" dynasty in the region gave way to the Turkic rulers who have been dominant in Central Asia until today. Crucially, Tajikistan's elevation in 1929 to the rank of union republic gave its people the right to full independence when the USSR disintegrated.

1

CENTRAL ASIAN IDENTITIES
BEFORE 1917

As the only people in Central Asia whose language is not Turkic, present-day Tajiks proudly claim to be descendants of the early pre-Islamic inhabitants of the region. Over the last 1000 years, it is claimed, successive waves of invading Turkic nomads gradually ousted them, first from the best grazing pastures and then, as the invaders adapted to the conditions of settled agriculture, from the best arable land also. This process was summed up in a long document or "working paper" prepared for the study of the region in advance of the new Soviet government's so-called National Territorial Delimitation of 1924 which divided Central Asia into new republics on ethnic lines. In this document, Tajik history was described as follows:

> The Tajiks are the only people [in Central Asia] of Iranian origin, who since time immemorial have been living in the frontiers of Bukhara and the Turkestan Autonomous Soviet Socialist Republic (see below for a description of this polity). The conquering Turkic peoples enslaved them. Part of them became totally Turkicised and adopted the language of their conquerors, while the rest, although they kept their language, took refuge in the mountainous and semi-mountainous regions of Samarkand Oblast' and Bukhara, and in the valleys of the mountain rivers and the basin of the Syr Darya and the Zeravshan where they were driven by their conquerors.[1]

According to the great Russian orientalist, Academician V.V. Bartol'd,[2] the use of the word "Tajik" was first recorded in the literature on Central Asia by the historian Beikhaki who reported a senior

Iranian so describing his nationality when speaking to Mas'ud of Ghazni in 1039. The possibly related word "Tat" was also used to define Iranian peoples, although originally it may have been used by the nomads of Central and Inner Asia for all settled peoples. Compare Mahmud al Kashgari's mysterious quote "There is no man without a hat and no Turk without a Tat". Despite attempts by Tajik nationalists and others to link the name Tajik to the Persian word for crown "taj", the usually, but not universally, accepted explanation of the origin of the word "Tajik" is that it stems from the Persian word "Tazi" i.e. "Arab". In the early Islamic period in Iran and Central Asia, this came to be applied in a general way by the locals to all the newly arrived Muslims. But, as time went on, this application was refined and, eventually limited to the Persian element which had come to the region with the Arab army. The true origin of the word "Tat" is even more uncertain.

The Tajiks' claim to be the region's oldest inhabitants has a superficial ring of truth, although it simplifies the issue somewhat and deserves closer examination.

Many of the 8th-century texts unearthed in the excavations of Mount Mug near Panjikent in the Zeravshan valley, are written in Soghdian — an Eastern Iranian language — which suggests that the dominant culture of the period was indeed Iranian. Nonetheless, the names of Turkic rulers are recorded as having defeated the previously dominant regional power, the Hephthalites, in a battle probably near Bukhara, in the 560s AD. After that defeat, the Hephthalite kingdom (as to whose ethnic identity there is still considerable uncertainty) appears to have split up into different princedoms. Some owed allegiance to the Turks in the north, others south of the Oxus to the Sasanians, while others maintained an independent existence in Kashmir and adjoining regions until the late 7th century. Soghdian coins also mention the Turks in the early 8th century.[3] Bactrian documents discovered in Northern Afghanistan over the last ten years also confirm that, before the Arabs arrived in 739 AD, Bactria (largely in present-day Northern Afghanistan) had already been under the at least sporadic control of Turkic overlords.[4]

It therefore seems plausible that the invading Muslim Arabs and their Persian-speaking allies found on their arrival in Central Asia in the early eighth century AD a mixed population using Eastern Iranian languages as the medium of cultural and official communication, and dominated successively by a mixed Sasanian, Hephthalite and Turkic aristocracy.

One of the puzzles of Central Asian history is why the Tajiks of the region's cities and plains have, since the Islamic conquest, spoken a Western Iranian language (Persian i.e. the language of Fars) rather than a descendant of Soghdian, Khorezmian or Bactrian, all languages that appear to have been in common and official use locally up to that conquest. One of today's Eastern Iranian languages, Yaghnobi, spoken by a small community living until recently[5] in the mountains of Tajikistan alongside the Yaghnob river (a tributary of the Zeravshan), is a clear descendant of ancient Soghdian. If the Yaghnobis are to be regarded, on these linguistic grounds, as the true descendants of the Soghdians, and the speakers of Pamiri languages in Gornyi-Badakhshan as descendants of other pre-Islamic Eastern Iranian peoples, what does it mean that most Tajiks speak the language of Fars, some 1000 miles to the southwest? Indeed, is their language any sort of guide as to their ethnic origins?

The commonest explanation of how the Central Asian Iranians replaced their own languages – Soghdian, Khorezmian, Bactrian etc – with the language of Fars, is that the latter was brought by the large Persian element in the invading Arab army which settled throughout the region after the advent of Islam in the 8th century. Given the strong (Sasanian) tradition of imperial administration, it was natural that they took over the management of the new provinces of the Arab caliphate. Their own language became the language of officialdom and the court ("Dar" from where "Dari" – the usual name for the Persian dialect spoken in Afghanistan and, by extension of the terminology, in Central Asia) throughout the region, right up to the Soviet period. With the passage of time, it is surmised, the bulk of the populace of the region also adopted the language. The Iran scholar Richard Frye attributes some of the dialectical difference in modern Tajik to the fact that Kulyab, the mediaeval Kuttal, in the south of the country, was ruled for a long time by the Middle-Persian-speaking Sasanians. They therefore adopted the New Persian language faster than the peoples of the north of what is now Tajikistan, who formed part of various Soghdian-speaking kingdoms.[6]

Once Islam had taken firm root in Central Asia in the 8th century AD, it was not long before a dynasty of local governors, who became known as the Samanids, established a strong local state, owing nominal allegiance to the distant Abbasid caliphate in Baghdad but to all intents and purposes independent. The Samanids, whose rule lasted approximately from AD 819 to 999, established New Persian (Farsi) as the language of administration and culture. As already noted, it is to the Samanids that today's Tajik nationalists look back when seeking historic inspiration for the non-Turkic legitimacy of their contemporary state. The fact that the Samanid capital Bukhara is now in Uzbekistan has, since the establishment of Tajikistan, rankled with many nationalist Tajik historians. For their part, Uzbek patriots react to this Tajik grievance with a mixture of irritation and suspicion. This potential bone of contention was kept reasonably well buried during the Soviet period but, since independence, has again surfaced to cause tension between the two nations.

Over the thousand years following the arrival of Islam, the original Pre-Islamic population of Central Asia was gradually either driven from the better land, or assimilated, by a succession of invaders, starting with the Arabs and Persian-speakers, and continuing with ever more successful and numerous waves of Turkic peoples. The best known of these were led by dynasties such as the Karakhanids (who overthrew the Samanids) and Seljuqs. Others arrived as assorted tribes fighting with the Mongol armies in the 13th century and, finally, arriving in the 15th and 16th centuries, as the confederation that became known as Uzbeks. By the middle of the 19th century according to the early Russian traveller Khanykov, the Uzbeks were already the dominant group in the area.[7] The dominance of the Uzbeks was also noted by other authorities before the revolution.[8] However, although from an ethnic point of view the local population became increasingly infiltrated, diluted, and dominated by Turkic-speakers, the position of Persian as the traditional language of government and continuing contacts with the heartland of present-day Iran ensured that Persian culture and language were to prove resilient in the administration and in social life. This was especially true of large centres like Samarkand and Bukhara, even where the ruling dynasty was Turkic. In the mountains of western Tajikistan, Persian continued to be spoken, while, in some remote valleys and in the Pamirs, Eastern Iranian languages also survived.

There is some evidence that, at least in the Middle Ages, relations between Tajiks and Turks were not always good. Bartol'd quotes instances of mistrust between the two nationalities in the Khorezmshah period around AD 1200.[9] However, by the first half of the 19th century, while the Turkic peoples still thought of the Tajiks as a separate group, they seem no longer to have regarded them as in any way hostile,[10] nor vice versa. The general consensus seems to be that, after centuries of living together in a society where ethnic distinctiveness was much less important than differences in way of life (i.e. settled as against nomadic communities) or Islamic solidarity, Tajiks and settled Turkic peoples got along perfectly well. Intermarriage was, for example, very common.[11] Indeed, in many communities, the notion of ethnicity, as later defined under the Soviets in linguistic or ethnic terms, was either very vaguely formulated or did not exist at all.

In this Islamic Central Asian environment, where ethnicity was of little consequence, the process of assimilation between the latest arrivals, the Uzbeks, and the Iranian/Persian/Turkic/Arab cocktail of peoples whom they found, produced in due course a composite identity of mixed ethnic make-up. In terms of language, its representatives were usually bi-lingual, but eventually preferred a Turkic language strongly influenced by Persian in both vocabulary but also in vocalisation (e.g. lack of characteristic Turkic vowel harmony). This composite identity became known as "Sart".[12]

The meaning of the term shifted over the centuries. By the Mongol/Timurid period, "Sart" had come to mean "Tajik" and, at the end of the 14th century, the language and literature of the Sarts was described as being what wasn't Turkish i.e. Iranian. That this identification with Tajik lasted even as late as the 19th century, is supported by the account of J. Klaproth, a German traveller journeying in Kazan and Siberia in mid-century. The numerous Bukharans he spoke to told him that the Turkic peoples called them "Sarts" although they called themselves Tajiks.[13]

By the late 19th century, possibly as a result of the increasing influence of Pan-Turkic ideas, the term was sometimes given derogatory connotations, including a popular etymological derivation from the words "sari it" i.e. "yellow dog". However, this contemptuous attitude was by no means universal. Many groups were perfectly happy to call themselves "Sarts" even though they did not always understand what this meant. This is clear from the observations of the Russian orientalist I.I. Zarubin, made while studying the so-called "Turks" who had been identified in various censuses in the rural areas of Central Asia in the late 19th and early 20th centuries. The Russian scholar S.N. Andreev had earlier identified them as a mix of various Turkic elements (Temir-Kabuk, Bakhrin, Burkut). "But," says Zarubin, "they do not really know what they are. They call themselves Turks. But their Turkmen and Kyrgyz neighbours call them "Sart" which word they also use for Tajiks. A.D. Grobenkin regards them as Uzbeks and indeed their language is very similar and they admit to Uzbek origins".[14]

The same author noted that the inhabitants of Zaamin and Kaisma, whom the census of the Jizzakh Uezd (District) (situated in what is now Uzbekistan) identified as either Uzbeks or Tajiks, could be classified as "Sarts". He added that P.S. Skvartskii (of the 1913 Imperial Russian Land Commission) had called them Tajiks, albeit Turkicised, but added: "On the other hand they themselves deny this saying 'we are Sarts' ".[15]

Again according to Zarubin, Andreev noted on 25 May 1915 that "Uzbek-Sarts" live in all the settlements (in Bishkent) together with a small admixture of an assimilated Tajik element, who have lost the conception of any sort of division into tribes and no longer remember their ethnic origins, but who do not consider themselves to be "Turks". As they told Andreev "we call ourselves Uzbeks but the Tajiks call us Sarts".[16]

In this mist of uncertainty, by the end of the 19th century the generally accepted meaning of the word "Sart" had, as Bartol'd noted, come to mean "an Uzbekized urban Tajik".[17]

After the revolution, the term's lack of any clear national or ethnic label or of any glorious historic association, did not suit the new Soviet regime, which was keen to create clearer national divisions in the region. With regard to the name "Sart", the Russian scholar A.A. Semenov had noted that, "because of a misunderstanding . . . the locals sometimes did not see its origin as part of the glorious past of a great country".[18] In his recent article on the "Archaeology of Uzbek Identity",[19] Alisher Ilkhamov also suggests that the traditional image of the "Sarts" did not accord with the social engineering embarked on by the new communist regime. The mercantile, relatively prosperous urban background of the "Sarts" was harder to reconcile with the new progressive ideals than the poorer rural Uzbek tribal types. Contemporary observers had already noticed the change. Writing in 1925 about the population of Samarkand, I.I Zarubin attributed the small number of "Sarts" registered following the 1924 National Territorial Delimitation (see below) to the "lack of clarity as to the term's meaning". By then this designation was rapidly going out of use and had largely been replaced by the word "Uzbek", a process described in detail in Obiya Chika's essay "When Faizulla Khojaev decided to be an Uzbek".[20] Commenting separately on the ethnic make-up of Central Asia, A.A. Semenov noted that "the largest group are the Uzbeks, assuming that the mixed Iranian/Turkic urban and village population which in past times used to be called "Sart" and speaks a local Turkic dialect (with a significant admixture of Persian words), is counted with them".

On either side of this composite "Sart" nationality were as yet unassimilated representatives of both Turkic and Tajik groups. On the Turkic side were Kipchaks, "Turks", Kyrgyz and Kara Kyrgyz (up to the 20th century the Russian names for Kazakhs and Kyrgyz respectively), Karakalpaks, Turkmen, Uzbeks etc, many of whom still lived nomadic or semi-nomadic lives. On the Tajik side, stood so-called Tajiks and Ghalcha (see below), most of whom either lived in towns or were engaged in agriculture, often at a bare subsistence level in the mountains.

It also has to be remembered that, until the Russian conquest stabilized the Pamirs, the pattern of administration in the mountainous area of what became known as "Eastern Bukhara" was very fluid. Although these mountains were nominally part of the Bukharan Emirate, the Amir's authority was at best intermittent. Local khans, on either side of the Oxus, were usually in charge and, as often as not, in a state of war with one another. In the middle of the 19th century, Shahr e Sabz, for example, under its Keniges Uzbek rulers, united with Gissar to throw off the yoke of the Mangit (Uzbek) Amir of Bukhara. Although both Amirs Nasrullah and Muzaffar repeatedly tried to re-conquer the town, they were unsuccessful. The English explorer Alexander "Bukhara" Burnes describes the town as independent of either Bukhara or Kunduz. Mir Muhammad Murad Beg, Khan of Kunduz in the first half of the 19th century, extended his rule north of the Oxus by defeating Mir Yar Beg of Badakhshan, and remained in at least informal control there until the 1840s. In the 1880s the Amir of Afghanistan Abdulrahman Khan sent his army north across the Amu Darya to occupy the Pamirs. Bukhara, Afghanistan, and Kunduz were not the only claimants in the Western Pamirs. The

Khan of Kokand also intermittently exercised some control there, while the Eastern Pamirs were more or less continuously under his at least nominal rule.

These changes in ruler, and the economic chaos they engendered, frequently prompted part of the local population to move elsewhere. The two attacks on Shughnan and the Wakhan (1883 and 1889) by the Amir Abdulrahman Khan, and likewise the union of Karategin and Darvaz with the Bukharan emirate, sparked considerable migration of Tajiks from the mountains into the Ferghana valley. The harsh rule of Muhammad Murad Beg of Kunduz also caused intense impoverishment amongst the Tajiks of the region many of whom preferred to move elsewhere.

If one feature was common to all these khans, big and small, it was a total lack of interest in the welfare of their subjects or, as a corollary, in the ethnic composition of their population. As we shall see below, the only attempts to gauge these matters were undertaken by visiting Russians – usually military officers – whose research was neither exhaustive nor reliable. In the late 19th century, Staff-Captain Stetkevich attempted a rough count of the mountain population of the Karatagh Darya valley of Eastern Bukhara. According to his estimate, in the Karatagh and Sary-Jui "Amlyakdarstvos" (districts) the Tajiks predominated; in Regar and Sary-Asiya, the Uzbeks. Not only were these very rough estimates. It is also hard to check them against other statistics, because different census-takers chose different combinations of districts. For example, the National Territorial Delimitation's Commission of 1924, drawing on the Bukharan census of 1913, but subtracting a good number because of the assumed losses during the revolution and civil war, concluded that Karatagh/Sary Assiya was more than 66% Uzbek. But what about Regar and Sary-Jui?

If Stetkevich and other Russians had a reasonably clear idea in their minds as to the difference – at least in the mountains – between Tajiks and others, the Tajiks themselves were not always so sure. Nor were they a homogeneous community.

As S.N. Andreev discovered when he visited the region as late as the 1920s, the local Tajiks at that time still had rather unclear ideas of their own identity. When asked to describe themselves, the (Eastern-Iranian-language-speaking) inhabitants of the reaches of the Upper Pyandzh (now in the Mountainous Badakhshan district of

Eastern Tajikistan) described themselves as "Tajiks" and the Persian speakers as "Farsigu" (Persian speakers). On the other hand, the Yaghnobis of the upper Zeravshan described themselves as Yaghnobis and their Persian-speaking neighbours, like the Falgartsy, as "Tajiks". For their part, the Falgartsy described themselves as Tajiks and the Yaghnobis as "Ghalcha", a word widely used in the region (including incidentally by the Chinese imperial administration in Altishahr, probably to indicate an Ismaili mountain Tajik from Badakhshan[21]) for the Tajiks of the mountains. In short, Persian-speakers who used the word "Tajik" to describe themselves were generally the mountain-dwellers of areas like the Zarafshan mountains, Karategin, Darvaz and the hilly parts of Khojand.[22] The Persian-speakers of the cities in the plains, such as Samarkand and Bukhara, were more inclined to identify themselves in regional terms, e.g. as Samarkandis or Bukhara'is.

In his study, "The Ethnography of the Tajiks", Andreev emphasised the difference, both in language and physical appearance, between the Tajiks of the mountains (including Ghalcha) and those who had succeeded in keeping their position in the plains. In the second group he included both the inhabitants of the cities of Samarkand and Bukhara, which remain to this day largely Tajik-speaking, and of Khojand, which was not part of the Tajik ASSR under the 1924 dispensation, but was to be transferred to the Tajik SSR in 1929.[23] The physical appearance of the former struck him as remarkably "European", while the plainsmen were obviously of much more mixed racial origins. Lt Colonel Snesyareff of the Russian General Staff, in his Description of Eastern Bukhara dated 1906, also noticed the physical difference between the Tajiks of Karategin and Darvaz (i.e. the mountains) and those of the plains. The former looked "European" while the latter were mixed with Turkic stock. He also noticed a difference in the way of life as between Tajiks and Uzbeks, with the former being mainly settled and engaged in agriculture, while the latter were still at least semi-nomadic and engaged in stock-raising. Like most outside observers of foreign peoples at the time, Snesyareff was not shy about subscribing to national stereotypes. In his summary, the Tajiks were "sympathetic, kind and patient" but "deceitful and miserly". As for the Uzbeks, they were "horribly lazy, lovers of freedom, proud, hospitable, kind, thriftless, simple and straight". He concluded that, while the Uzbeks were more political than the Tajiks, they had not yet developed an overall national identity. As we shall

see, Soviet rule was to change this, often to the continuing dis-
advantage of the Tajiks.[24]

The conclusions of the Soviet sociologist O.A.Sukhareva, who was
researching in Bukhara city as late as the 1950s, pointed to two
propositions: first that, as in many large and internationally famous
cities, which for centuries have acted as a pole of attraction for the
inhabitants of the surrounding countryside and beyond, the urban
population was very mixed. Over the centuries, the main obstacle to
intermarriage had been religious rather than national or racial. Tajiks
and Uzbeks, and most other Turkic peoples, were Sunni Muslims for
whom intermarriage presented little or no problem. On the other
hand, neither group would normally have given their daughters to
(Persian-speaking) Shi'i or Jewish families, of which there were also
large numbers in the city. Sukhareva's second conclusion was that
many Tajiks, even as late as the 1950s, still had a weak feeling of
national identity. Numerous Tajik-speakers still identified themselves
as Uzbeks, often citing long family traditions and specifying from
which Turkic tribe their forebears had originated. She further found
that, even within families, some members would call themselves
Uzbek and others, often the female members, Tajik. She wondered
whether this division might be due to a masculine inclination to
identify with the prestigious military caste in the former Bukharan
emirate, which was mainly drawn from families of nomadic Uzbek
background. She was probably aware of Tajik claims that the Uzbeks
had, during Soviet-sponsored censuses, forced Tajik families to
register as Uzbeks. To encourage Tajiks to identify themselves, she
therefore stressed that hers was an academic survey which had nothing
to do with the government. There must be some doubt as to whether
these Bukharans would have believed that a Russian conducting such
an enquiry could have been totally independent of the official and
Communist Party world. Nonetheless, her conclusions about the
Tajiks' lack of clear national identity to some extent chimed with the
earlier findings of Dr M. Gabrielyan of the Institute for Tropical
Diseases in Bukhara. Working in the city from 1928 to 1930 in the
districts of Khauz e Nau and Akhtachi, Gabrielyan found that, in the
former, nearly three quarters of the population described themselves
as Uzbeks and, in the latter, over 90% as Tajiks; this despite the fact
that they all spoke Tajik for preference. Moreover, she could discern
no difference in their appearance or way of life.

When Sukhareva asked those Tajik speakers who identified themselves as Uzbeks why their mother tongue was Tajik the reply was often that their forebears had come to Bukhara, a Tajik-speaking city, and had, over the generations, adopted the language of their environment. Asked further whom they considered to be Tajiks, such respondents would often either reply "the inhabitants of Tajikistan" or the "Fars" – Persian speaking Shi'i immigrants from Iran or Merv. Those "Fars" whom she interviewed did indeed often identify themselves as Tajik. Other Tajik-speakers who identified themelves as Tajiks (rather than "Fars"), often told her that they were descended from immigrants from the countryside, especially the mountains. Her conclusion, therefore, seems to have been that Muslim Tajik-speakers often thought they were Uzbeks, but, when asked to describe Tajiks, thought they were either immigrant mountaineers, or Shi'i "Fars".

As for the Tajik-speakers still in the mountains, although they seem to have been generally more clearly aware of their Tajik identity, in isolated cases confusion reigned here also. Sukhareva quotes the research of B.Kh Karmysheva who, working in the hilly Urgut district above Samarkand, found several instances of Tajik-speaking villages which associated themselves with Uzbek tribes – and were accepted as such by their Uzbek neighbours.[25]

If these findings from the second half of the 20th century show a good deal of vagueness as to national identity still surviving in Bukhara city amongst the Tajik-speaking population, these feelings will have been even vaguer and weaker before the advent of the Soviet regime. As one old man put it to Sukhareva "before 1926 no one ever asked us whether we were Tajiks or Uzbeks". The findings also seem to show that there is at least an element of truth in the claims of Uzbek nationalists that some Tajik-speakers are in fact of Turkic origin but have for various reasons adopted the Persian language. The pre-Soviet "Sart" identity had after all been bi-lingual Uzbek and Tajik. This is not to say that the efforts of Soviet censuses of Central Asia to divide the population into ethnic groups were always free of political manipulation (in this case by the Uzbeks). On the contrary, the evidence for manipulation, indeed falsification, is strong. But, for many of the inhabitants of Bukhara city, language was not and continued not to be a clear indicator of national identity. Irrespective of people's language or their genetic origins, they reached conclusions as to their own identities for a range of different reasons. Sukhareva and Gabrilyan's research suggests that there were Tajik-speakers who genuinely believed themselves to be Uzbeks. And who was there to tell them they weren't? However, as we may already have seen in Khojibaeva's account above, it was not necessarily the rank-and-file population who were to be the main players in determining Tajik identity but rather the intelligentsia – and here influences were at work which were to complicate still further not only the identity of individuals but the path to nationhood.

2

THE TURKIC ASCENDANCY

By the end of the 19th century a process had begun that was to promote a Central Asian Turkic national consciousness at the expense of the possible growth of similar awareness about Tajik identity. One of the elements in this process was the development of Chagatai Turkish rather than Persian in the official administration of the Turkestan Governorate-General. Was this change a cause of the growth of Turkic consciousness, or one of its symptoms? Probably both.

Direct Russian rule in the Governorate-General (Bukhara and Khiva were still separate autonomous states) boosted the use of Chagatai partly because many of the Russian translators were Tatars and Kazakhs who could understand a Turkic language more easily than an Iranian one. Bartol'd claims that, whereas Academician Radlov heard nothing but Persian spoken on the streets of Samarkand in 1868, in 1904 he, Barto'ld, heard much more Turkic. He also mentions that, when the former Qazi Kalan of Samarkand, Kemal ud Din, fell out of favour in 1871, he wrote his defence in Turkic because he thought it would be more easily understood by the Russian authorities. It is also significant that, when it was decided to print an annex to the official local Russian newspaper *Turkestanskie Vedomomosti* in native languages, the annex was initially published in Persian, Chagatai and Kazakh. In 1871 this was changed to "Sart" (i.e. Chagatai) and Kazakh, and from 1883 onwards it appeared in "Sart" alone.[1]

The presence in Tsarist Central Asia of Tatar translators and administrators was not the only cause of growing Turkic awareness in the cultural and educational development of the region. Other Turkic influences were making themselves felt from outside Central Asia.

The shock of the European conquest of much of the Islamic world in the 18th and 19th centuries had stimulated a wave of heart-searching amongst the intelligentsia of those countries most affected. Muslim thinkers tried to analyse the reasons for the weakness and lack of development of those governments, whether Moghul, Ottoman, Egyptian, or North African, which had been defeated by British, French, or, in the Caucasus and Central Asia, Russian arms, or, like Iran, had remained independent but fallen victim to Western influence and manipulation. It was natural that many of these thinkers should look for inspiration to the only surviving Islamic power, the weakened but still powerful and extensive Ottoman empire, and to the pan-Turkic ideas that flowed from this association. It was also understandable that, in the Russian empire, they should be led largely by Turkic-speaking Tatars, who, more than the Tsar's other Muslim subjects, had absorbed the principles of modern education. It was these intellectuals who championed the educational reform movement known as the "Usul-e-Jadid" (new principles) promulgated by the Tatar writer and journalist Ismail Gaspirali (also known as Gasprinskii). Strongly influenced by reformist thought and pan-Turkic ideas current in the Ottoman empire, Gaspirali devoted himself to the reform of the Turkic peoples of the Russian empire. The two pillars on which he built his programme of reform were the press and education, both to be propagated in a simplified version of Ottoman written in the Arabic script which he hoped would be comprehensible to all speakers of the different Turkic languages found in the Russian empire. The vehicle he chose for his ideas was the newspaper *Terjuman* (The Interpreter), which he founded in Baghchesarai in 1883 and which became widely read amongst Muslims throughout the empire. His educational reform started with the advocacy of new (phonetic) methods of teaching the language, in preference to the strict memorisation that had been in use in the traditional religious schools ("maktab"s) up until then. He also proposed a modernised syllabus including subjects such as geography and arithmetic, and advocated a new lay-out for classrooms, complete with desks and blackboards in the Western style. The "Jadids", as they came to be called, made less headway against the resistance of conservative Muslims in Central Asia than in their own lands of the Crimea and the Volga, and in Azerbaijan. Nonetheless, their influence was felt in Central Asia, and local exponents, whatever their mother tongue, absorbed these new teachings in the Turkic idiom rather than the Persian one. The message was taken up by Central Asian thinkers and literati such as Mahmud Behbudi, Munawwar Qari, Abdul Qader Shukuri, Sayyid Ahmad Siddiqi (Ajzi) and Abdulrauf Fitrat, all of whom, in good "Sart" tradition, were bi-lingual in Chagatai Turkish and Persian but saw themselves as working within a Turkestani reform movement. These reformists had more success in establishing their new schools and newspapers in the Russian-ruled Turkestan Governorate-General than in the more conservative atmosphere of the Bukharan Emirate. Here a number of Jadid schools were set up, both by the Tatar community and by home-grown Jadids such as Sadruddin Ayni and Abdul Wahid Munzim. However, many of these institutions eventually became political footballs in the intense competition between different factions within the religious and political establishment of the Emirate, closing and re-opening as this or that group gained a temporary ascendancy. Worse was to come. Immediately after the February 1917 revolution, as the Tsarist Russian political agency in Kagan, which had on balance supported the reformist schools, lost its authority in the face of growing Soviet power, the conservative clergy temporarily gained the upper hand. Under their pressure, the Amir Sayyid Alim Khan abandoned all earlier pretence at reformist policies and the Jadids were forced to flee the country.[2] By the time they were able to return, power was shifting to an entirely new type of government with a quite different agenda.

In the Jadid movement, whether under the Tsarist dispensation or, after the revolution, in the Turkestan Autonomous Soviet Socialist Republic (TASSR), which was set up on the territory of the former Governorate-General, this identification of pan-Turkism with progress tended to relegate Tajiks and Tajik culture to a secondary place in the new Central Asia. The description of the Tajiks of Bukhara in the Tatar magazine *Shura* of February 1910 is quoted by Adeeb Khaled as fairly typical: "Their faces are straight . . . their women renowned for their beauty. They are assiduous and masters of commerce, but deceptive and have low morals."[3] It was also argued, then as now, that the Tajiks, at least those in the plains, were in fact of Turkic stock but had been obliged to adopt the Persian language by the (unjust and feudal) rule of the Bukharan amirs and Kokand khans who relied on that language in their administration. As an unknown writer in the journal *Turkestan* put it in 1920:

wanting to use the Tajik language is only moving further away from the modern world, using a language which has become rare and superfluous. It is vital that the Tajiks *revert* [note the use of this word] immediately to the Uzbek language and stop using the specific Tajik language, for the Socialist movement has settled its fate.[4]

Interestingly, while this argument is now largely the stuff of Uzbek supremacist discourse, in those days, many Tajik intellectuals accepted it.

Guissou Jahangiri has referred to the polemics between Ismoilzoda, who wrote in the new journal *Ovoz e Tojik e Kambaghal* (*The Voice of the Poor Tajik*), and Bektosh,[5] both of them Tajik intellectuals, in which the former argued for and the latter against the need for Tajik language education. Sh. Jabbarov, in an article written for the journal *Za Partiyu* in 1929, describes how even the Tajik intelligentsia was under the influence of the Jadids and looked to Istanbul and the Ottoman empire for inspiration in their reformist ideas.[6] It must also be remembered that, in the immediate aftermath of the establishment of Soviet power in the TASSR, Persian was still the official language of the Emirate of Bukhara, regarded by all "progressive" intellectuals as the embodiment of unjust feudal despotism. Furthermore, the mountains of Tajikistan became in subsequent years the main bastion of the armed anti-Soviet insurrection known as the "Basmachestvo" (see below). The Persian language was seen as the language of reaction, while Chagatai Turkic, and its relative and literary descendant the Uzbek language, symbolised progress and reform.

Meanwhile, pan-Turkic organisations like the "Chagatai" group conducted an energetic campaign to put Tajiks under pressure to abandon their language and culture. The pan-Turkic press backed these activities. The newspaper *Turkestan* in an article of the 3 January 1924 again wrote:

Any inclination to use this language [Tajik] indicates a desire to distance one's self from life, because life and the flow of history are against it. Secondly, accepting it is to accept, not a useful, but a useless and superfluous language.[7]

The Tajik communist Abdulkadyr Muhieddinov,[8] had represented the

Tajiks during the national delimitation of 1924. He was later to admit that he himself had been under the influence of pan-Turkic thinkers at the time. During the meetings of the Uzbek Sub-commission of the Territorial Commission set up in 1924 to decide on implementing the National Territorial Delimitation (hereafter referred to as the NTD) in Central Asia, Muhieddinov spoke at length on the disputes between the Uzbeks and the Turkmen and Kyrgyz (i.e. Kazakhs) over the allocation of Tashkent, but said nothing about the details of the formation of the Tajik Autonomous Oblast'.[9] When judging the position taken by Mudieddinov and others, one must remember their youth. At the time of the NTD in 1924, Mudieddinov, later widely regarded as one of the "elder statesmen" of the Tajik state, was thirty-two. Bektosh was twenty-four, and Ismoilzoda twenty-three. Most, like their "young Bukharan" colleagues Abdulrauf Fitrat[10] and Faizulla Khojaev,[11] had been in their teens when they were swept up in the Jadidist underground movements of the First World War period, which were heavily dominated by pan-Turkic sentiment. They were at an impressionable age and for some, like Muhieddinov and Faizulla Khojaev, there was plenty of time to change their minds under the influence of later events.

3

THE REVOLUTION AND AFTER

The revolutionary period had been a miserable time for the Central Asians. The local population had been decimated by a series of catastrophes. In 1916, the imperial government, desperate to free Russian soldiers from auxiliary service to strengthen the combat units fighting against Germany, issued a decree mobilising the Central Asians, who until then had been exempt from military service. Although the mobilisation was not for enlistment in fighting units, the move was interpreted locally as both a betrayal and a threat. Particularly in Semirechye, Russian encroachment on Kazakh and Kyrgyz land had anyway raised resentment there to fever-pitch. Disturbances in Khojand and Jizzakh developed into a full-scale uprising which then spread to Semirechye. Russian and local officials of the imperial government, as well as Russian settlers, were attacked and killed. Russian troops were dispatched to bring the situation under control, while Russian settlers organised themselves into self-protection vigilante groups. By the time order was restored, some 3000 Russians had been killed. The Central Asian, especially Kyrgyz, losses were far higher. Exact figures are not available but according to some estimates the population of Turkestan fell by 275,000 during this period, while another 300,000 are thought to have fled to China. Hard on the heels of the 1916 uprising and its consequences came the Bolshevik revolution, misguided Soviet agricultural policies and the civil war, aggravated by the Basmachestvo. By the winter of 1919, Turar Ryskulov,[1] the Kazakh Bolshevik, reckoned that half the population of Turkestan was starving. The imperial Russian government's emphasis on cotton cultivation had made the region fatefully dependent on Russia for grain, which could not be delivered once communications with Central Asia were cut off by the White Armies. In Bukhara, the Amir's boycott of trade with the new TASSR devastated his country's rural economy. The civil war had also decimated the livestock population. Throughout the first half of the 1920s, famine continued to plague the region, along with typhus and malaria. Even in the winter of 1923, Soviet investigators estimated that in the Ferghana Valley 400,000 people were starving.[2]

The disruption in communications that had interrupted grain deliveries had also prevented Moscow exercising strict control over political developments. Initially, in 1917, the local Soviet regime, dominated as it was by Russians, seemed determined to exclude the locals from government and behaved towards them with intolerance and even brutality. In his report to the Presidium of the All-Russian Central Executive Committee, about the situation in Turkestan, I.A. Alkin was later to write:

> In the early days, as a result of a distortion of Party policy in Turkestan, the local population was not permitted to enter the organs of Soviet power or the Red Army . . . this forced them to the conclusion that they were regarded as untrustworthy and that the European population, in the accustomed fashion, intended as before to lord it over them".[3]

By mid-1919, P.A. Kobozev, the Chairman of the TASSR, which had been set up in April 1918 to replace the Governorate-General of the same name, decided with Moscow's agreement to open up the Communist Party to locals. The result was a flood of new Central Asian members who swiftly began to exert a profound influence on the direction of party policy. At the 5th Regional Congress of the Party held in January 1920, the locals secured a majority in the Party's so-called Muslim Bureau and, in conjunction with the Third Conference of Turkic Communists, voted to turn the TASSR into an Autonomous Turkic Republic. Parallel with this decision, they created a new Turkic Communist Party whose aim was the unification of all the Turkic peoples of Central Asia in a new communist but Turkic state.

This tendency was mainly led by Turkic Communist Party members who had been close to the Jadid movement and had been influenced by the same pan-Turkic ideals – people such as Turar

Ryskulov, Tursun Khojaev and the Bashkir Zaki Validi Togan. There was no room in these leaders' thinking for Tajik national aims.

This was the situation when a so-called "Turkkommissiya" (Turkestan Commission) was dispatched by Moscow to the Turkestan ASSR in late 1919 to tackle the problem of Russian chauvinist attitudes, which had been reported as prevalent in the Communist Party. On arrival, however, the Commission discovered that Russian chauvinism was not the only problem with which they had to deal. The Party was being infiltrated by an ideological tendency amongst local members, which, preaching as it did the need for an alliance with the (Turkic) nationalist bourgeoisie ran directly contrary to Lenin's ideas. Such had been the ignorance in Moscow of the true situation developing in Turkestan that the centre had failed to grasp this danger.

It was not until 1920, when the civil war was all but won and the position of the Soviet government throughout the whole former Russian empire had stabilised, that Lenin was able to devote more time to Central Asia. A re-staffed Turkestan Commission headed this time by the senior Bolshevik M.V. Kaganovich and with Georgyi Safarov[4] and the Latvian Communist Yakov Peters[5] as members, was dispatched to purge the local party of Turkic nationalist elements.

In theory at least, the TASSR undertook to protect the rights of ethnic minorities through a People's Commissariat for nationalities (Narkomnats). A statute issued on 16 January 1918 entitled "On the Regional Commissariat for National Affairs", declared that all the nationalities of the Turkestan ASSR had the right to appoint representatives to departments dealing with national affairs and to the above-mentioned People's Commissariat. In accordance with this statute, national departments were indeed established in this People's Commissariat, departments for the Uzbek, Turkmen, Kyrgyz, Azerbaijani, Armenian, Tatar, Persian, Ukrainian, Jewish and Bukhara Jewish communities.[6] No mention was made of the Tajiks, despite their well-known presence as one of the two or three leading elements in Central Asian society. Even the new TASSR constitution, approved in September 1920, seemed skewed against the Tajiks. As Bartol'd put it "When the Constitution of the Turkestan Republic was confirmed in 1920, only the Kyrgyz, Uzbek and Turkmen were recognised as indigenous peoples. The most ancient of the inhabitants of the region, the Tajiks, were forgotten."[7]

The question arises as to whether the Turkestan government intended that the cultural interests of the Tajik community should be taken care of under the provisions made for the "Persian" community whose existence was mentioned in the statute. Some modern Tajik historians are inclined to treat such a suggestion with derision, pointing out that, by the "Persian" community, Tashkent meant the small group of Persian-speaking Shi'is, most of whom had migrated to Turkestan from Merv in 1785. In that year, the Bukharan Mangit general Ma'sum Khan had attacked the Persian Qajar governor there and laid waste the city by destroying the famous Sultan Band dam on the Murghab river on which the city's agricultural prosperity depended.

A closer examination of the situation suggests that, while exclusive pan-Turkic nationalism may have been the "leitmotif" of social and ethnic politics in the Turkestan ASSR, the exclusion of the Central Asian Sunni Tajiks may have had as much to do with the Sunni Tajiks' own reluctance to associate with the "Persian" or "Ironi" community described above, as with any official desire to sideline the Tajiks. As immigrants and religious outsiders, indeed heretics, the Shi'i "Ironi" community was at the bottom of the social pile and thus a natural recruit to the Bolshevik cause. It was not surprising that it was an Ironi, Sayyid Reza Alizodeh (1887–1938), from the Ironi district of Bogh e Shemol in Samarkand, who started the first Persian language newspaper *Sho'leh ye Enqelob* (*Flame of the Revolution*) in the TASSR on 10 April 1919.

When an instruction arrived from the Communist Party centre in Tashkent in May 1919 ordering the formation of a "Persian Section" of the party, *Sho'leh ye Enqelob* carried a notice on 15 May with the following text:

> The Persian section [shu'beh ye fars], i.e. Ironi, Afghon, Tojik, which has been opened in our centre Tashkent in the Commissariat for National Affairs, has just sent a telegram to the Samarkand Commissariat and proposed the opening of such a section in our government office. Moreover, it recommends the opening of schools, clubs, reading rooms as well as the printing and publishing of literature for the "Fors" and in the Forsi language. In the name of all our Forsi-speaking brothers we express our gratitude from the bottom of our hearts.

The Persian Section was duly founded in July 1919 and its head was Alizodeh.

Neither this section nor the various Ironi institutions that were set up in Samarkand in those years enjoyed much success. There was the "Anjoman e muovenat e ironion" (Society for Assistance to Iranians) and the "Anjoman e donesh e Forsiyon" (Society for the Persians' Knowledge). Neither got off the ground. In "Sho'leh ye Enqelob" for 20 August 1919, Alizodeh complained that his efforts to establish a "Persian nation" on the basis of language had been fruitless. By October of that year, the local Samarkand Party Committee could no longer afford to support the newspaper *Sho'leh ye Enqelob* and it was obliged to close. It had never reached the circulation of 1000 readers required to break even. However, barely had it ceased to appear when it received a new lease of life. In the very same month of November 1919, the Turkommissiya set up by Lenin arrived in Tashkent. As part of their programme to put some life into the revolutionary movement and attract more members to the Party, the Turkkommissiya revived the newspaper.[8]

In its first incarnation, the paper had had very few writers and Alizodeh was obliged to write most of the articles under different names. The second time around, the leading Persian-language writers of the day, who were later to become lynch-pins in the development of the new Tajik linguistic identity, Hoji Mu'in[9] and Sadruddin Ayni[10] both took a very active part. Their work was encouraged by the Turkommmissya that visited the region in 1919/1920 and encouraged bi-lingualism as part of a plan to frustrate the pan-Turkic tendencies that the commission thought it had detected behind the local party's desire to co-opt the local bourgeoisie. However, in true Jadid tradition, these writers were active not only in the Persian but also in the Turki/Chagatai language press of the TASSR. Ayni wrote in both languages for the bi-lingual journal *Kutulush* (Liberation). The revived *Sho'leh ye Enqelob* continued to describe its language as Persian, but, unlike Alizodeh, both Mu'in and Ayni avoided appealing to any imagined "Persian nation" and repeatedly referred to themselves and their readers as "mo Turkestanion" ("we Turkestanis"). Despite this new initiative, the paper's popularity hardly increased. There were, at this time, numerous Turki-language newspapers in comparison with the single *Sho'leh ye Enqelob* in the Persian language. Ayni himself, like Alizodeh before him, complained of lack of interest in the paper and compared this unfavourably with the reaction of the Uzbeks to their papers.[11]

Various reasons have been proposed to explain the indifference of the local Samarkandi Tajik population to the main newspaper in their language. The most likely seems to be that the local Sunni Tajiks simply did not wish to follow the lead given by a despised group of Shi'i Ironi immigrants. It may also be that, as Lutz Rzehak has argued in his excellent study of the phenomenon, the Tajiks did not yet see language as an important part of their identity and were content to regard themselves as "Turkestanis" even if that meant preferring the Turki language which most of their literate members understood as well as Persian.[12] Turkestani nationalism had as much appeal for the Persian speakers in the state as for the Turkic speakers. Ayni even wrote the words for a patriotic "Turan March". Some modern Tajik historians such as Rakhim Masov see the exclusion of Tajiks from the political process as part of an intentional policy developed by pan-Turkic members of the political elite in the TASSR, an expression of the Turkic ascendancy described above. In their view, this elite was determined, with the help of Tatar, Bashkir and other Turkic representatives of the new Soviet regime, and with co-opted Turkish prisoners of war still stuck in the region after the end of the First World War, to create a new Soviet but Turkic state in Central Asia on the ruins of the pre-communist structures. In his classic work on Soviet Turkestan, G. Safarov mentions the leader of the Turkish officers in captivity in the region, Effendiev, who became People's Commissar for Education in the TASSR and had a profound influence on the reforms in that field during his incumbency.[13] Pan-Turkic designs certainly existed in the TASSR. Moscow had belatedly recognised this danger and the dispatch of the newly staffed Turkestan Commission was the Central Committee's answer to it. However, the failure of the policy of bi-lingualism was also due to the lack of solidarity amongst Persian speakers (Sunni Tajiks feeling antagonistic to Shi'i Ironis and Bukhara Jews) and the indifference of the Tajik community to the fact that the new message of Marxism was being propagated in their own language. As long as the Emirate of Bukhara existed, the Persian language retained a stronghold. But that reactionary bastion was soon to be overthrown.

In Bukhara, the question of ethnic identity did not exert much influence on the thinking of the Amir Sayyid Alim Khan, who was struggling to defend his country's independence against what he suspected was an unholy alliance between the Jadid-dominated pan-Turkic movement of Young Bukharans and the Bolsheviks in the TASSR. His fears were well founded. He had witnessed events in neighbouring Khiva. By February 1920, effective power in Khiva had passed from the Khan Sayyid Abdullah to a Turkmen warlord Junaid Khan. Junaid's arbitrary rule had alienated the progressive element in society, led by the reformist Jadid-orientated Young Khivan group. By the end of 1919, the Young Khivans asked the TASSR to intervene. On 22 December, General Frunze, the regional commander of the Red Army, launched a successful attack and drove out Junaid. Sayyid Abdullah Khan abdicated and the People's Republic of Khwarezm was proclaimed. The Amir of Bukhara will also have remembered that, in March 1918, the Tashkent Soviet had attempted to conquer Bukhara using a military force backed by members of the reformist Young Bukharan movement. That attempt had been defeated by the Amir, and the Soviets had been obliged to sign a humiliating treaty recognising the independence of Bukhara and even promising to return to the Emirate territories taken from it by the Tsarist government in the 19th century. This did not mean, however, that the Soviets had abandoned their plans to dispose of him. Intrigues continued with the aim of radicalising Young Bukharans and undermining his government. In September 1920, the Red Army under Frunze invaded. Bukhara fell on 2 September 1920 and the Amir fled into exile in Afghanistan (in the imaginative description of the diplomat and historian Fitzroy Maclean, dropping favourite dancing boy after favourite dancing boy in the hope of distracting his pursuers).[14] As in Khiva, a Bukharan People's Soviet Republic (BNSR) was declared within the old frontiers of the Emirate. These included the mountainous region of East Bukhara, later to form a substantial part of the Tajik Autonomous Soviet Socialist Republic.

In the new Bukhara, established on 20 October 1920, the Tajiks fared if anything worse than in the TASSR, although they constituted the majority of its population. As far as language was concerned, on 2 September 1920, the new government of the People's Republic, led by Faizulla Khojaev, declared Uzbek to be the official language of the state and instituted a conscious campaign to downgrade the Persian language. There was no provision for describing one's self as Tajik in Communist Party or Komsomol (Communist Youth Organisation) documentation. In the People's Commissariat for Education, headed now by Abdulrauf Fitrat, use of the Tajik language was punished by a fine.[15] Paradoxically, Fitrat had been educated in the "Sart" tradition and his knowledge of Persian was at least as good as his Uzbek. Indeed, he was later to find himself one of the scholars chosen to adapt the new Latin alphabet for Tajik. His anti-Tajik policies during this early Soviet period would prejudice Tajik nationalists against his proposals.

Under this sort of pressure, combined with the influence of Jadid reformists, many Tajiks fell into line and went along with the programme of Turkicisation. In order to be able more easily to enter political life, many registered as Uzbeks. Those who did so included leading figures like Ahmadbek Mavlanbekov and Abdulkadyr Muhieddinov, of whom the latter in particular was, as already described, to play a leading role in building Tajikistan – although much later. According to the Tajik historian Rakhim Masov, Stalin himself, in a conversation after the Second World War with B.G. Gafurov, the First Secretary of the Tajik CP, recalled that, in 1924, it had been the Tajiks themselves who had done most to prevent the formation of a separate Tajik union republic. Stalin regarded Abdullah Rahimbaev,[16] Secretary of the Central Committee of the Communist Party of Turkestan, as the most guilty in this regard. In 1924, at the joint congress of the Central Committee of the Communist Party of Turkestan and the Presidium of the Turkestan Central Executive Committee (TsIK), this same Abdullah Rahimbaev, a Tajik, had described the population of Central Asia as Uzbek, Kyrgyz and Turkmen and "various insignificant nationalities".[17] With the Tajiks' potential leaders in thrall to pan-Turkism, there were no voices to speak for a Tajik nation when Moscow took the step that was to determine the shape of Central Asia for the rest of the century and beyond. However, before addressing this step, it may be worth briefly reviewing the uprising which for a while formed the main threat to the survival of Soviet rule in the region.

4

THE ROAD TO SOVIET POWER

THE BASMACHESTVO

As has already been noted, this was a harsh time for the inhabitants of the region. Now the Soviets were to learn that it was one thing to overthrow the old regimes but quite another to establish peace and order. Following the violent destruction of the autonomous government in Kokand in February 1918, they had to contend with growing resistance from the local guerrilla movement known as the Basmachestvo. At its greatest extent this insurgency involved military operations with several thousand men operating all over the Ferghana Valley, throughout the mountains of so-called Eastern Bukhara, as well as in broad areas of Western Bukhara and Khorezm. Scholars disagree as to the reasons for the revolt and the aims of the insurgents. Soviet historians have tended to attribute the uprising to the machinations and support of British interventionists and American capitalists. The Basmachi leaders, such as Ergash, Madamin Beg and Kurshirmat, according to this interpretation, are former criminal elements and bandits.[1] At the other end of the scale, Turkic and Uzbek nationalists such as the academic exile Baymirza Hayit see the uprising more as a manifestation of the growing pan-Turkic consciousness of the Turkestanis.[2] There is also some disagreement as to the origins and commencement of the uprising. Traditionally, the violent suppression of Kokand's autonomous government has been taken as the trigger for the revolt – the moment when the political route to express the nationalist aspirations of the Turkestanis was closed and a violent uprising was all that was left. There is some evidence at least for a sort of connection in that the Kokand Minister for War, Ergash, subsequently became one of the Basmachi commanders. But this could be interpreted the other way around. When the political leaders in Kokand faced a military threat, it was natural that they should turn to a local war-lord/gangster who happened to be available even though he had no political credentials. The importance of Kokand's destruction as a trigger has recently been revised in favour of more practical and economic explanations as to why the Turkestanis, particularly the people of the Ferghana Valley, took up arms.[3] Certainly the failure of the different Basmachi bands to coordinate their tactics, and their ultimate resistance to Enver Pasha's attempt to achieve this (see below), suggest that they were primarily motivated by local aims, often in response to the severe economic situation, and the collapse of the Tsarist administrative structures. No doubt also, resentment at Christian Russian rule had in many minds been compounded by fear of a new atheist regime. For his part, Sayyid Alim Khan hoped that the revolt would lead to his restoration as Amir. But his control over the different Basmachi groups was tenuous to say the least. One thing seems clear. Although some of the Basmachi commanders may have been Tajiks,[4] none of them was fighting for the establishment of a Tajik state. Not only was such an idea far from Basmachi aims, Sayyid Alim Khan himself seems to have been rather hazy as to the "nationality" of those he thought were fighting for his cause. In his manifesto published in 1929 by the anti-Soviet Riga newspaper *Segodnya*, the Amir announced that "Junaid Khan – leader of the Tajiks (sic) – has joined forces with me, and at the head of all is the brave Uzbek Prince (sic) Ibrahim Bek".[5] Ibrahim Bek [Beg] may have been Uzbek (though hardly a prince) but the Turkmen leader Junaid, was certainly not Tajik nor in any sense the leader of that nation. There were virtually no Tajiks in Khiva/Khorezm[5] where his unenlightened rule had earlier hastened the Soviet take-over. Perhaps the Amir simply wanted to give the impression that the Uzbeks were not the only ones who were fighting the Soviets, irrespective of the facts. But a slip of this sort will certainly have raised eyebrows amongst the British intelligence officers sitting in Meshed and observing Junaid's operations on the other side of the frontier.

In September 1919, the Red Army defeated the anti-Soviet Cossack commander Ataman Dutov whose blockade had cut off communications between Moscow and Central Asia. Once these communications were restored, Red Army reinforcements could be dispatched to

Tashkent and more effective operations conducted against the
Basmachi. By 1921, the two main Basmachi commanders in the
Ferghana Valley had surrendered or fled into the mountains. However,
late that year, the Basmachi received a short-lived boost to their
fortunes and more especially their profile, when they were joined by
the former Ottoman Minister for War, Enver Pasha. This charismatic
if flawed character, fleeing his country after the defeat of the Ottoman
forces at the end of the First World War, had made his way via Berlin
to Moscow and offered his services to the new Soviet state, promising
to reconcile the Central Asian rebels to Soviet rule. Moscow responded
by sending him down to Bukhara. Once there, Enver absconded to
join the Basmachi. His reception by Ibrahim Beg, the main Basmachi
commander, was not encouraging. He was arrested and imprisoned.
It took the intercession of Sayyid Alim Khan, by now living in
Afghanistan, to get him released and entrusted with overall command. For eighteen months Enver tried to unite and coordinate the
different warlords under his command. To begin with, he scored some
spectacular successes, even capturing Dushanbe (an achievement
which sounds greater than it was; Dushanbe was at the time little
more than a village). But in due course his pompous and authoritarian
style made him enemies amongst the other local commanders and his
authority began to wane. Enver made great play with the fact that he
had married the Ottoman Sultan's daughter, describing himself in
official despatches as "the son-in-law of the Caliph of Islam". His
character was summed up in the immortal words of Harold Nicholson
who described him as combining the cruelty of a Kurd with the looks
of a Berlin barber.[6] His reputation as a general had suffered severely
after the Ottoman military disaster of Sarikamish in 1914 for which
he was largely responsible – but perhaps the Amir of Bukhara was
unaware of this. In 1922 he was trapped by a Red Army unit near
Kulyab and killed. His death did not end the insurrection, which was
continued by other Basmachi commanders, both Turkish and local.
Enver's Ottoman comrade Salim Pasha fought on for a few more
months, while Ibrahim Beg and others continued the struggle after
Salim Pasha, too, had been killed. Nonetheless, by massively
increasing the strength of their forces, and by occasionally deploying
aircraft imaginatively, the Soviets gradually gained the upper hand,
first in Khiva and then in East Bukhara. One by one the Basmachi
leaders had to abandon the struggle inside the Soviet Union and flee

abroad: Ibrahim Beg in June 1926 to Afghanistan, Junaid Khan in June 1928 to Iran, and Fuzail Makhdum also to Afghanistan in May 1929 after the failure of his final attack on Garm. Both Ibrahim Beg and Junaid continued to mount cross-border operations from Afghanistan and Iran respectively but ceased to be a serious threat to the establishment of Soviet power.

During these turbulent years government in the mountainous regions of the Bukharan People's Soviet Republic (known as "Eastern Bukhara") was in the hands of the "Extraordinary Dictatorial Commission" (all of whose documents incidentally were written in Russian and Uzbek) with draconian powers to deal with the military situation. There was little time seriously to address social reform or consider the position of the Tajik inhabitants of the region.

THE CONSOLIDATION OF SOVIET RULE

The imposition of Soviet rule in the area that was to become Tajikistan proceeded unevenly. An important obstacle to uniform progress was the quite separate administrative status of the western and eastern parts of the region. As a former part of the Ferghana Oblast' of the Governorate-General of Turkestan, the Eastern Pamirs had been absorbed into the latter's successor formation, the TASSR. The political trajectory of the western part had been quite different. Until September 1920 part of the Bukharan Emirate, this territory had been inherited by the People's Soviet Republic of Bukhara. Even here, the demarcation between Russian and Bukharan territory was not straightforward. Officially, Bukhara included the so-called "Western Pamirs" districts of Darvaz, Shughnan and Wakhan. However, as we shall see, in the early years of the 20th century, the several Russian officials working there became incensed at the extremity to which the local population had been reduced by the iniquities of the Amir's rule. Their lobbying was to lead to a de facto Russian annexation of some of these districts.

The Basmachi uprising, which enveloped the whole region, made even military control weak and unreliable. Neither in the Russian – nor in the Bukharan – administered areas, could the development of Party and Soviet organs get properly started, but if anything the situation was worse in Bukhara. In April 1922, when the revolt was in full swing and Enver Pasha's intervention was at its most troubling,

Moscow had prompted the Bukharan republic to establish a so-called Extraordinary Dictatorial Commission of the Bukhara Central Executive Committee. This body had full legislative, financial, executive and judicial powers in Eastern Bukhara, including the right to dissolve the Executive Committees, which were the principal organ of civilian government, and, in their place, to create Revolutionary Committees. It continued to rule the region almost up to the implementation of the NTD and the formation of the Tajik ASSR (TaASSR) in 1924. The development of any parallel Party or Soviet organisations here was complicated by the exceptionally difficult circumstances. Until the NTD, therefore, it was paradoxically to the most inaccessible part of the region, the ex-Russian, now Soviet, Eastern Pamirs, that Tashkent (the capital of the TASSR) decided to pay most attention; first, because the TASSR and its Communist Party were administratively responsible for it; and second, it was thought necessary to pre-empt Basmachi use of this mountainous region by promoting political change there.

The "working paper" on the Tajiks prepared for the NTD (referred to in Chapter 1 of this study) also touched on a consideration which, when the delimitation came, would require the advancement of Tajikistan from the level of Autonomous Oblast', as originally suggested, to Autonomous Soviet Socialist Republic. This was the first step on a ladder that might eventually lead to union republic status, and, many years later, to independence.

Noting the fact that many of the Eastern Iranian peoples living in the Pamirs were Ismailis, whom he described as "one of the most rational of the Muslim sects" (sic: perhaps he saw them as "least fanatical"), the anonymous author of the "working paper" went on to wonder whether, in view of their separateness from the rest of the Muslim mass, they might not be formed into a separate Badakhshan "raion" within the Tajik Autonomous Oblast' (AO). This seemed all the more desirable as these Ismailis were in constant touch with the mass of their co-religionists[7] who lived in the frontier regions of Afghanistan.[8]

The Pamir region, with its spectacular scenery of 7000 metre-high peaks, its strategic location between British India, China and Russia, and its "exotic" mountain peoples with their rare Eastern Iranian languages, had long occupied the imagination of both Russian and British politicians, linguists and anthropologists.

As already indicated, the Eastern and Western Pamirs had followed different historical paths, dictated largely by a quirk of geography which made the eastern part more accessible from the north than from the west. The eastern region, on the high plateau around Murghab[9] was thinly populated by semi-nomadic Kyrgyz and had been annexed to the Khanate of Kokand in 1776 by the then Khan Narbuta Bii. The western part, consisting of the "volost's" (districts) of Rushan, Shughnan, Ishkashim and Wakhan,[10] had been more vulnerable to the depredations of aggressive and greedy neighbours to the west. The last and most vicious of these had been Abdul Rahman Khan, ruler of Afghanistan, who, as already described, twice laid the region waste, in 1883 and again in 1887. After the Anglo-Russian frontier settlement of 1895, both parts had been allocated to Russia. When the Khanate of Kokand was dissolved in 1876, its territory was incorporated into the Turkestan Governorate-General, and thus, after the revolution, into the Ferghana Oblast' of the TASSR. The fate of the Western Pamirs had been less fortunate. Perhaps daunted by its remoteness, but also apparently anxious not to give an example of annexation that the British might want to follow in immediately adjoining territories, the Russians had initially handed its administration to the Emirate of Bukhara. The transfer had also been seen as a consolation prize to the Amir for those territories South of the Pyandzh (Oxus) which he had earlier claimed but which had been handed to Afghanistan as part of the Anglo-Russian frontier agreement. The Amir was not impressed by the offer, indeed he had pressed for the grant of some territory in the Samarkand oblast'. But, when this request was brushed aside, he had ultimately and with bad grace accepted a region that he regarded as poor and unrewarding.[11]

Those in the Tsarist administration of Central Asia who had misgivings about the possible impact of Bukharan misrule on the local population consoled themselves with the thought that there were Russian frontier posts scattered throughout the region and the commander of the Pamir detachment would intervene to stop Bukharan excesses. They were soon to be disabused of such comforting misconceptions. The Amir's Sunni representatives regarded the local Ismailis as heretics and treated them appallingly. This state of affairs was noted with alarm by a series of Russian visitors to the region, including commanders of the local frontier detachment such as Eduard Karlovich Kivekas[12] and A.F. Snesarev during the early years of the 20th century. These views were confirmed in 1904–6 by Baron A.A. Cherkasov who was sent on a fact-finding mission by Lyutsch, the Russian political agent in Bukhara. These observers were not only shocked by the extreme poverty of the local popu-lation but concerned at the impact such a dire state of affairs might have on Russia's reputation as a benevolent ruling power, should details of the situation ever leak out. This seemed quite possible since, as Snesarev noted, large numbers of the Ismailis of the region were fleeing across the frontier into Afghanistan and British-ruled Chitral. Indeed, the Russian political agent in Bukhara reported to the governor-general A.A. Polovtsov that Ismaili ishans (holy men) such as Sho Zoda Lais were spreading pro-British propaganda that highlighted the arbitrary nature of the Amir's rule.[13]

For their part, starting in 1901, the Ismaili population of the Western Pamirs repeatedly sent letters to the authorities in the Turkestan Governorate-General asking to be rescued from the Bukharan begs (local officials).

The pressure generated by the adverse reports from local Tsarist administrators such as Kivekas eventually forced the Governor-General of Turkestan to consider how to rescue the Western Pamiri peoples from the arbitrary rule of the Buhkaran Amir's repre-sentatives.

As a first step, in 1904, the commander of the Pamir Detachment, stationed in Khorog, was given instructions to dismiss the Bukharan Beg Mir Yoldash Bii, whose rule had apparently been particularly oppressive, and to replace him with another official from the Gissar administrative centre located further west. Moreover, he was to keep the new man under close supervision and not allow him to take any decisions without clearing them first with him. The local Ismailis almost immediately felt the consequences of this change. In 1905 for the first time for many decades, they were freely able to send their zakat contribution to the Aga Khan in Bombay. One may wonder whether gaining the right to pay taxes to one's religious leader can be regarded as a popular achievement, especially as, in this case, the tax-collection process was corrupt. At the time, though, it seems to have been regarded as such.

The next Governor-General, Tevyashov's, first move, in January 1905, was to call a meeting of regional experts in Tashkent to discuss the future of the Begstvo (district) of Shughnan. This meeting finally decided on the transfer of Shughnan from Bukharan to "temporary Russian administration". The population of the Pamirs would be free to elect their own "elders" under the watchful eye of the detachment's commander, while the Bukharan representative was to retain a purely symbolic role with the title of "Acting Representative" but in fact functioning simply as a rubber-stamp for the Russian decisions. De jure the frontier remained unchanged. The Russians could claim to the British that the territory still belonged to Bukhara. But de facto the Western Pamirs were annexed. After some debate, on the recommendation of the Russian agent in New Bukhara and the Governor-General, it was agreed that no special permission was required from the Amir but that his tax-collector's office should be informed in a laconic note from the political agent. It is not clear what the Amir thought of this unilateral move but, given his earlier complaints that the region would not bring him much in the way of taxes, the fiscal loss cannot have been that serious.

After the February 1917 revolution, the Khorog garrison had set up a "Shughnan Soldiers' Committee" under a certain T.N. Belov. Perhaps as a cosmetic measure, a leading local notable, Haidar Sho, was elected "Comrade Chairman". By June, the new provisional government in Tashkent created a Pamir Regional Civil Commissariat to replace the Soldiers' Committee. The Commissariat's members included experienced Russian orientalists like I.D. Yagello[14] and I.I. Zarubin.[15] However, as the aim of the re-organisation was to combine civil and military responsibilities in one unit, Lt Colonel Fenin, the then commander of the local Pamir Detachment, was also made a member.

In May 1917 the committee had taken the opportunity offered by the death of the local Bukharan beg Mirza Kasyrmirakhur, to decide "not to appoint any further representatives of the Bukharan government in consequence of the transition to self-government". The decision was not unopposed. The former local administrator, Aziz Khan, tried to summon the Amir to retake control but his letter was intercepted and he was arrested by the Pamir Detachment and exiled.

The October revolution was followed by five chaotic years. On 5 December 1917 there was a joint meeting of the Soldiers' Committee of the Pamir Detachment, the Shughnan Volost' Committee, and the Regional Commissariat. They dissolved the Commissariat of the Provisional Government, and elected a new committee under the

leadership of Haidar Sho and a certain Guminski (first name unknown) the military medical attendant.[16]

In the middle of November 1918, Fenin, who had pretended to
accept Soviet power, seized the detachment's money and arms and,
with a group of like-minded officers and soldiers, fled to India. In the
vacuum left by his defection, a group of revolutionary soldiers and
some officers founded the first Pamir Revolutionary Committee
(Revkom).

By 1921, as they consolidated their position in Central Asia, the
Soviets needed to establish a firmer grip on this remote area, particularly as it was being used as a base by the Basmachi, whose rebellion
was in full swing The Turkestan Committee (Turkkommissiya)
decided in the summer of that year to send a military-political
expedition to the Pamirs to set up regular Soviet organs of power and
to organise the defence of the frontier with Afghanistan. This so-called
"Troika" consisted of a Russian, Tarijan Dyakov,[17] representative of the
"Extraordinary Commission" ("Cheka" – forerunner of the Committee
of State Security or KGB), an Uzbek, Kh. Huseinbaev (representative
of the Communist Party of Turkestan), and Shirinshoh Shohtimur
(representative of the Turkestan Executive Committee i.e. government), himself a Shughnani from the Pamirs.[18] Dyakov's elder brother
Aleksei,[19] a qualified doctor, also accompanied the expedition. It took
them more than a month to make the journey from Tashkent, but,
once there, the "Troika" was able to claim some success in setting up
new governmental structures. Khorog, the local capital, had been
lucky in that the Tsarist officers posted to this wild and romantic spot
had founded a "Russian-Native School" with a boarding annex, where
Shohtimur had himself been a pupil. Using his contacts, Shohtimur
was able to recruit a number of his former school comrades into the
new political and Soviet organs, including the frontier troops. By
October, the "Troika" had finished its work and decided to return to
Tashkent. Shohtimur was left behind to head the new administration.

In view of the volatile situation arising from the Basmachestvo, the
"Troika" had to act fast. It was decided that, in the Eastern Pamirs,
rather than arranging elections, they should appoint Revolutionary
Committees (Revkoms) in each kishlak or aul (village or group of
"yurts") consisting of three members and one candidate member. Each
kishlak revkom would then choose a representative to send up to the
next administrative layer – the volost' revkom. Each volost' revkom

would then choose a representative to send to the raion revkom. In contrast, the situation in the Western Pamirs was deemed stable enough to allow the revkoms to be elected by the people at each level. Meanwhile, the old titles of "mingbashi", "aksakal" and "amin" were abolished.

Theoretically, the Western Pamirs were part of Bukharan territory right up until the 1924 incorporation of the Bukharan People's Soviet Republic into the Uzbek Soviet Socialist Republic (UzSSR) as a result of the NTD.

In 1922, Tarijan Dyakov and Shohtimur proposed to the Turkestan Commission that the eastern and western parts of the Pamirs be united in a single "Pamir Raion" and subordinated to the TASSR. In response, on 15 August 1923 the TASSR presidium created a Pamir Oblast' within the TaASSR.[20] Meanwhile, the Military-Political Troika was officially replaced with a Revolutionary Committee (Revkom) with Shohtimur at its head.

In the same year, it was felt expedient once more to tackle the task of constructing a Soviet administration. This time, the Western Pamirs were judged more suitable than the East to start the process. In each "kishlak" (village) the principle adopted was that one Soviet member would be chosen for every 100 inhabitants, although no Soviet should have less than three members whatever the size of the population. The reforms progressed fast enough for a first Raion Congress of Soviets of the Western Pamirs to be held on 25 July 1922, while a second such Congress was held from 1st to 5th April 1924. However, although the unification of the two parts of the Pamirs into a single oblast' had been approved in August 1923, the security situation had still not settled down sufficiently for Soviets to be introduced uniformly throughout the region. In the Eastern Pamirs the "revkoms" had to be preserved and it was not until 27 May 1923 that a Congress of Soviets was held there.

Writing to the Party's Central Executive Committee (TsIK) in Tashkent that same month, Shohtimur recommended strongly that the military detachment that was stationed in Khorog be reduced in size and that the Russians in it be replaced with locals. The 200-strong force, with their horses placed, he argued, too big an economic burden on the local population. Reading between the lines of Shohtimur's letter, it is clear that he also found it humiliating that the Communist Party and Soviet organs in the region were obliged to rely on the military detachment for financial support. It also rankled that the detachment provided the finance for the local school. He felt this sent the wrong message to the local population as to who was the main source of power in the new government. According to a British intelligence report from the political agent in Gilgit dated 7 June 1927, the "Bolshevik detachment" in Khorog numbered 150, of whom a hundred were Russians and fifty locals. Even four years after it was made, Shohtimur's request does not seem to have borne much fruit, at least as far as reducing the preponderance of Russians was concerned. It must have been clear to the Party in Tashkent that, without the organisational and political support of the detachment, and the stiffening provided by the Russian presence, the newly established Soviets and Revkoms would simply crumble under pressure from the Basmachi. The commander of the detachment was to be an officer of the Chief Political Directorate (GPU).[21] Indeed, in the absence of strong and reliable Party structures, the GPU representatives were destined to play the dominant role in the government of Badakhshan right up to the formation of the Tajik Soviet Socialist Republic in 1929.

5

THE NATIONAL TERRITORIAL
DELIMITATION

In 1924 Moscow decided completely to reorganise Central Asia by dividing it into different Soviet republics on the basis of ethnicity. The reasons for this decision have been the subject of speculation and analysis on numerous occasions. I shall not rehearse the arguments here in detail. However, it may be worth briefly recapping the administrative set-up in Central Asia on the eve of the NTD in 1924. As we have seen, in 1918 the Governorate-General of Turkestan (which since 1898 had included Transcaspia) had been transformed into the Turkestan Autonomous Soviet Socialist Republic (TASSR). The Governorate-General of the Steppe was remodelled as the Kyrgyz Autonomous Soviet Socialist Republic in 1920. Both polities were formally part of the Russian Soviet Federated Socialist Republic (RSFSR). Responsibility for the decision to carry out the NTD in 1924 has usually been attributed to Stalin, the then Commissar for Nationalities. Certainly, Stalin's disenchantment with the existing arrangement is well attested. In June 1923 he had described the People's Soviet Republic of Bukhara as having "nothing popular about it".[1]

Knowing the man as we now do, Stalin's irritation is unsurprising. Moscow had been content to support the Young Bukharans and Young Khivans who were working for reform in the Khanates, since the communist parties there were weak and small. They were to play an indispensible role in setting the scene for Frunze's military attacks and the overthrow of feudal rule. However, once in power, these Jadids came face to face with the social and political realities of their situation. When they came to draft constitutions for the People's Soviet Republics of Bukhara and Khorezm, the concessions they had to make to local conservatism, or perhaps their own "bourgeois" tendencies, were swiftly revealed. In Bukhara, for example, the new republican constitution enshrined the right to private property, guaranteed freedom of speech, writing and assembly and ruled that no laws might be passed that conflicted with Islamic law. Having come to power with Bolshevik backing and the support of the small group of local communists, Young Bukharans such as the president Faizulla Khojaev and his foreign minister the writer Abdulrauf Fitrat, both very much followers of the Jadid tradition, had found themselves increasingly caught between the revolutionary expectations of their communist backers and the reservations of the old elites.

Apart from this disappointingly unrevolutionary trend in Khiva and Bukhara, another reason usually attributed to Stalin for making this decision was anxiety about the growth of pan-Turkish nationalism and about the possibility that the new secular but "bourgeois" revolution of Mustafa Kemal in Turkey might prove a more attractive model for self-consciously Turkic peoples in Central Asia than the Soviet variant. Stalin will have remembered the earlier attempts by Ryskulov and co. to turn the TASSR into an independent Turkic communist state with its own Turkic Communist Party (see above). Abdullah Rahimbayev, later chairman of the Council of People's Commissars of Tajikistan, remarked at a session of the Central Asia Office (Sredazburo)[2] of the Central Committee of the Russian Communist Party[3] on 4 June 1924 that the National Territorial Delimitation was intended to prevent a "Central Asian federation which, it was feared, would lead to the extension of Turkestani intrigues over all of Central Asia as far as Siberia". What subtler way to frustrate the influence of the pan-Turkists than to create new "nationalities", each with its own language, which might indeed be of Turkic origin, but whose differences from Turkish could be emphasised in the linguistic engineering of Soviet philologists?

However instrumental Stalin may have been in taking the final decision, the idea of dividing up the region in this way was not totally new in 1923–4. Already in June 1920, the Turkestan Commission had recommended to the Politburo of the Central Committee of the Russian Communist Party that dividing the region into separate national units would simply help the nationalist bourgeois elements in the population. They advised that a united Turkestan republic be formed. The Politburo was not convinced. Minute 22 of the Politburo

Session of 22 June 1920 with the title "The Inner Organisation of Turkestan" stated:

> It is regarded as necessary to give the national groups of Turkestan the possibility to organise themselves in autonomous republics and their national minorities in municipalities. The Central Executive Committee (TsIK) of Turkestan is to convoke a congress of Soviets of Uzbek, Kyrgyz (i.e. Kazakh) and Turk-men workers finally to decide the question of the organisational forms of their existence. Until the convocation of these congresses a partition of Turkestan into provinces corresponding to their territories and ethnographical composition is to be carried out.

Lenin added his own proposal that a map of Turkestan be drawn up showing divisions into Uzbek, Kyrgyz and Turkmen areas and that the conditions for merging or partitioning these parts be cleared up in detail. Ultimately, the Politburo seems to have had second thoughts, ruling at the end of the session that "the partition of the republic into three parts is not to be decided in advance". The proposal remained a possibility but was not to be hurried.[4]

According to Faizulla Khojaev, the first President of the Revolutionary Committee of the Bukharan Republic, Georgyi Safarov, a member of the Turkestan Commission, had suggested as early as 1921 that the only way to get rid of the ethnic tensions which were endemic in the region was "Sovietisation" through the creation of autonomous republics for the different ethnic groups.[5] These ethnic tensions did not at the time seem to exist in relations between Tajiks and Uzbeks. Where they did exist most strongly was in Khorezm, between the settled Uzbek population and the nomadic Turkmen. It is noteworthy that, at this stage, neither the Turkestan Commission nor, more surprisingly, Lenin, saw fit to mention the Tajik areas.

So, the idea of a new delimitation of Central Asia on ethnic lines had been first mooted in the early 1920s. While the first formal steps towards this goal were not to be taken until 1924, Moscow could see the sense of preparing the ground by tying the nominally independent Bukharan and Khorezm People's Republics more closely to the areas administered by Russia. The republics' economic, and transport systems were integrated into the Russian system in March 1923 with the formation of the Central Asian Economic Council. Agriculture, commerce and planning were also brought into line with the Russian arrangements. Meanwhile, the ground was prepared for a political transformation. The Bukharan Communist Party had been united with the Russian one in February 1922. Thereafter, it was possible to purge the Bukharan party and prompt its remaining leadership to force through draconian legislation barring class enemies from holding office in the government.

On 31 January 1924 the Central Committee of the Russian Communist Party decided to re-examine a proposal for a division of Central Asia on national lines. Ya. E. Rudzutak[6] was charged with studying the matter and producing concrete proposals. By 3 March the Central Committee of the TASSR had approved the idea in principle, while the political establishments in Bukhara and Khorezm followed in short order. The Politburo of the Russian Communist Party approved the proposal on 5 April 1924 and, on its recommendation, in early May 1924, a Special Commission for the National Territorial Delimitation was set up within the Central Asia Office. Within this Special Commission, three sub-committees were established: Uzbek, Kyrgyz (i.e. Kazakh) and Turkmen. In addition, should they wish to set up a sub-committee to discuss the question of their own national delimitation, the Tajiks were invited to entrust Abdullah Rahimbaev, the head of the Uzbek sub-committee, with this task. Another Tajik, Chinor Imomov[7] was appointed to supervise the delimitation of a Tajik autonomous oblast'.

By 10 May the Special Commission for the NTD had decided on its recommendations: to conduct, on the basis of ethnic identity, a delimitation of the Central Asian republics.[8] At the time, these were: the TASSR, and the People's Soviet Republics of Khorezm and Bukhara. No doubt mindful of Stalin's guidelines, the commission was at pains to stress that the new dispensation should not be imposed in such a way as to form any sort of federation of the newly-formed units. These should be: an Uzbek and a Turkmen Soviet Socialist Republic each with the right of immediate entry into the USSR, a Tajik Autonomous Oblast' within Uzbekistan and a Kara-Kyrgyz (i.e. Kyrgyz) Autonomous Oblast' within the Russian Soviet Federative Socialist Republic (RSFSR).

The subsequent and definitive meeting of 28 May 1924 unanimously approved the decision to create, within the UzSSR, a Tajik

Autonomous Oblast' (AO) and to form a Tajik Communist Party within the Uzbek Party with the status of an Oblast' Party Organisation. It was confirmed that the Tajiks, in the shape of Imomov, would be invited to join in a commission to define the frontiers of their new AO. It was also decided to retain the economic arrangements in place until the end of the financial year in October so as not to cause confusion. In its final form, the relevant part of the Uzbek sub-commission's text ran as follows:

> "To create, within the structure of the Uzbek republic, a Tajik Autonomous Oblast' out of the mountainous part of Bukhara, Guzar, Kulyab, Matchi and other regions".

NTD. THE METHODOLOGY

As later efforts to divide up the region on equitable ethnic lines were to confirm, the sheer presence of a majority of one or the other nationality in a given area was not the only, or indeed the prime, factor that needed to be taken into account when deciding to which republic it should be allotted. As Krasnovskii of the Commission for the "Raionirovaniye" (redrawing of local administrative boundaries) of Turkestan reported, a number of factors influenced the thinking of those responsible when deciding how to form administrative units:

> "Raions" need a big centre from which it is easy to reach all parts of the "raion". They should also, where possible, enjoy a degree of self-sufficiency. The biggest agricultural factor is water, which is also the most frequent cause of inter-community disputes. The parts of each "raion" should be united by use of a common water resource and should ideally not have to share it with a neigh-bouring "raion". Unfortunately, "aryks" [underground irrigation channels] are often long. "Raions" cannot all be long and thin, so it is not often possible to implement this requirement, how-ever desirable.
>
> Secondly, "raions" should be oriented towards a particular bazaar town, which will secure their requirements and take their produce. In densely populated areas like Ferghana there will be more than one city competing for the loyalty of a particular "raion".
>
> Thirdly, there is the ethnic factor.

In practice, the larger the unit the greater will be the influence of the economic factors, whereas the ethnic factor will be in inverse proportion to the size of the unit. In other words, it is easy to make ethnically homogeneous volosti but less easy to satisfy the ethnic aspirations of oblasti which may find themselves attached to republics they don't like.[9]

The committee responsible for carrying out the NTD faced formidable tasks. These tasks replicated many of those experienced by the British in the censuses they carried out in Malaya in the late 19th and early 20th centuries, the nation-building purpose of which had been rather similar.[10] As we have seen, the concept of national identity was not uniformly well developed amongst the local population. The vague "Sart" identity, included in the 1897 census, was not yet totally abandoned. There were numerous Turkic communities who identified themselves by their clan names rather than as Uzbeks, Kazakhs or Kyrgyz. The term Uzbek had until then mainly been used to denote those Uzbek speakers still living a nomadic or semi-nomadic life. Many Tajiks, whether for reasons of self-advancement, a lack of a developed sense of national identity, or under various other pressures, thought it expedient to identify themselves as Uzbeks. The Soviet authorities themselves were not always clear what they were looking for. Until the mid-1920s, the people later to be known as Kazakhs were called Kyrgyz and the Kyrgyz, Kara-Kyrgyz. All this was made no easier by the lack of any reliable census statistics to show exactly which nationalities predominated in which areas. As we have already noted, in the mid-19th century, limited and somewhat amateurish censuses had been attempted by visiting Russian scholars. Both D.N. Sobolev and I. Vivorskii published statistical information on the Zeravshan Okrug in 1874 and 1876 respectively. But this information only gave numbers of households rather than population statistics. The Tsarist government had conducted a census of the Governorate-General of Turkestan in 1897. However, this census did not cover the then autonomous Emirate of Bukhara nor the Khanate of Khiva, the territory of both of whose successor states was now to be included in the 1924 NTD.

Before 1924, the best censuses had been those of 1917 and 1920 carried out in the area of the Governorate-General and its successor the TASSR, but the 1917 count did not specify ethnic affiliations.[11] Like the previous 1897 census, these censuses were not exhaustive even in

Russian-ruled Central Asia (in Samarkand Oblast' only Kattakurgan was properly covered), and anyway failed to cover Khiva (by 1924 renamed Khorezm) or the Bukharan People's Soviet Republic. In Bukhara, a census had been attempted in 1913 and revised again in 1917 but was very patchy. I.A. Zelenskii (1890–1938),[12] the then head of the Central Asia Office (Sredazburo), admitted in 1924 that there were no reliable data concerning the ethnic composition of the population of Bukhara. Last but not least, a limited demographic census had been carried out by the military in 1913. In 1923–24, in the run-up to the NTD, the Central Asian Economic Council had conducted a census of all those involved in the economy of the region but this only completed its work in 1925, after the delimitation was over. The first comprehensive census of the whole region was only carried out by the Soviet government in 1926 –well after the NTD. As we shall see, this 1926 census was to become a serious bone of contention between Uzbeks and Tajiks once it was decided to upgrade Tajikistan from Autonomous to Union Republic status.

NTD. THE TAJIK POSITION

Aware of the potential difficulties, those responsible for the NTD commissioned the "working paper" on the Tajiks, to serve as the basis for their consideration of Tajikistan's future as an Autonomous Oblast'.[13] On the basis of the available information, this study (the author is anonymous) identified the main concentrations of Tajiks as Samarkand, Bukhara and Khojand.

In the Samarkand Oblast' the study reckoned the Tajiks to be the second most numerous group after the Uzbeks, although it was unable to decide on their exact percentage, putting it at 29.6% of the population (234,500) on one occasion and 33% in another (with only 24% living in the countryside). They tended, the study said, to live in large towns, and were found in large concentrations in Samarkand, Ura Teppe, Khojand and Panjikent, where they formed the majority of the population. In the Khojand Uezd (then still part of the Samarkand Oblast') the Tajiks formed 56% of the population (including the towns), also forming the most numerous group in the countryside (43% of the population).

In the Ferghana Oblast' the Tajiks were mainly concentrated in the Kokand and, to a lesser extent, the Namangan Uezds, but were not as

numerous as those in the Samarkand Oblast'. In the towns there were
only 20,000 of them, but in the rural areas about 167,500. This figure
included the Pamir Tajiks (Ghalchas) who were once more seen to
differ from their brothers of the plains in language, way of life,
religion and physical type.

The study went on to remark that the remaining mass of Tajiks
lived in Bukhara and mainly in the mountain region of Eastern
Bukhara at that; i.e. in the former Begstvos of Darvaz, Karategin,
Gissar, Baljuvan, Kulyab and parts of Kabadian. However, Tajiks were
also present in considerable numbers in Western Bukhara also, e.g. in
the former Karategin and especially in the Old Bukhara Begstvos. The
Bukharan census of 1913 had put the number of Tajiks in the Emirate
at 390,000, but the report reckoned that number was unreliable,
preferring the larger estimate published in extract form by the
Turkestan Economic Commission (TEK) in its Compendium
(Sbornik) of the "Central Asian Economic Raion". This was based on
military-statistical records, which estimated the Tajik population at
802,632 in all Bukhara.

Working on these data, the total figure for Tajiks in the two
relevant republics of Central Asia (Turkestan and Bukhara) was
estimated at around 1,240,000. In Khorezm there were no Tajiks.

The same problems haunted those managing the NTD as had
concerned the designers of the earlier "Raionirovaniye" described
above. Often specifically Tajik areas might be connected to established
irrigation networks in an Uzbek area. At others, the position of high
mountain ranges separating Tajik-settled areas from the rest of
Tajikistan argued in favour of connecting those areas to the Uzbek
zone, despite their ethnic make-up.

In the Samarkand Oblast' the Tajiks accounted for all the population
of the three volost's in the upper reaches of the Zeravshan: Iskandarov,
Falgar and Kshtut. The first two were linked to Eastern Bukhara by
historic and economic factors and were connected to it by what were,
by mountain standards, relatively easy and short communication routes.
On the other hand the Kshtut Volost' was more closely linked to the
Zeravshan Valley and could be joined to a Tajik AO only at some
economic cost to its inhabitants. The mountainous volost of Magia-
Isfara and the valley region of Avtoburin were in a way similar to the
Kshtut Oblast', gravitating as they did to the Uzbek parts of the
Samarkand Oblast' although their population was overwhelmingly

Tajik. As for the suburban districts of the Tajik volost's of Hoja Akhran, Makhalin and Sob, they were inextricably tied to Samarkand, which was (still) the dominant centre of the Uzbek republic, and could therefore in no circumstances be separated from it.

In the Matchin Volost' Tajiks formed the bulk of the population of Unjin and Ura Teppe and were in a majority in three others: Basmandin, Dalyan and Kostakov. In the others, they took second place after the Uzbeks with whom they lived completely intermingled. With the exception of Matchin itself, all the other areas inhabited by Tajiks were cut off from East Bukhara (i.e. the mountainous area of today's Tajikistan), indeed they were closely linked to the Uzbek-dominated Oblast's of Ferghana and Southeast Syr Darya.

Tajik oases like Sokh, Isfara, Kanibadam and mountainous localities in the northwest Ferghana Valley, the basins of the middle reaches of the Kassan river and the smaller streams from the outlying parts of the Chatkal range were in a rather similar situation. There, large Tajik centres and market towns were just as big as other towns in Turkestan and, moreover, were surrounded by an almost solid Tajik rural population. However, the study argued, even such solidly Tajik towns could not at present be attached to the Tajik AO since they were too isolated from it and too deeply buried in Uzbek territory with which they formed a single economic unit. The local Ferghana Tajiks were so used to relying on the large urban centres of Kokand and Namangan, which were inhabited mainly by Uzbeks, that it would be premature to tear them away from these centres in the name of ethnic self-determination and unite them with distant and unfamiliar Eastern Bukhara.

On the basis of all the information gathered, the study concluded that, of the territories inhabited by Tajiks, the only areas which could be formed into a Tajik Oblast' were:

from the Bukharan People's Soviet Republic.

— the solid area of East Bukhara.

from within the TASSR:

— the adjoining mountainous areas of the Samarkand uezd: Iskanderov, Falgar, Matchin;

- Western Pamir, Ravshan, Oroshov, Shughnan, Ishkeshim, Wakhan (which had been provisionally under Russian administration although legally part of Bukhara);

- the Eastern Pamirs, which had been part of Turkestan's Ferghana Oblast'.

All these places were inhabited by a Tajik population, which was uniform in its composition and occupation. They were also linked together by mountain routes which were shorter than those that led to the settled Uzbek regions of Samarkand and Bukhara Oblast's or to Ferghana.

The paper concluded with a resounding message;

The offer of autonomy to this Oblast' is especially significant, since no nation in the world has been subjected to such a long and heavy oppression as has the mountain-Tajik nation. Driven by the victorious Turks into the inaccessible mountainous ravines, they were forced to lead a half-starved existence, to suffer a shortage of land and to struggle against the exceptionally harsh climate. Scattered into small groups, they were permanently victims of unjust and tyrannical khans usually of non-Tajik origins. Although part of one of the most cultured nations in Asia, the possessors of a centuries-old culture and rich literature, they themselves were exceptionally ignorant. Even amongst the men, literacy was a rarity, while the women are almost universally illiterate. The national liberation of the mountain Tajiks will give a significant boost to their cultural level. At the same time the Tajik Autonomous Oblast' will be the first Iranian Soviet state in Central Asia on the frontiers of Afghanistan and India.

It is clear that the author of this paper felt considerable sympathy for the Tajik nation and had a certain conscience about the fact that the NTD was likely to leave hundreds of thousands of Tajiks within the frontiers of Uzbekistan. He reassured himself with the thought that this represented no threat to the Tajiks since they lived together with the Uzbeks in peace and harmony, sharing the same economic way of life, tilling the land and using the same water supplies. It was also reassuring that the Tajiks who remained outside the frontiers of the new Autonomous Oblast' could serve as a reservoir of trained cadres who could work to educate their kinsmen in the mountains and contribute to the development of the new Tajik homeland.

The paper also reveals something of the political motivation behind the creation of the new statelet. A strongly unified and culturally developed Tajik Autonomous Oblast' could serve as a centre of attraction and target for emulation by the neighbouring Afghan Tajiks whose numbers were variously estimated to be about a million. (See Appendix A for the frontiers of the Tajik Autonomous Oblast' and Appendix B for how the different districts of the previous state formations were allocated to Tajikistan).

NTD. DISPUTED ALLOCATIONS

At the 28 May meeting of the Central Asia Office (Sredazburo)'s Special Commission, violent arguments had broken out around the future position of Tashkent, which, though a predominantly Uzbek (or at least "Sart") city, was surrounded by land where the dominant ethnic group were the Kazakhs, who claimed not only the city for their new republic but also the Hungry Steppe to the south, even as far as Baisun, which was later to become a bone of contention between the Uzbeks and the Tajiks. Faizulla Khojaev, who had gone to Moscow in June for the 13th Congress of the Communist Party, had claimed on return that the various squabbles about the NTD had been resolved. Amongst the questions which had been raised had been: "given that the main cultural and administrative centre in the region is Tashkent, to which republic should it be allocated?" Moscow had decided in favour of Uzbekistan.

During this dispute, the Uzbek delegates like Islamov argued that, although the capital of Uzbekistan was currently Samarkand, it was clear that this was a temporary arrangement and before too long Uzbekistan would require Tashkent as its natural capital. At one stage, Faizulla Khojaev intervened to shut Islamov up, indicating that this subject could be embarrassing. In later years, some Tajik historians were to take this intervention as proof that the Uzbeks had only chosen Samarkand as their capital as a ploy in order to strengthen their arguments against Tajik claims to it.

At this early stage in the delimitation, by comparison with the temperature of Uzbek/Kazakh arguments, relations between the Uzbeks and Tajiks were harmonious. Abdulkadyr Muhieddinov was present throughout the sessions and never seems to have spoken for the Tajiks. The only person to intervene on their behalf was Usmankhan Ishanhojaev[14] who said, "with regard to the Tajik Autonomous Oblast', I want to point out that no Tajik has participated in the commission and there has not been a Tajik sub-commission". To this the Chairman O. Karklin replied "I can give the reference: in our first meeting, our commission appointed three sub-commissions and the Uzbek one was to enrol Tajiks to work in it." At this, one of the Uzbek delegates, Hamutjanov, intervened to say: "When we discussed this matter in Samarkand, it was resolved unanimously." This was enough for Karklin who then moved on to discuss the Party Centre.

We have seen how tensions arose over Tashkent between Uzbeks and Kazakhs. There were disputes with other Turkic neighbours. In April 1924 in connection with the separation of an autonomous Turkmen oblast' in Charju'i (Leninsk), the Soviet plenipotentiary representative in Bukhara reported to Karklin that Turkmen and Kyrgyz workers were "once more" reproaching the basic circle of figures among the Bukhara Uzbeks of "great power chauvinism".[15]

Rows over the NTD were the subject of another letter dated August, this time more reassuring, written by O. Karklin to Stalin and Rudzutak (then head of the Central Asia Office) after his return from a visit to Bukhara and Khorezm:

I returned a few days ago from Bukhara and Khorezm. In Bukhara the questions related to the NTD are moving ahead more smoothly than anywhere else. I spoke to numerous (Party) workers – both local and European – and could not identify a single case where this question took a disorganised turn – discontent or frictions or the like. Before I left for Bukhara, I had been informed that ordinary Party work in Bukhara and the course of life in general had gone off the rails, but this turned out not to be true at all. My impressions are shared by the responsible instructor of the Central Committee of the Russian Communist Party (Bolsheviks) Comrade Ibragimov who had just been observing the Bukhara party organisation both in the city and in the countryside. You had for example heard that

Bukharan merchants were planning to up sticks and move to Samarkand, having heard that the capital was to move there. These rumours are unfounded. Nothing of the sort was mentioned and anyway the question of the capital isn't yet solved. [16]

Despite Karklin's reassuring tone, rows continued. On 2 September 1924, he wrote again to Stalin and Rudzutak, describing in detail not only the tensions between Uzbeks and Kyrgyz (Kazakhs) over Tashkent. Disagreements also began between Uzbeks and Tajiks about what sort of state they should be aiming for. Faizulla Khojaev had used a friend called Sa'id Ahrari[17] to write an article for the journal *Yunye Lenintsy* (*Young Leninists*) the drift of which was "Uzbekistan is for the Uzbeks. There should only be Uzbek communists there." In response, Abbas Aliev, the Bukharan communist[18] was induced to write a counter-blast in another paper *Ozod Bukhoro* (*Free Bukhara*).[19] Faizulla Khojaev, who combined both Turkic- and Persian- language knowledge in true "Sart" tradition, was already showing his true colours as an Uzbek nationalist.

Working at great speed, the commissions completed the bulk of the work of drawing the frontiers of the new states by September. On 19th of that month, the Vth All-Bukharan Congress of Soviets first declared Bukhara to be a "Socialist" (as well as People's Soviet) republic, and having formally prepared the way in this manner, accepted the NTD the following day. On 14 October, the 2nd Session of the All-Russian Central Executive Committee (XIth Convocation) accepted the recommendation of the Central Executive Committee of the TASSR concerning the NTD but introduced an important change: the Tajiks were offered the right to set up, not an Autonomous Oblast', but an Autonomous Soviet Socialist Republic, thus formally preparing the way to incorporate a Gornyi-Badakhshan Autonomous Oblast' into its structure as predicted by the author of the working paper. The thinking that led to this decision is discussed below.

As a note from the proceedings of the Territorial Commission for 21 August 1924 shows, although relatively peaceful, the process of dividing up the region between Uzbeks and Tajiks had not been simple. The fact that both communities were intermingled made the job of separating them well nigh impossible. Abdulrahim Khojibaev, the senior Tajik delegate, admitted that in Western Bukhara it would

not be possible to unite them with their compatriots living in the
Tajik Autonomous Oblast', while Imomov agreed that, "unfortunately, given Tajikistan's and Bukhara's geographical lay-out it is not
possible to unite all Tajiks in a single ?whole' unit. Even in the
mountain valleys they're all mixed up with the Uzbeks." The commission accepted in principle the 1913-based assessment of the Tajik
population at around 1,200,000, but reckoned that figure had since
probably been reduced by 40 to 45% because of the mass emigration
to Afghanistan occasioned by the Basmachestvo. All agreed that the
NTD would leave a large proportion of the Tajiks outside the Tajik
AO. S. Khojanov[20]complained that this could hardly be called self-
determination and he could not understand why the Tajiks had not
insisted on pushing their western frontier further south to include
Samarkand and the fertile lands around it. In his words "the Tajik
comrades may be satisfied but I'm not". The chairman of the
commission (I.A. Zelenskii) admitted that he was also having doubts
and wondered whether they should not look again at the whole
question. Alarmed, Islamov, the Uzbek delegate, reproved Khojanov
for being "more Tajik than the Tajiks" with whom the Uzbeks had
already agreed the frontier.[21]

The "fine tuning" of the frontiers and allocations made in 1924
continued for several years with the areas fringing the Ferghana Valley
proving the most disputed. Here pockets of settlement often found
themselves dependent for water and supplies on areas or towns
inhabited by a different ethnic group. It made no economic sense to
separate them. Sometimes the disputes could involve three parties. A
serious row between the Uzbeks and the Kyrgyz centred around the
overwhelmingly Tajik-inhabited enclaves of Uch Kurgan and Sokh. In
late 1926 a Parity Commission was set up under the chairmanship of a
certain Kul'besherov to adjudicate. The arguments deployed on both
sides were interesting when one considers the future relationship
between Uzbekistan and Tajikistan. The Uzbek representative
(Alihojaev) maintained that the population was 90% Tajik and, as
there was no discernible difference between Tajiks and Uzbeks, the
two nationalities should be considered as one united Uzbek one and
the volost' allotted accordingly. The commission disagreed. It
recognised that the majority of the population were Tajiks but argued
that, since they received next to no cultural support from the UzSSR
(interesting that this was already obvious), they might as well be part

of the Kyrgyz ASSR within the RSFSR. Likewise, although the Tajiks and Uzbeks were similar in their way of life, their languages were as different from one another as Tajik was from Kyrgyz. So, the Tajiks might as well be in the Kyrgyz ASSR. At the time, the population was 96.1% Tajik, 3.8% Kyrgyz and 0.1% Uzbek.[22]

One such debate, which was to become important in later years, was the question of Khojand. Asked by the chairman why the Tajiks from Khojand had not been included (in the new TaASSR), Khojibaev agreed that the population of Kanibadam, Asht, Sokh, all "raions" of the Chust-Fergana Oblast', was 100% Tajik. However, this time round, both sides had had to content themselves with allocating Khojand to Uzbekistan as a Tajik "national okrug" based on ethnic criteria, on the grounds that it was unacceptably distant and inaccessible from the Tajik central heartland in Eastern Bukhara.[23] The same argument applied to the Zeravshan Oblast', which had been reorganised to include Bukhara city. Tajiks amounted to 95% there too. But they were separated from Eastern Bukhara by a great distance and uniting them with the new TaSSR would be inconvenient.

Another example of the complications that arose for those trying to divide up the region on ethnic lines was the implementation of the Central Asia Office's 1927 directive that, following the allocation of both "viloyats" (provinces) to Tajikistan, Ura Teppe and Panjikent should be united in one new okrug. This decision, which was designed to save money by rationalising their administration, caused much dismay, especially among the inhabitants of Panjikent, who had traditionally received all their supplies from Samarkand, just down the Zeravshan river. One dares to imagine that the ethnic factor hardly loomed large with the local Tajiks, especially remembering that the population of the then Uzbek capital was largely Tajik anyway, when weighed against the inconvenience of having to struggle to Ura Teppe over an extremely high mountain pass, which was usually closed in winter. Aleksei Dyakov's refutation of the locals' arguments showed how artificial the whole NTD could be. It was true, he said, that there were no existing economic links with Ura Teppe but then there weren't any with Dushanbe either. He also argued that in fact the communications between the two towns were quite good, as those involved could travel between the two using the Soviet railway system via Samarkand. And, just in case anyone felt inclined to use these arguments to ask why the two towns should be included in Tajikistan when life would be so much simpler if they were in Uzbekistan, Dyakov replied that these arguments were unacceptable since the reasons for their inclusion in Tajikistan were "political".[24]

In fact, outside the borders of the TaSSR, some districts in the Ferghana Valley with majority Tajik populations seem to have been granted a measure of autonomy long before Khojand was detached from Uzbekistan or even before it was granted "national okrug" status in 1927. The first to benefit in this way were Kanibadam and Isfara, following a visit by the Soviet Head of State, Kalinin, in 1924. According to a letter written by the orientalist M.S. Andreev to Bartol'd in 1925, the inhabitants of these two areas had woken up to the fact that they were Tajiks and were demanding that all official correspondence should be in Tajik. By then they were about to celebrate the first anniversary of their autonomy and Andreev expected the Tajiks of other Ferghana Valley centres to join them in this.[25]

Yet another commission including Sanjar Asfendiarov[26], but under Beliyarov's chairmanship, was set up on 25 May 1926 to continue work started by the "Petrovski Commission", which had studied the territory around Osh. Its mission was to adjudicate the Uzbek claim to the city and its surroundings, which was based on the fact that 97% of the population of both town and oblast' was Uzbek. Ultimately the claim was rejected on the grounds that Osh was an important economic centre for the Kyrgyz living in the region.

So the Uzbeks did not always win.

6

THE NEW TAJIK ASSR –
ADMINISTRATIVE PROBLEMS

The decisions and delimitations of 1924 may have established the new TaASSR on paper. In practice there was still a long way to go before the new government could function at all normally. As important as, indeed in most senses more important than, the establishment of Soviet governmental structures, was the need to set up a Communist Party apparatus in the new ASSR. As a mere autonomous republic within the UzSSR, Tajikistan did not rate a republican Party organisation of its own. The Party there was ranked as an Oblast'-level Party subordinate to the Uzbek Party. The Pamirs' unusual status again called for special arrangements. Because of the remote and unstable position of the Oblast', until the summer of 1924, all Party activity was conducted by the Pamir Frontier Detachment in Khorog and all Party members were listed on the books of the military Party cells. In August of that year, the Central Committee of the Turkestan Communist Party agreed the establishment of "The Pamir Okrug Party Bureau" under its control. With the foundation of the Mountainous Badakhshan Autonomous Oblast' (Gornyi-Badakhshanskaya Avtonomnaya Oblast' – GBAO) in 1924, after one failed attempt in 1925, Tashkent finally appointed the membership of a new Oblast' Party Bureau in October 1926. M.K. Dudnik was the local secretary. But progress was slow, the region remote and membership extremely small. A fully fledged Oblast' Party Committee was not to be approved until 1930.[1]

On 28 May 1924, the Bukhara government had dissolved the Extraordinary Dictatorial Commission and transferred its authority to the Revolutionary Military Council of the 13th Army Corps.[2] However, after the foundation of the TaASSR, in October 1924, civil power was immediately re-invested in a Revolutionary Committee (Revkom), which enjoyed similar powers to the Dictatorial Commission – the reason being given as the continuing unstable situation especially in the south of the country where Basmachi bands were still operating. Four months later, in February 1925, the Revkom moved from its previous base in Tashkent to the new Tajik capital Dushanbe.

By October 1925, sufficient stability had been restored for Moscow to announce that the Basmachestvo had been defeated and that new Soviet government structures would be put in place. After the devastation of nine years of revolution and civil war, the work of rebuilding the country and developing the economy had to begin. The Tajik Revkom remained the supreme governmental organ in the ASSR until December 1926, when it handed its authority over to the Central Executive Committee, newly elected by the First All-Tajik Constituent Assembly of Soviets meeting in Dushanbe. Looking ahead, the Assembly instructed the Executive Committee to draft a new constitution for the republic. In its first session, the Executive Committee set up the new Presidium of Soviets, with Nusratulla Maksum[3] as chairman. It also appointed a new Soviet of People's Commissars (ministers) to succeed those appointed by the Revkom in early 1925. One can gain an interesting albeit anachronistic picture of the elite that made up the government of the new autonomous republic from the list of 27 names who signed the "evidential note" protesting over Uzbek treatment of the TaASSR and asking for the separation of the two republics (see below and see also Appendix C for list of names of the signatories). No date is given for this unusual and bold protest, which became notorious in early Soviet Tajik history, but it was probably drafted some time in 1928.

While the foundations were being laid for the creation of Soviet government structures throughout Tajikistan, the political development of Mountainous Badakhshan (GBAO) had as usual been following a slightly independent path. The original "working paper" on the Tajiks (see above) had suggested that the preponderance of Ismailis in Badakhshan might be a reason for granting the region special status within whatever state structure was eventually agreed for the Tajiks. This proposal seems to have been elaborated into the idea of an autonomous oblast'.

Official accounts describe how, on 5 October 1924, the inhabitants of the Pamirs used the Tajik Sub-commission (of the NTD commission) to send a request to the Central Committee of the Communist Party in Moscow that the Pamirs, which had been part of Russia since 1893 (sic), be united with the Tajik ASSR that was about to be formed. This request is said to have been supported by Chicherin,[4] who was well informed about the Pamirs. Given the top-down nature of Communist Party decision-taking, it is much more likely that this request was stimulated from on high to create the impression that the decision to unite the Pamirs with the new TaASSR was in response to the will of the "toiling masses". Whatever the truth, the idea of autonomy for the Pamirs had profound significance for Tajikistan as a whole. As Kalandarov puts it, "There is a suggestion that the submission of such a request became one of the reasons for the formation of the Tajik ASSR instead of a (mere) Tajik Autonomous Oblast', since two autonomous oblasts could not be contained within the structure of one autonomous formation."[5] Only six days later, on 11 October 1924, the Central Committee set up a special commission under Kuibyshev,[6] Rudzutak and Chicherin "to discuss the question of the Pamir and to form an Autonomous Republic of Tajiks within the Uzbek Republic". The decision of the Central Committee of the USSR of 2 January 1925 brought final confirmation of this.

Tajikistan presented uniquely difficult problems for those trying to construct a new government and Party apparatus there. Apart from the geographical and climatic challenges that beset the country, the exactions of Bukharan misrule and the devastation caused by civil war had reduced the population to penury. Local landowners, usually referred to in Soviet documents as "beys", and religious leaders, whether Sunni or Ismaili, retained near absolute influence and authority over an intensely conservative, indeed apathetic populace. Large numbers of refugees had fled to Afghanistan to escape the Basmachestvo. What was left of the economy was still overwhelmingly pastoral and agricultural – and even here it must be remembered that less than 5% of its territory was cultivable. There was no industry. Educational and health facilities were almost totally absent. Against this background, recruitment of Party and government cadres with anything approaching the right social and educational background was exceptionally difficult. The lack of acceptable living conditions also made it very hard to attract cadres from outside – even from otherwise dedicated Party workers.

Activists from outside the new republic were reluctant to face a posting to what was regarded as the back of beyond, and, if they went, did their best to ensure that their posting was as short as possible. By 1925 it was clear that whatever they themselves might feel, Party activists had to be made to stay in Tajikistan for more than one year. The then military commander of the Pamir Detachment, K.M. Gerasimov, wrote to the Orgburo of the Uzbek CP in the TaASSR asking that it should be made clear to activists that they were to stay for two years.[7]

Once there, the lack of comforts often drove people to drink. During the 1926 census, stories abounded of the Uzbek census authorities threatening to deport people to Tajikistan if they did not register as Uzbeks. Clearly Tajikistan had the reputation of a "hardship posting" even for Tajik speakers. Time and time again, Party leaders in Tajikistan complained to their superiors in the Uzbek Communist Party in Tashkent (its HQ was in Tashkent, although Samarkand remained the official capital until 1929) or direct to Moscow, that those posted by the party from outside Tajikistan were of poor quality. As late as 1928, Gotfrid, the Director of the Organisation Office (Orgburo) of the Party's Provincial Committee in Tajikistan,[8] complained to Zelenskii (1st Party Secretary of the Central Asia Office), Gikalo and Kirkizh,[9] that the Tajik Provincial Committee paid 600–800 Roubles for each Party worker only to find that they had to expel them for being picked up drunk or put in gaol.[10] Later on the same year, at the 2nd Plenum of the Provincial Committee, complaints were heard that most of the party workers sent from outside had been very bad —mischief-makers and drinkers. Even the staff of the committee, who had been chosen at the previous Plenum, turned out to be 23% "defective". Three had been expelled from the Party for a range of crimes, as well as for anti-communist or even anti-Soviet activity.[11]

An extreme example of the type of Party worker sent in from outside and the situation he found in Tajikistan, in this case in Garm, came to light when the Party intercepted a letter written by a certain Osin ((first name unknown) to a friend in the Ural region. Osin had been banished to Garm as punishment for staging a drunken orgy with a couple of Russian nurses in Samarkand. On arrival in Garm, he did not find the locals particularly receptive to the Party's message. One of his first tasks was to organise a meeting of local worthies and preach the benefits of the Soviet regime. As he wrote in his letter, when he started his speech with the rhetorical question "surely at least the Soviet regime is better than that of the Amir of Bukhara", the audience responded with "a deep silence".[12] As the Responsible Secretary of the Organisation Office of the Uzbek party, B.V. Tolpygo[13] and the deputy chairman Aleksei M. Dyakov said in a letter to the Central Asia Office, the Uzbek party was only prepared to send to Tajikistan those members it wanted to get rid of. Even the most dedicated tended to look on a posting to Tajikistan as the equivalent of exile.[14]

If attracting good Party and government workers from outside was a problem, finding suitable candidates inside Tajikistan was even harder. The local Party organisation pointed out that, in a country without an industrial proletariat, it was virtually impossible to find candidates for Party membership from the right proletarian background. In 1926, the Party had only been able to find eighty-one Tajik factory workers in the whole Uzbek SSR as opposed to 7684 Uzbeks of that social category.[15] In the absence of a clearly identifiable industrial working class, the Party divided the society it found into different categories of impoverishment to use as a rough yardstick for assessing people's suitability for Party membership and jobs in the government. The poorest peasants were classified as "bednyak"s, the richer as "serednyaks". Anyone richer than that was a "bey" and automatically unsuitable for recruitment (although as we shall see, the filter system often failed). At the lowest level came a category of "batrak"s, or casual hired labourers. These were the social reservoirs from which the Party aimed to draw its workers. Such people might be useful as raw recruits for basic Party work but, without further training, not for more responsible jobs.

The Provincial Committee in Tajikistan reported as late as 1928 that there were still practically no Tajik cadres. The number of Tajiks in the party leadership could be counted on two hands. There was only one Tajik party secretary in the republic (in Ura Teppe). The working-class background that was a sine qua non for appointments of this level was a rarity in a country without an industrial proletariat. The committee had hardly a single Tajik, nor did other Soviet and Party organisations like the Koshchi, Komsomol and the Ministries.[16]

For non-Tajiks, who made up the bulk of the senior levels of the Party and who shouldered the task of seeking out suitable candidates for membership, it was hard to tell friend from foe in the unfamiliar fabric of Tajik society. People from "bey" families repeatedly succeeded in smuggling themselves into Communist Party organisations disguised as "batraks". In December 1928, Tarijan Dyakov, head of the local OGPU (United State Political Directorate),[17] and Alekseevskii (fnu), who were on an inspection trip to Dushanbe, found that Nusratulla Maksum and a certain Abdujabbarov had appointed one Mulla Rustam, from a "bey" family, to be in charge of "supplies" in Sarai Kamara. Questioned about this choice, the Tajiks defended themselves saying they had earlier chosen a "batrak", only to find he had absconded with the cash.[18] Around the same time, Dyakov, in a report on the emancipation of women in Khojand, commenting on the relatively high numbers of women in the local Komsomol apparat, warned that the readers should not be misled by the figures. The social background of most of the members, female or male, was quite unsuitable. In Garm for example, a certain Ziya Sharifov took over the whole Komsomol organisation on the grounds that he had been a soldier in the Red Army and a candidate for full Party membership. He promptly placed friends in paid positions in the Komsomol structure, creating, for example, eight new positions in Darvaz. His appointees included two former Basmachi, five former officials in the Amir's government, and, as his assistant, a certain Arkanzada who was the son of a big "bey".[19]

As the vanguard of the revolution, the Party naturally attached great importance to the ideological commitment and proletarian credentials of its members. But this was not all. One of its other tasks was to choose cadres for government (Soviet) institutions and here, too, the social background of those being chosen left much to be desired. In 1927, the Party had instituted a reform of local government, introducing a three-tier system, the smallest unit of which was, in the northern provinces at least, the "jamagat". The government launched a massive campaign to revive the activity of the local councils of this level – the Jamsoviety – and purge them of hostile elements. More than a hundred members were expelled. There were then two big campaigns for the Jamsoviets in 1927–8 and 1928–9 in which a big growth in the participation of hired casual labourers ("batraks") and poor peasants ("bednyaks") was the target. The statistics show limited success. The percentage of "bednyaks" and "batraks" in the Jamsoviets was 96% in 1927–8 and 97% in 1928–9. However, the proportion of peasants actually fell, because a number of them were revealed to be nothing more than "bey" elements in disguise. The Party was pleased that the numbers of "batraks" had increased, although the cynic may be forgiven for wondering how many of them were people placed in other categories in previous assessments, who had simply been reclassified.[20]

For the whole period from 1924 to 1929, when Tajikistan became a union republic, the south of the country suffered from Basmachi attacks launched from across the Afghan frontier. However, then, as now, the part of the country that was the most difficult to reach was the remote region of the Pamirs. In 1928 A. Shirvani, Joint Secretary of the Tajik Provincial Commitee (Obkom)[21] wrote to I.A. Zelenskii in the Central Asia Office (Sredazburo) in Tashkent: "We are losing sight of the Gornyi-Badakhshan Oblast' [Communist Party]". Firm links ought to be established between Tajikistan and the Oblast'. At one stage, he said, parallel instructions were being sent there from both Uzbekistan and Tajikistan. Exchanges of representatives and correspondence had been haphazard.

Shirvani then announced the establishment of a government commission to set out on 10 May 1928 for a study trip on how to raise standards in the Pamirs and to develop communications. The Party was, he said, even considering the possibility of uniting the Garm vilayat (Darvaz) with the Pamirs in order to strengthen the latter. The Commission would have a limited sum in cash to solve immediate problems that may come to their attention. The members of the team were to be: Nusratulla Maksum (Chairman of the Central Executive Committee (TsIK) of the TaASSR), A.. Gotfrid (Director of the Organisation Department of the Provincial Party Committee (Obkom)) and Dailyami (Member of Narkompros – People's Commissariat for Education). In December 1928, Kuprian Osipovich Kirkizh, Secretary of the Central Committee of the Communist Party of Uzbekistan, returned from visiting the region with the commission, and submitted his report to the Party's Executive Committee. He saw the main aim as the struggle against starvation, the fight against opium and anasha, and against smallpox.[22] At the same time the local party, which he described as "hopeless", needed taking in hand. The Party should embark on a more intensive programme of "Tajikisation", which should include introducing the Tajik language in government business. Although no doubt well-intentioned and in line with the general Party Line of linguistic "korenizatsiya" currently in vogue,[23] this recommendation was a little perverse for a part of the country where the locals spoke Pamiri languages and Tajik was for many as foreign as Russian. With regard to the performance of the local government in Badakhshan, Kirkizh identified the usual problems found elsewhere: "a large part of the governing officials stems from the prosperous classes and other elements which, however devoted their work [an admission this], must affect it". So, not only was the party "hopeless", the government, although effective, was made up of class enemies and "politically incorrect" elements. The Tajik government was not the last to suffer from this phenomenon.

In early 1929, a protocol of the Tajik Provincial Party Committee regretted the current weakness of the Party in the Garm vilayet (province) and its seeming inability to counter the influence of "beys" and former Emirate officials who still enjoyed their old privileges and were openly conducting activities aimed at disrupting Party work. The priesthood was also actively obstructing the emancipation of women.[24]

Faced with the related difficulties of an unappealing environment, a politically uneducated, indeed hostile semi-feudal and often deeply religious society, the Party resorted to a combination of stratagems.

On the one hand, initially at least, the sheer lack of talent obliged the Party to show flexibility in the selection process. During the period of the NTD, the Party had to grit its teeth and make do with non-proletarian support. In the GBAO for example the local Party was given authority to select candidates for Party membership without reference. In an undated letter (though presumably written before August 1924) the Soviet plenipotentiary in Bukhara, Znamenskii[25] wrote to Karklin, Deputy Chairman of the Central Asia Office, that the situation in East Bukhara was so sensitive and the hostility to the new regime so strong, that the locals (he specifically mentions those from Darvaz and Rushan) were not just resisting Sovietisation, which they saw as a manifestation of Western influence, but had declared war on it. "There is a need", he continues, "to proceed with great tact and to try and recruit people from good clans and families. It would be quite mad to break with the long-standing networks of relationships, the solid social structure and the traditions and experiences of the local people . . . in order to construct the new Soviet building." The head of the government, Nusratulla Maksum, he added, "is well respected and comes from a good family". At least he was no "bey" (a Party inspection of 1929 described him as of peasant stock).[26]

Once chosen, the vanguard of the revolution had to be educated. Quite apart from the "class" problems described above, the educational level of those being inducted into the Party was very low. Already in 1925, the Party had identified the complete illiteracy of its local members as a major problem. The Party had estimated that, in 1924, only 1.39% of the total population was literate. The Party decided on a campaign to eradicate illiteracy amongst the "organised part of the population" i.e. the Party's ranks. On 27 February 1927, the Organisational Office (Orgburo) of the Party ordered work to start counting the numbers of illiterate Party and Komsomol members and attracting them into schools for the eradication of illiteracy (Likbez). As part of the campaign to improve the situation, all party workers engaged in teaching literacy were exempted from other work; and, to spread the word and encourage reading, a newspaper was started in the spring of 1925 called *Sharoraye Inqilob* (*the spark of revolution*), no doubt named after Lenin's newspaper, *Iskra*. The problem could not be solved quickly. In December 1928 the Ura Teppe Party was still able to note that, of 368 local members, 191 were illiterate.[27] The previous year the Executive Committee of the Tajik Provincial Party had asked the Uzbek Central Committee to expedite the dispatch of Tajik party workers from the Ferghana Valley, where the level of education was perceived as higher. The same Ispolkom recommended an extra effort to improve school education for national minorities in Tajikistan by providing teaching materials in their languages from neighbouring republics.[28] With effect from 1927, as part of the general policy of boosting national cadres, 486 Party members were sent from the UzSSR (including the TaASSR) for training to various Communist Higher Educational Institutions (Komvuzes), and Workers' Faculties (Rabfaks), while six (of whom four were Tajiks) had gone for practical training to industrial districts in Moscow. However, even amongst such a select bunch, many of their social backgrounds were dubious.[29]

Meanwhile, in addition to the Central Asian Communist University in Tashkent, efforts had to be made to set up Tajikistan's own institutions for the education of Party cadres. According to Nikolai Porfirovich Arkhangelskii, the chairman of the Soviet for the Education of National Minorities within the Narkompros (People's

Commissariat for Education) of the Turkestan ASSR, there had, in August 1923, still been no department within the ministry with responsibility for establishing a Tajik institute of education; and this at a time when other minorities already had such departments. In Arkhangelskii's words, no one paid any attention to the education of the Tajiks. It was left to Shirinshoh Shohtimur to invite the Afghan communist Nissor Muhammad [30] to set up a tiny operation called Tajikinpros (Tajik Institute of Enlightenment (sic)) in a couple of rooms in the Tashkent Central Asian Communist University. Its targets were candidates for Party membership. However, the high illiteracy rate amongst Party members reflected the general lack of education throughout the Tajik-speaking population. There was a pressing need for school-teachers trained in the Tajik language. In late 1924, Nissor Muhammad's small unit in the Communist University was turned into the first Tajik Paedagogic Institute, where a five-year course was offered for 200 Tajik teacher-trainees. Nonetheless, those fighting for an improvement in the educational facilities for Tajik speakers continued to experience obstruction from the Uzbek authorities. This prompted Shohtimur to write a direct letter to Stalin in June 1926, complaining of the Uzbek behaviour. In particular, he drew attention to Uzbek attempts to obstruct the circulation of *Ovozi Tojik* (*The Tajik Voice*) and also to the persecution of Tajik school teachers who had completed the course at the Paedagogic Institute and were trying to teach in the Tajik language. The letter produced results. The Uzbek Central Committee was instructed to tackle the question of Tajik education. In 1927 the institute was placed under the authority of the Tajik People's Commissariat for Education. In Samarkand, where the first training course for Tajik teachers had been started in June 1925, the first Teachers' Training College (Tekhnikum) seems to have been opened in October 1926.[31] Already in 1926, the People's Commissariat for Education (Nizorati Mo'aref) had also started publication in Dushanbe of a journal for teachers called "Donish va Omuzigar" (Knowledge and the Teacher). In 1927 another such journal was started in Tashkent first called *Donish-Binish* (*Knowledge and Perception*) though its title was later changed to *Rahbari Donish* (*Guide to Knowledge*). This was to become one of the organs where many of the arguments around the formation of the new Tajik language would be aired (see below).

Eventually, a small Communist Institute of Higher Education (Komvuz) was established in Dushanbe to take students over from the Tashkent Communist University. The effort even reached Badakhshan, where, in 1926 the Central Asia Office decided to found a limited Party School in Khorog staffed by a school director with four teachers. Instruction was to be in Tajik and Russian. By 1928 there were twenty-five students, and by 1930 the figure had risen further to fifty-three (forty men and thirteen women). Of these, seven were batraks, forty-one bednyaks and ten serednyaks.[32] Despite the efforts to eradicate illiteracy, at the end of 1931, the proportion of Party members who could not read or write was still 34%.[33]

7

PURGING THE PARTY'S RANKS

General nervousness, perhaps because of the smouldering threat of the Basmachestvo, combined with a desire for ideological conformity, and the problems of checking its members' background, dictated that the Party's favourite tool for ensuring purity should be the purge. Within four years of the NTD, it became clear that, in its enthusiasm for expansion and construction, the Party had recruited large numbers of opportunists whose commitment to the revolution was suspect. Throughout 1928 and 1929, the Party underwent a series of sanitisations.

The problems over the proletarian credentials of the members of the Tajik Communist Party came to a head with the purge of the senior membership carried out in late 1928 and early 1929, presumably as part of the first union-wide purge of national cadres. Grigoryi Sigin, Chairman of the Provincial Control Committee[1] was made responsible. As he himself observed, in the "viloyats" (oblast's) and "raions" the work of the local Party committees did not match up to the tasks they had been allotted. In most cases, they had only undertaken propaganda and agitprop work and ignored the organisational and technical aspects. In many places no preliminary work was done on the basic briefing materials. Only the Dushanbe and Kurgan Teppe Party Organisations had followed the Party's directives. Sigin blamed these shortcomings on the lack of instructional materials which had been expected from Uzbekistan. As far as practical guidance was concerned, which might have offered something on the ideological or organisational aspects of how to prepare for the purge, only one letter had been received from the Uzbek Party's Central Committee.

The shortage of suitable personnel even affected the choice of the inspectors who were to carry out the purge. Sigin had difficulty meeting the demands of the Centre with regard to "Partstazh" (Party Service Record), social background and nationality. Although about a third could be found who had had experience of "stazh" work, and some 80% could be described as of working-class origin, none of the Tajiks came from the "shop-floor" (presumably because in Tajikistan at this time there were no "shops"). Some areas simply could offer no one suitable. Searches were made in Ura Teppe and Panjikent but no one could be found, thanks to what Sigin described as their "absolute political and literal illiteracy". In the end, staff for the auditing committees ("proverkoms") had to be sent from Uzbekistan's Central Control Commission office. Of those chosen, four persons were Tajik, two Persian, fifteen Uzbek and nineteen European.[2]

Again, in late 1928 the inspection of the Party "aktiv" in the administrative/penal and judicial branches, and in the cooperative organs, showed that, even amongst the senior ranks, in the former, 53.1% of the workers were of unsuitable background and, in the latter, 44.4%. All would have to be removed. The only district organisations that escaped censure were Garm and Ura Teppe, although the latter was also criticised, but unfairly in the view of the chairman. Three Party organisations, Kulyab, Panjikent and Kurgan Teppe, were definitely unhealthy, especially Kulyab where 30% of the whole organisation appeared before the control commission. The Party secretary, the deputy chairman of the Executive Committee and other members were all expelled from the Party. In a move to correct these phenomena which betrayed a certain measure of desperation, the Party proposed to ask all Party members to respond to a questionnaire which included the questions "Do you drink spirits?" and "Are you a trouble-maker?"

Although the critical review of Party activity of July 1929 had recommended a similar clean-out in the Soviet structures, it was recognised that, given the circumstances in Tajikistan, it would not be possible to conduct a thorough purge of the institutions. For the time being the purge of government organs would be confined to the People's Commissariats for Agriculture (Narkomzem) and Justice (Narkomyust).

All in all, the composition of the Soviet apparat was seen in the review as no better than in the Party, indeed probably worse, as it was infiltrated by undesirable social elements: "beys", former servants of the Amir and even criminals. The Tajik Provincial Committee had not "pursued with sufficient vigour" the expulsion of these people from the Soviet, cooperative or other organisations along the Afghan frontier. To overcome this problem, the Party organisation once more resorted to trying to attract "batraks", "bednyaks", and medium peasants "serednyaks" to build up the Soviet structures. Poor peasants (bednyaks) should be offered tax reductions of up to one third, and consumer credits should be introduced. At the same time, peasants should not be pressurised into taking out loans they could not afford – a mistake that had been made in the past. Finally, public opinion should be educated to vote in local elections against "beys" or people linked to "beys", the traditional leaders of the past, or the Basmachis. There should be put forward in their place "trusty supporters of Soviet power and comrades from the batrak, poor and middle peasant classes". The inspection also revealed that mistakes had been made in the government's resettlement programmes designed to boost cotton production in the southern valleys. Repressive measures had been used against peasants who did not want to move and, in the re-settlement areas selected, tensions and even conflicts had arisen between settlers and old-established inhabitants. More of this below.

Not that the situation in the relatively more developed north of the country appears to have been any better than the south (it will be remembered that Khojand and neighbouring districts were to be transferred to Tajikistan in 1929). A commission studied the impact the unsatisfactory state of the Isfara party organisation was having on the autumn campaign to boost cotton-sowing in October 1929. The whole Party structure seems to have been rotten, starting with the secretary Nazarov, who was accused of being well-disposed to "beys" and elements of the priesthood who had gained control of entire cells. The peasantry and the "batraks" reported being terrorised by them. In particular, they were being prevented from sowing cotton, since the "beys" foresaw greater profits from planting grain, especially rice. Having heard all this, the Khojand District (Okrug) Party Executive Office decided that:

1. The "raion" party committee be dissolved.
2. An extraordinary "raion" party conference be held to elect new staff.
3. A member of the District Executive Committee (Okrug Ispolkom) be posted to Isfara to prepare this conference.

4. Details of Nazarov's activities be passed to the Control Commission, which would decide whether to call him to account.

The report added that all this should be undertaken with great speed as until very recently the Basmachestvo had been operating in this area.[3]

Inevitably, such a small and remote group as the Communist Party membership in Tajikistan suffered from internal tensions as different members jockeyed for position. For many the work no doubt brought great social and personal pressures, not only between individuals but between Russians and locals. In 1927 for example, Dyakov and Alekseevskii complained that Nusratulla Maksum and Abdujabbarov were trying to discredit the frontier troops by claiming that they had been robbing and even killing the local population and then pretending they had been operating against bandits from Afghanistan (plus ça change).[4]

Both Gotfrid, deputy head of the Provincial Party's Executive Committee, and A. Shirvani, Joint Party secretary, reported separately on tensions in the ranks of the Party and agreed that the main source of the in-fighting and trouble-making was Shirvani's colleague as joint secretary, Muminhojaev,[5] who they thought should be removed for obstructing Party work. The Party activist who received the most praise from Gotfrid was Muhieddinov. To judge by Manzhara's[6] complaints about the intrigues within the main Uzbek Party against Faizulla Khojaev, the situation there was no better. By January 1929, things had reached the stage where the 2nd Tajik Provincial Party Conference relieved both Muminhojaev and Shirvani of their jobs.

At the First Plenum of the Provincial Committee held on 10 February, the Party chose as its next Party secretary Shirinshoh Shohtimur who at the time was away studying at the Communist University of the Toilers of the East (KUTV) in Moscow and no doubt clear of internal intrigues. By July of 1929, the Party was still unsatisfied, but this time the axe was to fall on the very top ranks of the Provincial Party Committee and the government organs (Soviets). The Uzbek Party (to which the Tajik Party was subordinate) had been "too slow to implement the orders of the Central Committee of the All Russian Communist Party in Moscow". It had "tried to discredit senior members and to set younger party workers against them, and had tried to cover up mistakes". The purge that followed in July and August 1929 brought about a deep change in the Tajik Party's leadership. Gotfrid and Rossov[7] were removed, while Aleksei Dyakov was relieved of his duties as chairman of the Khojand Organisation Office (Orgburo). Zelenskii was dispatched to Dushanbe to chair an extraordinary plenary session of the Provincial Committee at which two entirely new figures were appointed: Georgyi Yevseevich Chicherov and Vainer (no further details). Chicherov was a seasoned but uneducated Bolshevik whose previous posting as Party secretary in the Vologda governorate had only lasted three months. Shohtimur was demoted to second place on the committee and allowed to stay in Moscow. Chicherov's incumbency as secretary of the Tajik party hardly lasted longer than his Vologda posting. On 26 December of the same year, the Central Asia Office had him recalled to Moscow and for the next six months Shohtimur seems to have led the Tajik party from there. This lack of decisiveness can hardly have helped a Party that was already struggling. By June 1930, Moscow had decided what to do. Mirza Davud Guseinov, an Azerbaijani, was appointed secretary with Shohtimur continuing as number two.

In some cases, particularly in the senior ranks, Tajik party members' unsatisfactory class credentials were to prove fateful in the later purges of the 1930s, when Stalin determined finally to root out all signs of nationalist or bourgeois deviation. For example, Abdulkadyr Muhieddinov, who reached the top of his career as Chairman of the Council of People's Commissars of Tajikistan, was eventually arrested in 1934. He was accused of anti-Soviet activity, cooperation with foreign powers and other heinous crimes, and shot, probably in 1937 (although, in his collected works, Faizulla Khojaev gives the date of his death as 1934). Muhieddinov had been the son of the leading Bukharan millionaire merchant Muhieddin Mansurov who had been involved with the Jadid movement in 1916 and 1917. When the chips were down, his early commitment to the revolution and the high praise he received from the likes of Gotfrid counted as little in comparison with his bourgeois origins. While the knives were being sharpened, the new secretary of the Tajik Party, Shaduns (nfd), set the scene by describing him as a "wild Tajik chauvinist, old Jadid, and well-known businessman who was continuing his criminal intrigues at a time when Soviet rule had already been established in Central Asia for eleven years."[8]

In the complicated process whereby Stalin dragged the Soviet
Union from the relative liberalism of Lenin's New Economic Policy
to the revived Russian dominance of the late 1930s, Terry Martin[9] has
identified a number of different campaigns: against the fellow-
travelling but opportunistic national bourgeois intelligentsia of
"smenovekhovtsy"; the "cultural revolution" of intensified linguistic
and educational "korenizatsiya" of the late 1920s; and the campaign
against "great power chauvinism" of 1930 onwards. The evidence
from Tajikistan reflects all of these obsessions. At the same time, local
conditions required a certain flexibility. Great power chauvinism was
relative. In Tajikistan the "great power" could not only be Russian,
but Uzbek, and that realisation seems to have dawned early.

The dangers from "nationalism" and "chauvinism", especially in
a mixed community like Uzbekistan, loomed large in the anxieties
of Party leaders in the Centre. Once Stalin perceived that Lenin's
New Economic Policy had done its work in restoring a measure of
prosperity to the people of the USSR, he began to tighten discipline.
The Party line reverted to stricter socialist principles. In November
1927, Yanson[10] reported to the Central Control Commission of the
Moscow Party on the situation in the equivalent commission in
Uzbekistan. The Party, he advised, should recommend to the commissions of Uzbekistan and of the Tajik Provincial Party that they
get together with all the Party committees throughout the Uzbek
SSR "in the struggle against the nationalist influence on different
party strata [and] of bourgeois democratic ideology [read Jadidism]
being spread by a radical bourgeoisie, which concealed its true
nationalist nature with leftist catchwords".[11] In debates at the
Centre, there was also much criticism of the Uzbek cadres for their
treatment of the senior cadres and for their chauvinism. In a resolution passed in March 1929, the Moscow Party criticised the Uzbek
Party for failing to liquidate non-working-class and landlord-
orientated enterprises, while all cadres in Kyrgyzstan, Tajikistan and
Uzbekistan were invited to examine their own actions in the light
of the danger from national chauvinism.[12] The plan of work for the
Uzbek Party for September 1929 to February 1930 specified the
need to counter "the growing national chauvinism which shows its
influence on individual groups within the membership of the Uzbek
party organisation, in connection with which elements of Great
Russian and on occasion Great Uzbek chauvinism can be observed

especially with regard to Tajiks, Jews and others". These attitudes were attributed to the national intelligentsia's hostility towards the dictatorship of the proletariat.[13]

The uncooperative attitude of the Uzbeks in the Party was also blamed for holding up the campaign of popular indoctrination in Tajikistan. By way of example, in a letter to the Central Asia Office in Tashkent, Mirsaidov of the Indoctrination Section of the Tajik party complained that the programme was going very slowly in the important south of the country – important because it bordered on Afghanistan for which Tajikistan was meant to become an example of socialist development. They had only succeeded in opening one so-called "Red Chaikhane", in Sarai Kamara, and had had to enlist the help of "non-party forces" (Red Chaikhanes were an attempt to build on the local tradition of the "tea house" to create centres for the dissemination of communist propaganda). The commander of the 48th frontier detachment had agreed to lend his mobile film units. The Tajiks had then sent a representative to Tashkent to negotiate the loan of suitable material, but the Uzbek State Film Agency (Uzbekgoskino) had insisted on charging 76 roubles for each film. With delivery costs, this amounted to 100 roubles per film, which was very expensive for a country as poor as Tajikistan. The Uzbek attitude was the main obstacle to organising mass indoctrination in the south of the country.[14]

Tajik/Uzbek relations had to be carefully managed on the ground. For example, the interests of those Tajiks being resettled from the mountains (often the Garm area) to the future cotton-growing lands of the south especially in the Jilikul and Kaizabad areas, conflicted with those of other groups. In the late 20s there were estimated to be some 700,000 refugees still living in Northern Afghanistan, of whom the majority were ethnic Uzbeks. The Party therefore thought it advisable to set up an Uzbek centre in the region to act as a pole of attraction and to counter anti-Soviet propaganda emanating from Northern Afghanistan. It was recognised that Soviet rule had deprived the Uzbek community of certain advantages they enjoyed under the Bukharan Emirate and that they were therefore likely to be hostile to the new regime (an interesting admission from a Communist Party trying to present the Emirate to the Uzbeks as the personification of evil). Such a centre would have to be in the Kurgan Teppe district, but, and this was important, not in such a way as to turn it into an Uzbek province (viloyat), since there were even greater numbers of Tajiks living there, and their number was likely to increase still further as a result of the resettlement pro- gramme. So the new Uzbek centre would be in Sarai Kamara and would also be responsible for Kabadian, south Jilikul, and Chubek Parkhar. Once this was established, the re-settlement of Uzbeks from Afghanistan should be encouraged and the settlement of new Tajiks discouraged.[15]

In fact the representation of minorities in the Soviets throughout the country seems to have been pretty good in the TaSSR. A review of the situation from 1927 to 1928 showed that the main three national minorities (Uzbeks, Kyrgyz and Turkmen), who accounted for 24.1% of the total population, held 28.8% of the seats on Soviets.[16] Even at the end of 1928, after four years of work, the numbers of Party members in Tajikistan was very small, though the Party appeared to be recruiting from more suitable backgrounds. The Executive Committee of the Provincial Committee of the Tajik Communist Party reported in December of that year that the figures for Tajik Party membership were as follows:

		1926–7
Members		614
Candidates		533
	Total	1147

		1927–8
Members		661
Candidates		602
	Total	1263

At least some increase was being recorded. According to another set of figures, in April 1928, Party membership amongst Tajiks stood at 1196.

At the time, the social structure of the Tajik communists was as follows:

Workers and casual labourers (batrak)	53.3% (of whom 29% workers)
Poor peasants	22%
Service work	27% (sic)[17]

In the GBAO, the Party had reported seventy communists in 1925. By 1927 the total had risen to 117 and by 1930 to 138. By then the social composition of the membership was also closer to what the centre was demanding. Seven were women (5%), twenty-six were workers (19%), seventy-two peasants (52%), forty service staff (29%). The continuing preponderance of peasants (engagingly referred to in Soviet literature as "dehqanizatsiya" i.e. "peasantisation") could be attributed to the fact that, here, society was even more solidly engaged in agriculture than elsewhere in the country.

8

THE TAJIK LANGUAGE

Throughout the UzSSR, including the TaASSR, the whole process of "korenizatsiya" (i.e. promotion of locals to administrative posts and the concomitant encouragement of education in local languages) was held back by the high levels of illiteracy. In 1926 the Central Asia Office (Sredazburo) noted what everyone knew – that literacy in the towns was more common (12.1% among Tajik males) than in the villages (3.1%) and much more widespread among men than among women (whose rates were 1.1% and 0.2% for towns and villages respectively).[1]

In the years immediately following the establishment of the TaSSR, except in Mountainous Badakhshan (GBAO), instruction in the new Soviet schools was conducted in the Uzbek language, whereas it was the old-method schools (maktabs) that used Tajik. The People's Commissariat for Education recognised that this was a serious obstacle to their aim of promoting Soviet education and reducing the influence of the clergy. This was particularly irritating to those who wanted to promote Tajik as a Soviet language bearing in mind that the government was offering all sorts of inducements to parents who sent their children to the new Soviet schools. They received a year's tax holiday, credit for buying stock and free medical treatment. But it was hardly surprising. In December 1924, the People's Commissariat only had seven schools with twenty-six teachers and 152 pupils under its authority within Tajikistan. In the Tajik areas of Uzbekistan the situation was no better. Haji Mu'in, one of the editorial board of *Shu'leh ye Inqilob* might agitate for the introduction of Tajik language schools in Samarkand and the surrounding area. But the resources simply did not exist.

During the first years of the 1920s, in both the TASSR and the BNSR, the Tajik language was banned from official correspondence. These were the years of Turkic cultural supremacy – a supremacy that many Tajiks did not question.

With the formation of the TaASSR, not only did many of those Tajiks who had acquiesced in Uzbek dominance begin to ask themselves what it meant to be a Tajik. At the same time the need arose for a Soviet version of the their language. In Stalin's analysis, national identity was closely bound up with language. This posed a problem for many Tajik thinkers bearing in mind that so many of their people were bi-lingual in Tajik and Uzbek. Clearly the creation of an acceptable version of the language was a matter of urgency.

I have briefly mentioned Nissor Muhammad's establishment of the Tajik Teachers' Training college in Tashkent and have noted the high illiteracy rate in the new republic. With the Tajiks' language the Soviets faced a problem that was quite different from those they faced in developing most other minority languages. Languages like Kyrgyz or Karakalpak, not to mention many of those spoken in the North Caucasus and elsewhere, had rarely if at all been written down and had virtually no literature, beyond an oral folk tradition. With Persian, the Party had to deal with a language that not only had a vast literary tradition dating back more than 1000 years in Iran, Central Asia and Northern India, but that had been the official language of successive dynasties in those regions. A debate at once arose. The revolutionary government might wish to distance itself from the old literary Persian encumbered as it was with feudal baggage. But what sort of language should replace it? The need to promote education amongst a largely illiterate population suggested that it should be a simple language.

Shohtimur had played a major part in organising the publication in Samarkand of the first Tajik-language newspaper in the Turkestan ASSR since the closure of *Sho'leh ye Enqelob* in 1921. This was *Ovozi Tojik e Kambaghal* (The Voice of the Poor Tajik), which first appeared on 25 August 1924.[2] Abdul Qayum Qurbi was the notional editor, but for all practical purposes, our old Ironi friend Sayyid Reza Alizodeh fulfilled this role. Haji Mu'in was on the editorial board and Sadruddin Ayni was a contributor. So, to outward appearances the same team as for *Sho'leh ye Enqelob*. However, the appearances were deceptive as the new journal was to become the vehicle for the great debate on the future course to be mapped out for the new Soviet Tajik language.

In his introductory article for this new journal, Ayni for the first time used the word "Tojik" to describe the language in which he was writing. This "Tojik" language, he proclaimed, should be simple like that spoken by the Tajiks of the mountains, in places like Falgar and Mastchi, rather than the language of the urban literary sophisticates of the plains, which was too mixed with Arabic, Turkic and literary Persian. This was in line with the Party's latest edict of 19 October 1924 on the "appeal to the village". Nonetheless, Ayni continued, the mountain people could benefit by being educated by the urban teachers of Samarkand "who know the Tajik language well" (but by implication are not Tajiks themselves). For those who wondered what Ayni thought the Samarkandis were, if not Tajiks, his article in the next number of *Ovozi Tojik* gave the reply. He called them "Farsiyon".

As Ayni played such an important role in the development of the new Tajik language, it may be worth briefly describing his life. He had been born on 15 April 1878 in Khoja Sohtare about twenty-five miles from Bukhara. His father was a poor farmer but, unusually for someone of this class, he had had a partial madrasa education in Bukhara and could read and write. In 1889 both his parents succumbed to cholera and Ayni was left in charge of the family. In due course he made his way to Bukhara and by working as a servant managed to support himself while studying. In 1907 the first reformed school for the children of Tatars was opened in Bukhara and from then on Ayni became increasingly involved in the Jadid educational reform movement. This set him on a collision course with the Emirate's authorities. By April 1917, the Amir came under strong pressure from the Russian Provisional Government to introduce reforms. His reaction was to clamp down. Along with a number of other reformers, Ayni was arrested and flogged. He would probably have died had it not been for the intervention of Russian soldiers from neighbouring Kagan who released him. After seven weeks recovering in hospital he moved first to Tashkent and then to Samarkand where, after the revolution, he took a job first as a teacher of Tajik and Uzbek and then as a journalist. During this time in Samarkand, Ayni learnt that his brother had been arrested and killed by the Amir. This tragedy seems to have prompted Ayni to work with the Communist Party preparing for the Soviet intervention and overthrow of the Amir in 1920. It also inspired him to write an elegy on the death of his brother, as well as his first substantial prose work *Jallodon i Bukhoro*

(*The Executioners of Bukhara*). With his first novel, *Odina* written in 1923,[3] Ayni began the career which was to make him perhaps the leading Tajik literary figure of the 20th century.

This raises an additional question. If it was the mountain people who were the Tajiks and the town-dwellers of the plains were "Farsiyon", what did Ayni think he himself was and why did he think he could speak for the former, whose dialects he did not speak? He was after all, a typical plains dweller, educated in the traditional way in Bukhara. He finally settled in Samarkand, which had been chosen by Zelenskii as the centre from which the educational campaign amongst the Tajiks was to be launched. Zelenskii had decided against Bukhara for that role on the grounds that the Bukharans were "darker and more backward and quicker to fall victim to the provocations and fanatical agitation of the mullahs". Once there, Ayni remained in Samarkand until the last year of his life. It must be a matter for regret amongst Tajik nationalists that their most famous literary figure preferred to spend his life in Uzbekistan. His mother tongue may have been Tajik but he was equally at home in Uzbek, both in poetry and in prose. He had also had close links with the Jadids for whom Turkic was the language of progress and Tajik that of obscurantism and feudal oppression. Why did he embrace Tajik nationality? Perhaps he was alienated by the extreme Uzbek nationalism of the circle around Abdulrauf Fitrat who had set up the Uzbek literature society "Chagatai Gurungi" (Chagatai Discussion) and whose policies in the Bukharan Republic penalised the Tajik language. Ayni's article "Tojiklar Mas'alesi" ("The Question of the Tajiks") in the 1923 edition of the Uzbek paper *Mehnatkeshlar Tavushi* (*Voice of the Toilers*) was an attempt to assert the Tajik position against this tendency. Whatever the reasons why he opted for being a Tajik, opt he certainly did and by the time the new TaASSR was set up he was one of the leading literary figures writing in the Tajik language.

It was therefore natural that, when the leaders of the new Tajik republic turned their minds to the question of language reform, they should think of Ayni. As a first step he was asked to prepare a compendium of Tajik literature. His response was the *Namunayi Adabiyoti Tojik, 300–1200 AH* a collection of Persian poems and prose writings dating back to the mediaeval poets Rudaki and Firdausi.

This compendium gave rise to intense debate, which was to encapsulate the argument over the type of language Tajik was to become.

Several Russian scholars objected to the contents on the grounds that the Tajiks as such had no literature. In their view, the language of the contents of the *Namuna* was Persian, which was the language of Iran, as well as being a historical and international language unconnected with the mountain peoples of Soviet Tajikistan. Ayni had defended his position by writing "just as both Tajiks and Iranians like to read the works of Sa'adi, Hafiz, Nizami *et al.* they also both understand and enjoy Rudaki, Kamol Khujandi, Ismat Bukhoro'i, Saifi Isfaragi and so on".[4] But his position was precarious. He had included a poem by Rudaki which celebrated the return of a Samanid governor to Bukhara. This was seized on by ill-wishers to indicate that Ayni was in fact a crypto-monarchist agitating for the return of the Amir. Akmal Ikramov, Secretary of the Central Committee of the Uzbek Party demanded that the book be banned. Even Bukharin attacked Ayni as a "reactionary monarchist". By 1930 the *Namuna* had been banned and in many cases destroyed. In the feverish atmosphere of the period, Ayni's position would have been extremely grave had he not produced his novels *Odine* and *Dakhunda* (published in 1930), which were seen as unassailably pro-Soviet.

There were two main points around which the arguments about the future of Tajik swirled. Should it, as the so-called "internationalists" advocated,[5] act as the vehicle for carrying the message of Marxism/Leninism to other Persian-speaking countries like Iran? Or, should it be directed at the people of the mountains of Tajikistan whose could not understand the refinements of the classical language. The arguments involved grammatical and syntactical questions, vocabulary and, later on, script. The language of the cities of the plains contained, as did Iranian Persian and the language of the Ironis of Samarkand like Alizodeh, many words of Arabic origin. Most reformers, including Ayni, wanted to reduce these, although Ayni himself had difficulty kicking the habit of using Arabic plurals. In the second version of *Shu'leh ye Enqelab*, Alizodeh also made an effort to reduce Arabisms. The town language was also much more influenced by Turkic grammatical structures. This prompted the Tajik nationalists among the so-called "language inventors" (known as "ekhtera'chion") to invoke the "Iranian purity" of the mountain language in their enthusiasm for putting as much distance as possible between their language and Uzbek. An additional complication in the debate was provided by a small number of "proletkult" supporters who favoured a very basic language which completely rejected any similarity with the non-communist past. In 1932, as the atmosphere in the whole Soviet Union became murderous, the writer Bektosh was accused of Proletkult leanings and eventually shot.[6]

In the end, while both sides made concessions, the supporters of a dialect-based new language had to concede most. Whatever their views, most of the Tajiks taking part in the debate were from the cities of the plains. Those who wanted to adapt their language to that of the mountains found they were not sufficiently familiar with it, nor had they any means of getting more closely acquainted, as no serious studies of it had yet been undertaken.

Aleksander Aleksanrovich Semenov, the famous Russian orientalist, chaired the decisive Linguistic Conference on 22 August 1930 in Stalinabad. His conclusion followed the three views which had earlier seemed to unite the most important group of literary figures and language experts in the country.[7] These were:

- the new Tajik language should emerge from the existing language of Tajik newspapers, journals and books and not be completely re-invented.

- this language should be comprehensible for all Tajik speakers in the Soviet Union. The necessary simplification of the language could be achieved by approaching the language spoken by Soviet Tajiks.

- the language would have to abandon certain forms which until then had been common characteristics of the Persian/Tajik written language both inside and outside the Soviet Union.

He was supported by his Russian colleague Eygenyi Edvardovich Bertel's who also recommended that leading writers like Ayni, Fitrat (see below) and Azizi should write in a style that was as close as possible to the spoken language. In contrast to the Russian "linguo-technologist" Niklolai Feofanovich Yakovlev, who believed that the development of language, like the economy, could be manipulated mechanistically, Bertel's saw little point in trying to dictate to poets what sort of language they should use.

Parallel with the debate over the sort of language Tajik was to become, ran another even more heated debate over the introduction of the Latin script. The original proposal had been made for the Turkic languages and the All- Union Central Committee for the New Turkic Alphabet (VTsK NTA) was formed. Following that example, throughout 1926 discussions were held both in the Tajik Party and People's Commissariat for Education on the desirability of replacing the Arabic script with one based on the Latin alphabet. In 1927, the TaASSR decided to go ahead and ordered two scholars to submit proposals. These were, paradoxically, the Uzbek Abdulrauf Fitrat and the Russian orientalist A.A. Semenov. Perhaps chastened by the accusations of Uzbek chauvinism levelled by Moscow at the Uzbek Party after Shohtimur's letter to Stalin, Fitrat had swung round in support of "bi-lingualism". After 1925 he wrote a lot in Tajik. In 1930 he wrote a grammar of the Tajik language and in 1927 he taught Tajik language and literature at the Samarkand Teachers' Training College. Whatever his feelings about Turkic supremacy, Fitrat was genuinely bi-lingual in the "Sart" tradition. Nonetheless, Tajik nationalists (interesting that such a phenomenon had developed so fast out of the apathy that had attended the NTD) at once criticised his alphabet proposal as too close to the one designed for the Uzbek language. The only Tajik to support Fitrat, Bektosh, was promptly labelled a "pan-Turkist" (and we know what happened to him). At a later date, the Russian Iran scholar A.A. Frejman was also invited to submit an alphabet.[8]

In the reformist and progressive atmosphere of the day, alphabet reform seemed the obvious answer to the literacy problem. The Arabic script, it was argued, was difficult to learn and ill-suited to the Persian language. It was also unfashionably linked to Islam. Soviet propaganda represented it as a "lame donkey" in comparison with the "aeroplane" of Latin letters. The Tajik Alphabet Committee actually sponsored a collection of money to build an aeroplane which was to be called "October Alphabet". The reasons for preferring the Latin alphabet to the Cyrillic seem to have been largely impressionistic. The Latin script symbolised international understanding, scientific and technical progress and industrialisation. The Cyrillic still carried a mild taint of Tsarism.

In some respects the dispute about the correct Latin alphabet for Tajik mirrored that about how to develop the Tajik language, in that it centred on differences in pronunciation in various dialects. The main feature of a phonetic alphabet like the one projected was that each letter would represent a specific sound. But what if different dialects pronounced that sound differently? This was likely to be particularly relevant with regard to vowels where the scope for dialectical variations was huge. Predictably therefore, the main disagreements concerned how to represent "u" and "i". In the end, after endless wrangling, the same Linguistic Conference of 22 August 1930 in Stalinabad decided that the phonetic base for the language had better be the dialect of Bukhara. Where there were still ambiguities it was recommended that these could be solved by putting the script to practical test and then agreeing on the best solution. The alphabet eventually chosen combined features from all three of those who had been charged with the task of creating it: Semenov, Fitrat and Frejman.

It took some time for the new alphabet to catch on. For several years, Party correspondence continued to be conducted in the Arabic script. It proved especially difficult for older people who had learned the Arabic script to adapt to the Latin one. Ayni himself used the Arabic letters until he died. Nonetheless, whatever the objections and difficulties, the new script did fulfil the promise of better literacy. In 1926 96.2% of the population was reckoned to be illiterate. By 1939, according to official statistics, 71% of men were literate and 65.5% of women. The statistics may not have been totally reliable and the criteria by which literacy was judged were not very demanding. But, even if the figures were half what was claimed, the achievement was still remarkable.

Already in March 1927, before the final alphabet had been agreed, attempts were being made to introduce it – and complaints were being heard about the slowness of the process. The Tajik Provincial Committee of the Party (Obkom) took note of the unsatisfactory progress being made. This was seen as due to the weakness of the VTsK NTA, which suffered from lack of funds, and to the uncooperative attitude of the Uzbek alphabet commission, which initially refused to approve the new alphabet on the grounds that it was inconsistent with the new unified Turkic alphabet.[9]

In line with the committee's decree, courses were started for Tajiks to learn to write properly and for non-Tajiks to learn Tajik.

But there were too few teachers and teaching materials. Compulsory universal primary education was introduced in February 1931 and huge progress was made in building, staffing and equipping new schools. However, it was realised that the campaign would be a long drawn-out one. To complicate the issue still further, the Cyrillic alphabet was introduced in the late 1930s and its adoption more or less complete by 1940. The reasons behind this last change are complex but seem to have reflected Stalin's view, in what he recognised was the run-up to war with Germany, that all Soviet citizens liable to serve in the military should be able to read the Russian script. With regard to the Turkic languages he also feared lest citizens of the Soviet Turkic republics might be able to read publications coming out of Ataturk's Turkey, where the Latin script had been introduced in 1928.

By early 1929, the Obkom of the Party was also exercised about the slow progress being made by non-Tajik Party workers in learning the local language. As many educated Uzbeks of the day would have known at least some Tajik, the concern seems to have targeted Europeans. It is likely that the Russians of that period were no keener on learning "backward" languages than in the period after the Second World War. However, the steps taken to encourage use of the Tajik language bear all the hall-marks of what Terry Martin has described as the "cultural revolution" phase of "korenizatsiya", which was being pushed through at that time in many non-Russian parts of the Soviet Union, including Uzbekistan. In an unrealistic attempt to meet Utopian Party targets sent from the Centre, a "Commission on Tajikisation" was established on 27 January 1929, which decreed that all members of the Party and the Komsomol should be obliged to learn Tajik within one year.[10] This was clearly unrealistic given the lack of teachers and teaching materials. In any case, by the mid-1930s, the Party line was changing. The programme of encouraging local officials to absorb the message of the revolution in the context of the regional language and culture was modified and the Russian language was given back its dominant position.

In the tense atmosphere of the time, the debate over the shape and structure of the Tajik language had inevitably been highly politicised and at times very dangerous. Many of those participating did so anonymously, like the person who scattered accusations of pan-Turkist tendencies and signed himself "Tojik" in the exchanges about dialect and alphabet. In 1927, the Uzbek writer Sanjar dared, in the discreetist possible terms, to regret the fact that introducing the Latin script for Marxist literature published in Tajikistan would deprive Persian and Afghan readers of the chance to study the great man's works. The social political journal *Rahbari Donish* (*Guide to Knowledge*), which had been set up in August that year in Dushanbe, immediately felt it expedient to distance itself from what it saw as a potentially subversive opinion. Iranians, Indians and even (sic) Afghans, it wrote, would be envious of Tajikistan's progressive stance and would shortly follow suit. Later writers and critics took great care to concoct reasons for allowing the publication of Persian literature from the "feudal" period. Firdausi's *Book of Kings* could be tolerated in view of his instinctively democratic decision to choose non-royal figures such as Rustam and Isfandiyar as his main heroes. His anti-Islamic tendency was also clear from the sympathy he expressed for the uprisings of Mazdak and Kova the blacksmith. Of 19th-century writers, Ahmad Donish was admirable for the themes of patriotism, and the fight against exploiters treated in his works as in the *Navader ul Vaqa'e* (*Rarities of Events*) which contained bitter criticism of the Bukharan amirs.[11] It was also convenient that Donish had also written in praise of the Russians in another of his works, *Nomusi A'zam*.

There is no doubt that Russian writers also had a profound effect on the development of Soviet Tajik literature. Ayni openly acknowledged his debt to Gorkii in prose and to Mayakovskii and Bednyi in poetry. Later Soviet literary critics see their influence in his work *Ghulomon* (*Slaves*) and also in the poetry of the Iranian communist Abdulqasim Lakhuti, and of the Tajik Mirshakar.

It is hard to overestimate Ayni's contribution to Soviet Tajik literature. Although a gifted poet, he was the first to establish prose as an acceptable vehicle for expression in a society that had until then seen poetry as the only genuine literary vehicle. He acted as advisor and guide to the next generation of Tajik prose writers such as Jalol Ikromi, Jalil Rahim and Badruddin Azizi.[12] Not that he neglected poetry or poets. He worked closely with contemporaries such as Lakhuti and Munzim,[13] and encouraged younger Soviet poets such as Pairav Sulaimoni,[14] Muhammadjon Rahimi,[15] and Muhieddin Aminzadeh.[16] For Westerners Ayni is perhaps most interesting in his role as historian of the last years of the Emirate of Bukhara. His autobiographical works like *Maktabi Kuhna* (*The Old-style School*) and *Yoddoshtho* (*Reminiscences*) and *Margi Sudkhur* (*Death of a Usurer*) give us a portrait of the time the value of which is not obscured by its Marxist perspective.

9

ECONOMIC RECONSTRUCTION

The government of the TaSSR faced colossal economic problems in trying to rebuild a country ravaged by civil war. The funds allocated by the centre were limited and there was intense competition for them. Already in December 1924, even before the NTD had been finalised, Karamysov and Orunbaev (no further details) of the Orgburo of the Kyrgyz Provincial Committee complained officially about a decision of the Central Asia Office (Sredazburo), to raise Tajikistan's financial allocation by 5%. Such an increase could only be met by cutting other republics' allocations. They felt especially aggrieved as, in the past, they had always supported Tajikistan's requests for extra support, knowing how poor the country was. If the Office failed to respond to their protest, they threatened to take the matter to the Central Committee of the Party in Moscow. On the Tajiks' behalf, a month earlier, Dadabaev, the chairman of the Tajik Revolutionary Committee, had written a number of identical letters to addressees such as the Central Asia Office, the Agricultural Bank (Selkhozbank), the Directorate of Water Management and the State Bank (Gosbank) asking for special attention for the problems besetting Tajikistan. He submitted plans for rebuilding the country's agriculture, which had been shattered by the Basmachi, and asked for a statement of how much of the 7 million roubles allocated by the Centre for irrigation would go to the TaASSR.

In early 1928, the head of the Tajik Provincial Committee's Organisation Office (Orgburo), Gotfrid, recorded a series of difficulties he was facing, for many of which he blamed the Uzbek Communist Party. Of the 300,000 roubles allocated for reconstruction in Tajikistan, only 7500 had arrived by the end of February when he arrived to take up his post. Likewise, the papers for the "loan" (he appears to mean government bonds, which he was to sell in the villages to mop up surplus cash generated by wage payments for work during the sowing season) had arrived late only on 10th March. Nonetheless he had succeeded in selling 112,000 roubles-worth – about 39% of the total.

At the time of Gotfrid's writing the sowing season was in full swing and the payment of wages unleashed a flood of cash into people's pockets. Unfortunately there were no goods on the market for people to buy. The small amount stored in Surkhan station was quite inadequate to satisfy demand. Gotfrid found the delays incomprehensible as Uzbektorg (the Uzbek trading agency) was getting the goods direct from Moscow. Gotfrid asked the Party to get goods from the Plenipotentiary Representative of the People's Commissariat for Trade (Upolnarkomtorg) reserve fund, especially as an additional loan and more wage payments were imminent (380,000 roubles' worth). There were already complaints coming in of insufficient goods, especially in areas where people were being resettled. He had written to the Central Asia Agricultural Supply Agency, the resonantly named Sredazselkhozsnab, about all this, but his telegrams had not been answered. Meanwhile, he had heard that the Uzbek party had made every effort to ensure supplies for Karakalpakistan, although the situation there, Gotfrid claimed, was much better than in Tajikistan. In the latter, moreover, the Basmachi menace was still real.

By 1929, indignation in Dushanbe had reached boiling point at the way the UzSSR was abusing its position by withholding funds meant for Tajikistan. This led to the creation of a special Commission for the Analysis of Budgetary Disputes between the TaASSR and the UzSSR, with Manzhara as chairman.[1] Having studied materials submitted by the Tajiks, which covered budgetary allocations for the period 1924 to 1928, Manzhara's report drew attention to a whole range of abuses. Funds sent from Moscow for passing on to Tajikistan were repeatedly either passed on only in part or not at all. On numerous occasions the Uzbek People's Commissariat for Finance (Narkomfin) simply seized credits bound for Dushanbe. These abuses occurred in virtually every field of the economic and social sectors: in infrastructure (electrification and construction), in agricultural development (expansion of cotton, flour-milling and dairy farming), in the rehabilitation of victims of the Basmachestvo, in resettlement of returnees from Afghanistan and IDPs, in poverty alleviation, in education. The target for the delivery of industrial goods was consistently under-fulfilled: for example, in 1928, in the first quarter by 40% and in the fourth quarter by nearly 50%. General subsidies for the domestic budget were on an average underpaid by between 35 and 40%. Meanwhile, taxes were levied on Tajikistan at a level around 60% higher than in Uzbekistan. The report was highly critical of the Uzbek government's record. It concluded that the Centre needed to clarify the meaning of "autonomous" especially with regard to budgetary rights, which should be increased "within the bounds of the Soviet understanding of the concept of autonomy". Otherwise, experience showed that the UzSSR tended to treat the TaASSR in the same way as it treated Okrug Executive Committees (Okrug Ispolkoms) and even, as far as decrees were concerned, Raion Executive Committees (Raiispolkoms). Finally, the report recommended the speedy establishment of an independent office of Uzbektorg in the TaASSR with a self-admini-stered account. Tajikistan should be able to manage this office independently of Uzbekistan.

The Uzbeks were also accused of manipulating the supply of goods to Tajikistan via Termez. Situated on the Afghan frontier and at the entrance to the Surkhan-Darya valley leading north to Dushanbe, Termez lay on the main all-weather route from Tashkent to the Tajik capital. It was a natural staging post. However, in reorganising the Termez supply base and giving it responsibility for supplying the whole of southern Tajikistan, the Uzbek Unification Agency (Uzbekbirlyashu) had failed to consult the Tajik authorities. The result of this reorganisation had been that 500,000 different industrial items were stuck in Termez where, by all accounts, they were being sold off. The Tajiks protested and considered it necessary to concentrate the job of supplying the whole of Tajikistan on the Tajik office of Uzbekbirlyashu and to subordinate the Termez office to it. The Tajiks also complained at the unsuitability of some of the goods supplied. Shoes had been undersupplied for example, while the levels for the supply of perfumes and wine had been exceeded.[2]

The Tajiks' own development plans sometimes brought their own problems. A big programme of re-settlement was already under way, aimed at bringing people out of the mountains to the valleys of the south where it was envisaged that they would work on the newly planned cotton farms. Gotfrid reported in June 1928 that between 500 and 600 resettled people were still on the road, while others had already arrived in Kurgan Teppe. Many had been robbed by the Basmachi, who came over the frontier from Afghanistan. The latter were becoming more active now that spring was approaching, stealing camels and robbing resettlement convoys. To counter their activities he had sent a militia detachment with two machine-guns and had organised village self-defence units of six to eight men each. In some regions, e.g. Panjikent (note how far north), the Basmachi were making political capital out of their criminal operations. As far as political work was concerned, the Uzbek People's Commissariat for Finance (Narkomfin) had sent the necessary "agitmaterials" via the normal post with the result that they were now stuck in Termez. The Uzbeks had also failed to live up to their promise to send the materials in the Tajik language.[3] Even here it seems, the Uzbeks were seen as letting the Tajiks down.

10

TAJIKISTAN'S FOREIGN RELATIONS

The National Territorial Delimitation in 1924 brought the unification of the territories deemed at the time to be both inhabited by
Tajiks and capable of being administered from the new republic's
capital Dushanbe. Until then these territories had been administered
separately, with the Eastern Pamirs having been inherited by the
TASSR from the Tsarist Governorate-General of Turkestan and the
western part of the new ASSR having been part of the Bukharan
People's Soviet Republic. The inhabitants of the former had only been
incorporated into the Russian empire after the Anglo-Russian frontier
agreement of 1895, while those living in the latter had legally been,
until that date, citizens of a foreign state.[1] In neither case had the
locals had much experience of Russian rule, whether Tsarist or Soviet.
Indeed, insofar as the inhabitants of the region had had any contacts
outside their immediate environment, it could be claimed that they
looked, not to the provinces of the infidel Russian empire to the north
and west, but to the adjacent Islamic regions to the south and east,
much of the population of which was ethnically, linguistically and
culturally similar. This is not to say that the rule of the Mir Muhammad
Murad Beg of Kunduz or the Amir Abdul Rahman of Afghanistan
was more benevolent than that of the "White Tsar". Far from it. But
the uneducated and intensely religious local population was not
familiar with the principles of what we would now call "good gover-
nance" and certainly not in the habit of demanding it from local
rulers. When the Amir Abdul Rahman launched his two attacks on
Badakhshan in 1883 and 1887, while a substantial part of the local
population took refuge in the Ferghana Valley, many of those who fled
his campaign did so to Yarkand in China and to Chitral in British-

controlled India. Later, many more thousands fled across the Oxus into Afghanistan to escape the instability caused by the Basmachestvo (much as they did during the Tajik civil war seventy years on). For people whose lands had for centuries been fought over by contending rulers the concept of the state defined by secure frontiers was incomprehensible.

Once Soviet rule over the Tajik ASSR was established in 1924, while responsibility for the new autonomous republic's relations with the outside world was theoretically taken over by Moscow, the Soviet capital faced extraordinary difficulties putting this responsibility into practice. Not only was the population unused to the very concept of "foreign relations", but controlling this remote and mountainous frontier represented a challenge that Moscow was not immediately able to meet. For all practical purposes the frontier with Afghanistan remained open for more than ten years after the formation of Tajikistan. It was not officially closed until 1936.

The Soviet government appreciated the problem early on and adopted a flexible policy. In 1926, for example, the Special Frontier Commission of the Central Asia Office discussed the fight against smuggling in the Pamirs. It advised that the government should be very careful not to introduce restrictions on travel and trade that they would be unable to enforce. Such measures would alienate the local population, which relied on smuggling for its supplies and its income. The commission also discussed the advisability of allowing the inhabitants of the Sarai-Parkhar district to cross the frontier into Afghanistan to purchase daily necessities. They had to remember that the Soviet system was not yet able to provide them with everything they needed. Confirmation of the situation came from the other side of the frontier. An intelligence report of the British Political Agent in Gilgit dated 1927 mentioned that movement across the Pyandzh (Oxus) was completely free and unrestricted.

After 1924, official relations between Tajikistan and the outside world were conducted via Moscow. For example, it was to the British embassy there that the Soviet government communicated the elevation of Tajikistan from an autonomous to a union republic in 1929. Commenting on the announcement, in a letter to London, P. Fitzpatrick thought that the aim of the move was to "settle the disturbance caused by the Bacha Saqao's regime in Kabul and to encourage refugees to return from Afghanistan".[2] This official announcement did not mean, however, that Moscow had a monopoly of contacts between Tajikistan and the outside world. The great majority of these contacts were direct and unofficial. First, Basmachi units continued to launch attacks on Soviet territory from Afghanistan at least as late as Fuzail Makhdum's incursion in 1929. Second, as we have noted, there was a constant flow of contraband across the Oxus. Third, there were regular contacts between members of families, clans, tribes and other groups who found themselves on different sides of the frontier.

The context in which many of these contacts took place was the relationship between the spiritual head of the Ismaili sect, the Aga Khan, and his flock in the Pamirs, who after 1924 found themselves citizens of the Soviet Union. In his encyclopaedic study of the Ismailis, Farhad Daftary writes that "in the twentieth century the Aga Khans have not had any contacts with their followers in Central Asia and Chinese Turkestan, following the establishment of communist regimes in those regions".[3] A closer study of the Russian and Soviet sources reveals that this was far from being the case. Given the extreme remoteness and inaccessibility, especially of the Autonomous Region of Mountainous Badakhshan (GBAO), the fledgling Soviet state was unable to mount effective patrols or controls until the mid-1930s. This, combined with the local Ismailis' interest in maintaining contact with co-religionists in Afghanistan and India, and with the Aga Khan himself in Bombay, meant that this part of Tajikistan at least conducted its own foreign relations quite independently of Soviet control. For their part, the Soviets were commendably flexible in the face of these realities. In 1925, the Special Frontier Commission of the Central Asia Office (Sredazburo) recommended that it would not be expedient to try and prevent the Badakhshani Ismailis from travelling to a conference with the Aga Khan in Bombay. As the commission concluded "even if we forbid it, they will almost certainly go illegally".[4]

The origins, history and detailed beliefs of the Ismaili community in the Pamirs lie outside the scope of this study. However, it may be useful to explain very briefly the way in which authority was exercised in the community. A class of holy men or "ishans" was responsible for the spiritual well-being of the community, supervising their religious observances and social behaviour. While in theory authority was invested in these ishans by confirmation from the Aga Khan himself, in practice, the remoteness of the region and complexity of Badakhshani society meant that the link with Bombay was often tenuous. Nor does there appear to have been any organised system for testing the doctrinal expertise of the various claimants to ishan status. Those ishans who achieved undisputed authority frequently controlled large groups of followers ("murids") spread over a wide area of Central Asia where Ismaili communities could be found – from Central Afghanistan in the west to Yarkand in Xinjiang to the east. One responsibility of those ishans who were in contact with Bombay was to collect religious tax ("zakat")[5] from the faithful and send it to the Aga Khan there. This task gave the tax collectors ample scope to siphon off some of the funds on their way to India. The right to collect zakat was therefore keenly contested by all who could lay a claim to the requisite status, with the sons of established ishans often claiming this right by inheritance. Candidate ishans would go to great lengths, including "personal" contributions to Bombay of large sums of gold and currency, to obtain "firmans" (decrees) from Bombay confirming their rights. For example, after the death of the prominent ishan Sayyid Mahmud Sho, his son Sayyid Oris found his claim to inherit his father's status challenged by the son of a rival of his father, one Khoja Badal. Despite urgent pleas from the Aga Khan to bury the hatchet, the feud worsened. Keen to consolidate his claim, Khoja Badal scraped together a large sum in gold and silver coins and ingots and dispatched it to Bombay as a supplementary zakat contribution. The grateful Aga Khan obligingly issued a firman giving Khoja Badal the title "mukki" (ishan). Sayyid Mahmud Sho, incidentally, had distinguished himself in May 1917 by joining Aziz Khan (see above) in calling on the Amir of Bukhara to re-establish control after his authority had been terminated by the Shughnan Soldier's Committee.

For one reason or another, during the late 19th and early 20th centuries, several leading ishans had been obliged to flee Badakhshan and seek refuge in neighbouring territories. One such was Sho Zoda Lais who fled the Amir Abdul Rahman Khan's attack in 1883 and moved to British-controlled Chitral. Russian and particularly Soviet writers have been at pains to show that he, and others who found themselves on British-controlled territory, allowed themselves and their networks of murids to be used by British intelligence not only to gather information but even to stir up insurrections against Soviet power in Russian-controlled Badakhshan and elsewhere. According to these claims, for example, the British used one Timur Khan, an Ismaili "pir" (holy man) from Chitral to ferment an anti-Soviet uprising in Badakhshan in the summer of 1922.[6]

Likewise, after trying unsuccessfully to establish Sho Zoda Lais in a listening post north of the Oxus, the British were said ultimately to have settled him in Zebak in Afghanistan from where he was able to control all movement to and from Badakhshan into India. Sho Zoda Lais' son Sho Abdul Moani had, like his father, murids and subordinate junior clerics, or "khalifas", scattered over the whole region, from the Tarim and Yarkand in Xinjiang in the east through both Tajik and Afghan Badakhshan, to Chitral and the Northwest Frontier District of British India.[7] Abdul Moani was described by L.N. Kharyukov, earlier a GPU officer in the GBAO, as one of the more energetic pirs in the pay of the British, who was active collecting information on Soviet human rights abuses for the Aga Khan to use in the League of Nations. As late as 1930 the Aga Khan issued a firman granting him the right to collect zakat. He was killed in a shooting accident in 1936.[8]

The same writers have also claimed that the British used the Aga Khan's whole Bombay-based network to gather information about the new Soviet administration in Central Asia and to spread anti-Soviet propaganda. Although such claims are rarely supported by firm evidence, it seems very unlikely that the intelligence bureau in India would have failed to profit from the possibilities offered by a well-disposed network, which enjoyed such easy access to Soviet territory. These and more general claims form a whole "genre" of Soviet literature, which accuses the British of every sort of anti-Soviet activity, from arming the Amir of Bukhara and supporting the Basmachestvo, to generally establishing intelligence-gathering networks throughout the region. Such activity was also seen as inextricably linked to British interference in the politics of Afghanistan, especially perceived conspiracies aimed at destabilising the position of King Amanullah Khan (ruled 1919–29) whom Simla regarded as unacceptably independent-minded and pro-Soviet.

While some of these claims of British interference in Central Asia appear rather far-fetched, there is ample unbiased evidence that, following the Bolshevik revolution, the British government of India was deeply concerned at what it saw, or thought it saw, going on the other side of Afghanistan's northern frontier, and was determined both to try and stop the advance of Bolshevism and to gather as much information as possible about the Soviet government. Indeed, it would have been regarded as extremely remiss if it had not done so. The Malleson mission to Ashkabad is well documented.[9] Colonel "Eric" Bailey, when escaping from Tashkent in 1918 after an adventurous but largely fruitless mission there on behalf of the Indian government, records having met two Indian army NCOs in Bukhara who had brought a hundred camel-loads of "supplies" up from Meshed.[10] However, such evidence as there is suggests that even before 1924, many in both London and Simla had become thoroughly disillusioned by the "Basmachestvo" and were keen to avoid close contact with the Amir of Bukhara, who since his flight from Bukhara in 1920 had been a guest of the Amir of Afghanistan in Kabul. In December 1924 HM Minister in Kabul Sir Francis Humphreys wrote to the Secretary of State for India about the Amir's request to travel through India on the "haj". Humphreys recommended imposing strict conditions on the Amir. He should only be allowed to transit British territory and with a small retinue. Commenting on this letter, P. Fitzpatrick of the Foreign Office wrote "it is difficult to know to what extent Basmachi activities are being restrained from Kabul".[11] Not exactly the comment of a senior member of the government machine which was masterminding them. Commenting later on a similar request from the Amir, J.G. Acheson, Deputy Secretary for the Government of India, wrote on 27 October 1927 of his "extreme anxiety not to lend colour to the belief that we are secretly in touch with the revolutionary (sic) elements in Bukhara. Haidar Hoja Mirbadaleff has already displayed a desire (*which was not encouraged*) [author's italics] to act as an Indian intermediary to such elements".[12] Bailey had been helped by Haidar Hoja in Bukhara in 1918 and the two had remained friends. Haidar had fled to Afghanistan in 1920. But, by 1927, he had clearly become something of an embarrassment at the official level.

Perhaps the main listening post outside India maintained by the British after the 1917 revolution, for keeping an eye on events in Soviet Central Asia, was the Consulate-General in Meshed. The mixed feelings about the Basmachestvo harboured by officials in this and other offices is illustrated by correspondence in April 1923 arising from the appearance in Meshed of a delegation claiming to represent Enver Pasha's lieutenant and successor Sami Bey of the so-called

"Turkestan Nationalist Committee" (Enver had been killed in August 1922). The leading members of this group, Ahmad Zaki Walidi and Abdul Qadir (described rather improbably as a "Cossack"), approached the Consulate-General hoping to attract British support for the Basmachi. Describing Sami Bey as a leading figure in the Turkestan pan-Islamist movement, Major D. Thompson, the Military Attaché, expressed anxiety lest, not content with exporting Islamic revolution to Russia, he might also wish to take it to India. The ensuing debate about how to react to this approach shows considerable difference of opinion amongst the various officials concerned. While Thompson was sceptical, HM Minister in Kabul Humphreys, whom Ahmad Zaki later approached, seemed more sympathetic, noting that "the Committee of Union and Progress is distinctly anti-Russian in sentiment" . . . and . . . " there is no proof that the Bolsheviks have yet captured the Pan-Islamic movement". Likewise, in June 1923, Monteith of the J and P (s) Department (of the India Office) wrote "Sami Bey seems to be keeping the flickering flame of anti-Bolshevik effort alive in Bukhara". Whatever the sentiments of the various parties, the correspondence engendered by this incident is hardly consistent with the reaction of British intelligence to an approach from a movement it was actively supporting.[13]

Throughout this period, the British Consulate-General in Meshed produced a regular stream of intelligence summaries on events in Soviet Central Asia, which are available in the India Office Library in London. In the main, they report the strength of Soviet military units and the incidence of Basmachi raids. There is very little political reporting. At a distance of ninety years it is hard to assess how valuable these reports were to government officials in India and London. It was natural that the former at least should try to follow the military strength and intentions of a neighbouring power whose hostility they had good grounds to suspect. Certainly the army department in Simla continued to regard Meshed as a very important post. Others were perhaps not quite so sure. In 1929, the Persian foreign minister Timurtash asked the British government to replace the military attaché in Meshed with a civilian. He explained that the Soviet government had asked Tehran's agreement to the establishment of a military attaché's post in Sistan. The Persians were reluctant to agree but found it difficult to refuse as long as Moscow could point to the equivalent British post in Meshed. The Foreign Office reaction was surprisingly muted. In March 1929, Fitzpatrick minuted that the value of the intelligence received from Meshed had "fluctuated considerably". While there had recently been a better coordination of the items of information recorded (whatever that might mean), there had also been an increase in the amount of intelligence of a purely military character. Faint praise indeed. As far as the value of the political intelligence is concerned, the reader of this material cannot but be struck by the fact that, as late as July 1929, the summaries were still referring to Soviet Central Asia as the Turkestan Soviet Socialist Republic, which had ceased to exist five years earlier! [14]

With the benefit of eighty-odd years' hindsight, British military intervention and support for anti-Soviet groups in Central Asia may appear to have been half-hearted and short-lived. Likewise, British intelligence-gathering operations across the frontier from Meshed may seem to have produced scant returns. On the other hand, the new and relatively weak Soviet government of the 1920s can be forgiven for seeing in these operations a considerable threat from a powerful and hostile neighbour, in whose overthrow, incidentally, it believed history had assigned it a major role. The busy and uncontrolled comings and goings of Ismaili leaders between the GBAO in the new TaASSR and British India naturally caused great concern in Tashkent and Moscow.

Whereas in the 19th century successive Aga Khans in India may not have paid much attention to the fortunes of their followers in Central Asia, the 1920s saw an increase of contacts. This quickening of interest arose as a result of the appearance of a reform movement in the Pamirs that became known as the Panjabhai movement. The coincidence of this movement's entry onto the regional stage with the advent of Soviet power in the early 1920s inevitably prompted some Soviet observers to regard it as a creation of British intelligence. For example, the Eastern Secretariat of the Executive Committee of the Communist International (IKKI) attributed its formation to the British. They thought that the latter had been worried to see zakat returns dwindling, and, equally important, the number of Ismaili faithful also declining, as British influence in the Pamirs was reduced.[15] Other Soviet historians attribute the genesis of this reform movement to the greater freedom of religious practice that became possible with Soviet rule in Badakhshan.[16] Picking one's way carefully between the different interpretations, it seems likely that a group of

Ismaili reformists chose the unsettled circumstances following the termination of Bukharan rule in the Western Pamirs to question the authority of some of the established hereditary ishans (holy men). Prominent amongst these reformists was Sayyid Haidar Sho, the same man who had been chosen as "Comrade Chairman" of the Shughnan Soldiers' Committee in May 1917. In 1921, Sayyid Haidar Sho travelled to Bombay to lay before the Aga Khan a charter of reform proposals.

This charter drew on mediaeval Ismaili teachings and practices dating back to the Fatimid period in Egypt when the Ismaili sect came into being. The proposals included a seven-tier hierarchy of the priesthood, and a governing Council of five to seven members in which the ishans role should only be an advisory one and restricted to religious affairs. The ishans should also be required to be well qualified in religious matters. In a nod to the new Soviet masters, the charter declared that no one should have the right to exploit the labour of others. Attention was also drawn to the need for self-improvement and mutual help. The charter recommended the establishment of prayer-houses where wise preachers were to put the flock on the right track on moral issues, basing themselves on the teachings of Nasir Khosrow [17] whose name was to be introduced into the communal "zikr" ceremonies. The reforms should be introduced by new "societies" ("anjomans"), which were to be set up throughout the region. The initial reaction of the Aga Khan seems to have been positive. In 1922 he sent one of his representatives, Sayyid Munir, to the Pamirs to supervise the implementation of the reforms while, the following year, another emissary, Sabza Ali, was sent with instructions to set up the anjomans.

Another of the reforms attempted by the Panjabhais in their charter was a change in the nature of zakat and the mechanism through which it was collected. They proposed to introduce accurate accounting methods. Instead of a compulsory tax, it was to be regarded as a voluntary contribution. One result of these changes was that the amount of money contributed by the faithful diminished, while the sum taken to Bombay actually increased; the reason being that the ishans who had hitherto collected it had creamed off a goodly portion for themselves.

The Aga Khan's positive attitude did not last. The ishans in the Pamirs swiftly identified in the Panjabhai movement a serious threat to their time-honoured privileges, particularly their right to collect zakat and send it to Bombay. Protests began to rain down on Bombay accusing the Panjabhai movement of heresy and of undermining the very structure of the faith. Simultaneously, voices began to be heard in the Aga Khan's entourage that warned that the reforms might encourage separatism amongst the Pamiri Ismailis, a trend which might be exploited by the Soviets. Particularly the promotion of Nasir Khosrow was seen as an indication of Pamiri nationalism and an attempt to distance the community there from the authority of the Aga Khan.

By 1927 the Aga Khan's entourage in Bombay had made up its mind. A firman was sent to two of the leading Badakhshani ishans commanding that the anjomans be dissolved. The following February, a further firman ordered that: "those who had been collecting zakat for us should no longer do so. The pirs whose duty it was to hand over all that was collected should do this as they did before". Parallel with these orders, Sayyid Arab Sho received a message via Sho Abdul Moani to the effect that the Aga Khan's mother had instructed that Naser Khosrow should no longer be invoked as "pir sho" during zikr but instead the invocation should be "Ya Muhammad, Ya Ali". Towards the end of 1928, the Aga Khan sent yet another firman saying that "every believer, especially those who collect zakat, should consider himself subordinate to his ishan in everything". Thus was re-established the authority of the ishans which the conservatives in Bombay had decided should be reinforced. As a final move to tighten control over this distant group of independent-minded Ismailis, the Aga Khan ordered that all leading ishans should visit Bombay once a year. Although this shows the confidence he had in the porous nature of the Soviet frontier at the time, this assumption was soon to be challenged, as the Soviets consolidated their administration in the region. In December 1927, the payment of zakat was forbidden for Party members.

Despite the obstacles set up by different opponents, the Panjabhais kept going well into the 1930s. In 1931 they even sent zakat to Bombay and were rewarded with the re-instatement of their right to collect it and with the "pir sho" invocation during zikr. But even in this remote part of Tajikistan, the days were numbered for their freedom to carry out these traditional rituals and to travel abroad. The frontier was closed in 1936, by which time the payment of zakat was dying out.

11

THE CREATION OF THE TAJIK SSR

Despite the misgivings in the NTD's sub-commission at leaving 60% of the Tajik population outside the confines of the Tajik Autonomous Oblast', the Tajiks had consoled themselves with the thought that these arrangements might be revised at a later date. Imomov pointed out that the cultural level of the mountain Tajiks was considerably lower than their co-ethnics or the Uzbeks in the big cities. Their main occupations were "collecting snow and thorn bushes to send to the markets of the towns" (for refrigeration and fuel).

Uniting the mountain and the city Tajiks might one day be possible but not immediately.

There also appears to have been hope that the large Tajik centres remaining in Uzbekistan would, until suitable new centres were developed in the TaASSR, serve as a training ground for Tajik cadres. When the chairman of the Territorial Commission's meeting of 21 August 1924 had asked where the Tajiks' main centre would be, someone in the room shouted "Dushanbe", but it then transpired that the most densely populated place was Karatagh, now a remote and insignificant settlement. Abdurahim Khojibaev added that the Tajiks' principal temporary cultural centre would in fact be Samarkand where they would have to set up schools etc. As they couldn't yet organise any cultural centres in the TaASSR, the Tajik cities within the UzSSR would have to fulfil this function. He confirmed that there were no further problems except some unfinished business in Ura Teppe, which they could sort out after the delimitation. Finally, he confirmed that, while Samarkand and Bukhara would be cultural centres, the administrative centre would be Karatagh. It isn't clear from the record at what stage this idea was dropped.[1] In view of the tiny size of today's village, it is hard to believe the proposal was ever serious, although the fact that it was made shows how modest a centre even Dushanbe was at that date.

The decision to form a TaASSR had at the time been greeted with pleasure by the local Communists, few though they may have been in number. Nusratulla Maksum, chairman of the Karatagh Ispolkom and shortly to be promoted to the temporary job of Executive Committee (Ispolkom) Chairman of Eastern Bukhara (shortly to be absorbed into the TaASSR), and Alimjan Akchurin,[2] who was to become his deputy in August, swiftly penned a telegram to Karklin and Rakhimbaev offering profound thanks.[3]

However, although obviously prepared to make the right noises publicly, Nusratulla Maksum (or Lutfullaev as he came to be known) soon began to have his own doubts as to the justice of the division of territory that had been agreed. In a note addressed to the Central Committee of the Russian Communist Party undated but written while he was still chairman of the Eastern Bukhara Executive Committee (so, presumably in 1924), Nusratulla Maksum challenged the earlier decree ordaining the entry of the Tajik Autonomous Oblast' into the structure of the UzSSR on the grounds that many places with Tajik majority populations had been left outside its frontiers. This, he claimed, violated the rights of the Tajik nation to self-determination at the same time as those rights were being granted to the Uzbeks and the Turkmen. He requested that the Central Committee review the decree and revisit the question of whether regions like Ura Teppe, Khojand, Kanibadam, Isfara, Sokh and Rishtam (sic) and other places with a Tajik majority should be included in the Tajik Autonomous Oblast'.

Invoking historical arguments, which were to become common currency in Tajik nationalist discourse, he reminded the Central Committee that "until the end of the 19th century many places in Tajikistan such as Darvaz, Karategin, Kulyab, Shughnan and Rushan were completely autonomous and independent from both the Bukharan Amir and the Khan of Kokand (both Uzbeks). It was only after the Russian conquest that the Bukharan Amir succeeded with Russian help in subjugating the free Tajik people."[4]

Protests like these were to grow in intensity in the years following the NTD as the awareness of a separate Tajik identity grew amongst an intelligentsia whose outlook had been shaped by association with the Turkic-dominated Jadid movement and who, in the past, had tended to see demands for independence and national self-expression in the context of a pan-Turkic agenda. As we have seen, these protests were to feed on injustices in Uzbek treatment of the subordinate TaASSR for whose development they were theoretically responsible. These injustices had been further demonstrated in the way the Uzbek authorities manipulated the census of 1926 to consolidate their dominance in regions that the NTD had allocated to Uzbekistan in 1924, but that they feared might be re-allocated at a later date. There was also intense resentment amongst the Tajik intelligentsia at the way the Uzbeks had, already during the existence of the TASSR, failed to fulfil their obligation to grant cultural rights to the Tajik minority within these regions.[5]

By 1928 the Tajiks were growing increasingly impatient with their lot as an ASSR within Uzbekistan. On the one hand, as even the Central Asia Office (Sredazburo) recognised, the Uzbeks turned out not only to be negligent of the obligations they had undertaken in 1924 with regard to the economic development of the TaASSR and the cultural advancement of both the Tajiks there and the large Tajik minority in their own country; there was also ample evidence that the Uzbek party and government was siphoning off for its own use funds and credits sent from Moscow which were expressly earmarked for Tajikistan. In view of the considerable progress made, despite these obstacles, in developing the small mountainous area allocated in 1924 to the TaASSR, there were voices in the Tajik leadership who demanded a re-examination of the status of centres of Tajik settlement such as Samarkand, Bukhara and Khojand which fell outside it. Such voices recalled that, at the time of the 1924 delimitation, these towns and their surrounding areas had been allocated to Uzbekistan partly because Tajikistan had still been devastated by the Basmachestvo and unable to administer these relatively large centres. Now that the Basmachestvo was defeated (the final serious incursion from Afghanistan, staged by Fuzail Makhdum in 1929, was to weaken the Tajik case somewhat, but that was still in the future and was anyway brief when it came) the time had come to call in the debt and claim these historic Tajik cities. The Tajik leaders of 1924 such as Muhieddinov, whose undeveloped sense of Tajik national pride had at the time led them to acquiesce in a solution that left the majority of their fellow ethnics outside the bounds of their ASSR, had had time to reflect on their misguided indulgence. As time went on, numerous Tajiks began to become aware that they were separate from the Uzbeks. As Rzehak has noted,[6] "the founding of Tajikistan was not the result of Tajik nationalism but the hour of its birth". With the formation of the ASSR, Tajik speakers began to dare to see their identity as different from that of Uzbek-dominated Turkestan. A significant part of this new awareness focused on the issue of language. Andreev noticed in 1925 that the inhabitants of Kon-i-Bodom and Isfara had started insisting that all official correspondence be addressed to them in Tajik. In the same year, at the Party-sponsored celebration of Tajikistan's first birthday, the ceremonies were held in Uzbek. This piece of tactlessness led to anti-Uzbek demonstrations, which seem to have had some effect. The Uzbek People's Commissar for Education Mu'min Khoja was obliged to advocate the opening of Tajik- language schools and clubs in Samarkand and Bukhara. Another important milestone along the route to Tajikistan's separation from Uzbekistan was Shirinshoh Shohtimur's letter to Stalin of 25 June 1926 complaining of attempts by Uzbek nationalists to block circulation of the newspaper *Ovozi Tojik*, and of threats to newly graduated teachers who wanted to teach Tajik in Samarkand.

Once the TaASSR had been established, the requirement for committed Tajik cadres grew. As we have seen, what with the shortage of suitable material, extremely young men found themselves in positions of authority. Some of these younger Party members came from a different tradition from the Bukhara-based former Jadids like Muhieddinov. The likes of Shohtimur and Ismailov,[7] both Pamiris, and the former's protégé the Afghan Nissor Muhammad, had not been exposed to the pan-Turkic influences of their older comrades.

At this time there was also hope that the "Raionirovaniye" would lead to a redrafting of the frontiers in Tajikistan's favour. At any rate, the initial Tajik demand at this stage seems to have been that the Tajik districts in and around Khojand, Samarkand, Bukhara and Surkhan-Darya be transferred to the TaASSR.

The new Tajik point of view seems to have attracted some support in Moscow, where Stalin was increasingly concerned at the nationalist aspirations of a Turkic Uzbekistan that had, thanks to the NTD in 1924, succeeded in uniting in one state all the former important regional centres, such as Bukhara, Khiva and Kokand. This was an achievement which the Amirs of Bukhara had long dreamt of but never been able to achieve. Perhaps Uzbekistan needed to be cut down to size.[8]

The archives currently available are silent as to the pressures that persuaded the Uzbeks to give Khojand up to the Tajiks. When one considers the determination with which they resisted the transfer of the other two great Tajik-dominated cities, Samarkand and Bukhara, it is hard to believe they surrendered without a struggle. Whatever the circumstances, on 31 March 1929, the Executive Committee of the Uzbek Communist Party reached the decision to transfer Khojand to the Tajik ASSR.

It is unfortunate that the key document that sets out the Tajiks' claim for the transfer of territory from Uzbekistan – the so-called "evidential note" submitted by the Tajik Obkom of the Uzbek Communist Party to the Central Asia Office (Sredazburo) and signed by twenty-seven members of the Obkom – is undated.[9] This note was read and commented on at length by Aleksei Dyakov who, ten days after the transfer was decided, had been made responsible for managing the transfer of the city and Okrug.[10] His comments are also undated, but suggest that he must have been in a position of authority to assess the Tajik demands for some time before then. Certainly he will have read the study of the historical background to the ethnic distribution within the Surkhan-Darya Oblast' which I. Alkin of the Communist University of the Toilers of the East (KUTV) had finished by 19 February, but which had presumably been commissioned some time before that, possibly as a result of the "evidential note".[11] Although there is no clear evidence, it seems fair to date the "evidential note" some time at the end of 1928 or very early in 1929.

Such documentary evidence as there is suggests that, while the Communist Party's Central Committee in Moscow was well aware of the irritation building up amongst Tajik leaders over perceived Uzbek maltreatment of their autonomous republic, the decision to do something about it was relatively sudden. In the decree of its IVth Session of the 4th Convocation called on the 15 December 1928 to review the UzSSR government's report (for the year) the Central Executive Committee wrote:

> In the field of securing the provision of the cultural, national and economic needs of Tajikistan, the Central Executive Committee of the USSR proposes to the government of the UzSSR that they

should pay special attention to the necessity for work and continuing assistance and cooperation with the toilers of Tajikistan
with regard to an accelerated establishment and development of
agriculture and a fuller satisfaction of the cultural requirements.[12]

There is no hint here that at the end of 1928 things had reached the
stage where Moscow was intending to hand a key part of Uzbek
territory to Tajikistan, let alone create an entirely new union republic
out of what was then part of the UzSSR. And yet, within a matter of
weeks, even days, the first steps were being taken to transfer Khojand.

The official announcement of the transfer was made in the name of
the Ispolkom at the All-Uzbek Congress of Soviets which followed.
(see Appendix D for the text of the Act of Transfer).

Although the Tajiks' initial claim had simply been for the transfer
of territory, as we shall see below, it was pretty clear to those involved
that they had more ambitious plans. Nonetheless, for the time being,
despite their suspicions that they would ultimately have to cope with
a Tajik demand for Union Republic status, the Communist Party
decided to concentrate on the immediate claims – for the transfer of
territory and cities. Assuming that Moscow accepted in principle that
the TaASSR had recovered sufficiently from the devastation of the
civil war to be able to administer large population centres like
Khojand, Samarkand and Bukhara, there had to be two conditions
governing the response to Tajik demands for their return: first, that
the majority of their population was indeed Tajik, and second that
there were no telling economic reasons why they should not be
transferred to the Tajiks' eponymous state. Dyakov was well aware of
Tajik complaints that the Uzbeks had manipulated the results of the
1926 census by using various forms of pressure to persuade Tajiks to
register as Uzbeks. One form of such pressure was a refusal to give
work to Tajiks, which compelled many to register as Uzbeks. As
Dyakov summed it up:

> The reason for this [electoral manipulation] is that, under the
> influence of a section of the Uzbek party and some workers in the
> Soviet apparat also, there has occurred a perversion of the
> nationalities policy of the Party and Soviet authorities regarding
> ethnic minorities in general and the Tajiks in particular, a
> perversion which expresses itself in a desire to Uzbekify the

Tajiks by whatever means possible. In support of this we can mention the following facts.

During the census of 1926 a significant part of the Tajik population was registered as Uzbek. Thus, for example, in the 1920 census in Samarkand city the Tajiks were recorded as numbering 44,758 and the Uzbeks only 3301. According to the 1926 census, the number of Uzbeks was recorded as 43,364 and the Tajiks as only 10,716. In a series of kishlaks [villages] in the Khojand Okrug, whose population was registered as Tajik in 1920 e.g. in Asht, Kalacha, Akjar i Tajik and others, in the 1926 census they were registered as Uzbeks. Similar facts can be adduced also with regard to Ferghana, Samarkand, and especially the Bukhara oblast's.

The differences in the interpretation of the 1926 census results and the methods used to achieve them were to form the core of the dispute that developed between the Uzbek and Tajik sides.

The "evidential note" had drawn attention to the difficult circumstances created by the Basmachestvo, which had obliged the Party to concentrate its work in the east of the area inhabited by Tajiks. In consequence, in the 1924 NTD some 740,000 Tajiks had been left outside the frontiers of the ASSR. At the time, the note continued, the members of the territorial commission on the NTD, the chairman of which was I.A. Zelenskii, and even some members of the Politburo of the Central Committee of the Communist Party of Uzbekistan, both Russian and Central Asian, expressed their bewilderment at this unsatisfactory solution to the Tajik problem. As the note put it with only a slight degree of exaggeration, it was only the categorical statement of both the Tajik and Uzbek comrades that this was a temporary solution, combined with an understanding of the problems then facing the Party in Eastern Bukhara and Turkestan, that dispelled this bewilderment. The commission stipulated that leaving the main body of the Tajiks with their cultural centres inside Uzbekistan by no means meant that these provinces should be out of Tajikistan's reach once it had achieved the status of a state. It likewise foresaw that these centres should become the main cultural and economic centres for the main body of the nation. Once the military operations in the country had ended and a Soviet government established, the commission anticipated the unification of those estranged parts of Tajikistan.

The Tajik argument continued that the Basmachestvo was now defeated. Zelenskii had himself declared in 1927 that it had been totally destroyed. As already mentioned above this was not strictly true. Fuzail Makhdum's incursion of 1929 and his attack on Garm still lay in the future. However, if Zelenskii had declared it to be true, the Uzbek communists could hardly deny it.

Furthermore, significant progress had been made in repatriating some 60,000 refugees of the approximately 250,000 who had fled to Afghanistan during the civil war. Meanwhile, more than 8000 Tajik households had been transferred from the mountains to the Vakhsh Valley (as part of the programme of resettlement in areas earmarked for the development of cotton production).

Perhaps mindful of their relative weakness and lack of influence and experience, the Tajiks seemed to have considered it would be counter-productive to dwell in too great detail on the unsatisfactory way in which the Uzbeks had discharged their responsibilities towards the Tajik part of their republic. They contented themselves with saying that relations between the two nations were "extremely bad" and that, in contrast to their treatment of Kyrgyz, Kazakhs and Karakalpaks, the Uzbeks had grossly neglected the cultural and economic rights of the Tajiks. Despite this, the Tajiks had not until then raised any territorial disputes against the Uzbeks. All this said, they continued that "without going into details of the inadequacies of the Uzbek performance in looking after the interests of Tajiks residing in the UzSSR, we declare that *we are now moving the territorial question into pride of place*" [author's italics]. That is to say, at this stage, in their "evidential note" the Tajiks were concentrating on territory transfers within the UzSSR, and not raising the question of the complete separation of the TaASSR from Uzbekistan.

What were the Tajiks' territorial demands? "The unification with the TaSSR of those areas with indisputable Tajik majorities, always taking into account that those areas where the Tajik population is more scattered, but where Tajik rights must be secured, may be made a special case at a later stage." In the opinion of the "evidential note", these areas were: the Khojand Oblast', northern districts (Raiony) of the Syr Darynskii Okrug, the city of Samarkand and its surrounding districts, the former Bukhara Begstvo and its city. According to the Tajiks' calculations the population of all these areas was divided as follows: Tajiks: 514,368; Uzbeks: 162,030; others: 94,563, leaving a total of 748,958. Amongst "others" the Tajiks had included Ironis (now definitely seen as separate from the Tajik community), local Jews (who incidentally were also Tajik speakers), Arabs and Russians. In the Uzbek total they had included Lokay and Karlyuks.

The argument that then unfolded between the Tajik and the Uzbek delegations (led respectively by Khojibaev and Islamov) revolved around the question of whether the 1926 census could be regarded as reliable. The Tajiks argued that the Uzbeks had falsified the results. Their evidence was that, whereas the 1920 census showed that, for example, the Tajik element in the population of Samarkand and Bukhara was 75–98%, the 1926 census showed a proportion of 15–20%. Such a change in such a short space of time could not be explained any other way – except by a massacre, which even the Tajiks did not claim. Enquiries showed that more than 50% of the Tajiks had been obliged by pressure from the Uzbeks to have themselves registered as Uzbeks. This pressure consisted mainly of threats to resettle them in Eastern Bukhara or to refuse them employment, if they did not relent, etc.

The Tajiks further argued that, given the serious doubts as to the 1926 census, a solution of the current dispute should be based on the same statistics on which the National Delimitation itself had been based, i.e. the 1920 census (in the TASSR) and the Military-Demographic census undertaken in 1913. These gave:

for the Bukharan Emirate: 210,000 (70%) Tajiks and 75,000 (25%) Uzbeks

and,

for the Turkestan Republic:

Former Ferghana Oblast': 450,000 Tajiks
Former Samarkand Oblast': 750,000 Tajiks
Other places: 100,000 Tajiks
Total 1,300,000.

This gave a grand total of Tajiks for both Bukhara and Turkestan of 3,400,000.

Dyakov's reaction to these demands casts an interesting light on what the Russians in the Party thought of the two sides' arguments.

As a starting point, Dyakov states that there is no doubt that the larger part of the population of Samarkand and Bukhara is Tajik. Clearly, the leadership was not impressed by the 1926 census figures, which had been massaged by the Uzbeks to produce a result in which they formed the majority. Nor were they inclined to accept what they seem to have regarded as a specious Uzbek argument that, while Tajik might be their mother tongue, many Tajiks saw themselves as of Uzbek origin. In this context, what mattered in Stalin's definition of nationality was the linguistic criterion. On the other hand, Dyakov considered that the transfer of these two cities was not expedient since, firstly, neither of them bordered on Tajikistan, indeed they were separated from the main body of the country by high mountain ranges, and, secondly, they were administrative and economic centres for areas inhabited largely by Uzbeks. So Dyakov continued to be swayed by the economic/administrative considerations ranked already by Krasnovskii in 1923 for the Raionirovaniye Commission (see page 53 above) as the dominant factor in deciding where to allocate territory.

Dyakov applied rather different criteria in formulating his recommendations regarding Khojand. On the one hand, he again dismissed the 1926 census as inaccurate. To quote: "the data from the pre-1926 censuses show that the percentage of Tajiks was actually higher than indicated, because many were recorded as Uzbeks in the 1926 census. The 1920 census gives 63.32% Tajik and 33.55% Uzbek, which is probably closer to the truth [than the 1926 figures of 59.94% Tajik and 38.88% Uzbek]". On the other hand, the undoubted physical separation of Khojand from the bulk of Tajikistan's mountainous territory was not allowed to weigh as heavily as it had with regard to Samarkand and Bukhara. From the economic standpoint, Dyakov held, it also made sense to reunite Khojand with the large fertile district of Ura Teppe which was famous for its production of fruit, cotton, silk and grain, and which, without a large adjacent centre like Khojand, was rather cut off from the rest of Tajikistan (indeed). Equally important, from the political point of view, Tajikistan would benefit enormously from the addition of Khojand, since the Party there had more members and was better organised than anywhere else in Tajikistan. At the time, the Party in Khojand had 1572 members, which would give a huge boost to the party's membership in Tajikistan.[13] It is still not entirely clear why these arguments were not accepted with regard to Samarkand, which could have increased Tajikistan's staff of communists even more substantially. Perhaps it was the fact that in Samarkand's surrounding villages the Uzbeks predominated so heavily. In any case, the illogicality of Dyakov's position was academic. The decision had already been taken and he simply had to give it symbolic approval and organise the practicalities.

Dyakov did not ignore the cultural angle either, noting that, despite the recognition that Khojand was a Tajik area, the instruction in most schools was still in Uzbek. Even in towns like Asht the correspondence with the Rural Council (Selsoviet) was conducted in that language. In the Soviet Administration of the Okrug the majority of workers were Uzbek and the recruitment of Tajiks was not proceeding satisfactorily. He had already written that, while prepared to refuse the unification of Samarkand and Bukhara with Tajikistan, he considered it important that the interests of the Tajiks there be secured by the establishment of Rural and Town Councils (Selsoviets and Gorsoviets) and by arranging instruction in the Tajik language, not only in those two cities but in "other Tajik-inhabited areas in Ferghana, Andijan, Kashka Darya and Zeravshan".

Dyakov next considered the proposal that Surkhan Darya should be attached to Tajikistan. It was hard to judge the accuracy of the 1926 census figures (which gave 202,213 Tajiks) because there had never been another census there (it having been a part of the Bukharan Emirate, which was not examined in earlier counts). The commission on "Raionirovaniye" had recognised a Tajik majority in Baisun Raion and a considerable presence in Denau and Sari Assiya, which had been attached to the TaASSR in 1925. Dyakov was reluctant to make a decision without further investigation but concluded that "as these regions adjoin Tajikistan and are similar to it economically, they might be joined to it".

As part of their demands regarding Samarkand, the Tajiks had proposed moving their capital there from the village of Dushanbe. Having refused the proposal to make Samarkand Tajik, Dyakov was bound to rule out this transfer also, adding, for good measure, that it would adversely affect the development of former Eastern Bukhara, which, being a sensitive frontier region, anyway deserved to have a strategically well-placed centre.

Finally, although concentrating at this stage on the question of the Tajik cities, Dyakov also tackled the implicit demand that the

TaASSR be separated from the UzSSR and promoted to the level of "Union Republic". He rejected the idea on three grounds: first, Tajikistan was not strong enough to have this status; second, it had only a small territorial link with the RSFSR (through the Kyrgyz ASSR, which at the time was part of it), and third, once Khojand was added to its territory, Tajikistan would of necessity continue to rely on close transport links via Uzbekistan. Dyakov's argument about the close link to Uzbekistan made good sense, especially in the 1920s when there was no reliable or regular civilian air traffic, and in winter communications between the different parts of Tajikistan were impossible without using Uzbekistan. As for the concept that all union republics should have a useful land connection with the "mother" republic of Russia, this was deeply embedded in strategic Soviet thinking. But, as Soviet power and with it Soviet self-confidence, strengthened, other ASSRs within the RSFSR would gain union republic status even where they had no common frontiers with Russia – e.g. Kyrgyzstan, separated from Russia by Kazakhstan when the latter became a Union Republic. Of another separated republic, Armenia, the Russians were doubtless confident that fear and hatred of Turkey would prevent any attempt by the Armenians to secede from the Union.

Dyakov was not by any means pleased with the outcome of his deliberations. When he sent his conclusions to Ostroumov[14] on 16 April 1929 he complained that there had been insufficient statistical and economic data and too few people to ask for advice. He described the outcome as "unsatisfactory".[15]

It was interesting that, in considering Tajik claims to Samarkand and Bukhara, the Centre, whatever misgivings there may have been about the threat of pan-Turkism or straightforward Uzbek chauvinism raising its head in Uzbekistan, (and the numerous references to these dangers in the records show that these misgivings definitely existed), it was not thought a realistic option to weaken the dominant regional power still further by depriving it of even one of the two most famous cities in the region. The chairman of the Commission of Inspection, who had been sent to Bukhara in the summer of 1929, wrote back to Makeev (chairman of the Central Asian Economic Council (EKOSA) and a member of Kirkizh's commission (see below) after two months in the region, expressing his amazement that Bukhara was not to be allocated to Tajikistan. The overwhelming majority of the inhabitants

of both the city and (interestingly as this is often denied) the surrounding villages, were Tajiks. The Organising Committee had even
ordained that all instruction in schools should be in Tajik. "Why" he
asked "is everyone shutting their eyes to the dangers of pan-Islamism
and pan-Turkism?". Makeev was at the time preoccupied with the
Tajik–Uzbek dispute over Surkhan-Darya and no acknowledgement of
this message is to be found in the archive.[16]

The Khojand Okrug was formally transferred to Tajikistan in May
1929 by a decree of the III All-Uzbek Kurultai (Assembly). However
some of the details of the transfer were fiercely disputed during the
autumn of 1929, while, as we shall see, the issue of Surkhan- Darya
was to drag on into 1930.

Although the Tajiks' initial demands had been limited to the
transfer of towns and territory, it was apparent to some that they had
further ambitions. In his comments on the Tajiks' "evidential note",
Dyakov made it clear that the Communist Party did not expect the
Tajiks to be satisfied with the transfer of the "lost cities":

> "This [the Tajiks'] line of argument suggests that, in addition to
> the demands openly expressed in their note, two other demands
> are implicit in the contents: the transfer of the capital from
> Dushanbe to one of the other Tajik centres; and the separation
> of the TaASSR from the UzSSR".

Dyakov also indicated that such demands had been brewing for some
time. Using the Party jargon of the day, he added:

> Recent demands for the separation of the TaASSR from the
> UzSSR have been put forward, not only by individual Tajik
> workers in the Soviet and Party "apparat", but such demands
> have been quite widespread amongst the non-party intelli-
> gentsia. For example, at the teachers' conference in Bukhara in
> January 1929, this demand was made quite openly by several
> delegates.

> Apropos the question of education, Dyakov added that, in
> Bukhara's schools with Tajik children, in 1928, only 68% of the
> pupils were being taught in their own tongue. An inspection of
> the "Uzbek" schools (again presumably in Bukhara) found that
> the mother tongue of 78% of the children was Tajik.[17]

Meanwhile, the Tajiks' implicit raising of the question of a separation from Uzbekistan had taken on a life of its own and the Party began seriously to reconsider Dyakov's initially sceptical reaction. In her book "Memories of a short life" Baroat Khojibaeva is unspecific about dates until the beginning of June. Up to then, she writes: "The Party "Activ" listened to [Nusratulla] Maksum and [Abdurahim] Khojibaev's presentation on the separation and regrading of Tajikistan as an independent Union Republic and decided on an application to the Party's Central Asia Office (Sredazburo) to approve this proposal." Again, she writes: "The Tajikistan leadership repeatedly directed requests about this to the Central Asia Office and to the Central Committee of the Communist Party of Uzbekistan". According to her record, her father Abdurahim went to Moscow at the very beginning of June 1929 and asked for a meeting with Stalin. The Tajik leadership had authorised him to meet the leader and persuade him of the need to establish an independent Tajik republic. Stalin agreed to the meeting and also invited a representative of the UzSSR to be present. According to this account, after a meeting which lasted an hour and a half, having heard the arguments of both sides, Stalin decided that a Tajik SSR should be established.[18] An interesting side-light on this interview is thrown by a letter written by Khojibaev to Shirinshoh Shohtimur from Moscow. Presumably he thought it safer to write since he starts the letter saying he prefers writing to speaking on the telephone or communicating by telegraph (displaying a healthy awareness of the activities of the state security agencies). Khojibaev's letter continues

> The Uzbek question is like vermicelli – without beginning or end. We still do not know the decision of the Central Executive Committee (TsIK). I have been with Comrades Rykov and Voroshilov and yesterday with Comrade Stalin. Comrade Stalin gave a series of directives, of which I can say that he and all the others support Tajikistan's direct entry into the Union.

Presumably this letter was written on or shortly after the meeting on 1 June.[19] Khojibaev does not reveal why Stalin favoured union republic status for Tajikistan. Whatever the internal considerations, the international scene to the south of the Soviet Union was changing in a way that perhaps made the proposition more appealing to the

Soviet leader. With the departure of the sympathetic Amanullah from the throne of Afghanistan, and the ascendancy of the nationalist Reza Shah Pahlavi in Iran, the attractions of establishing a Soviet model Iranian state in that corner of Central Asia became greater than ever. When the complex process of creating the new Tajik SSR was complete, Moscow's declarations celebrating its foundation gave special emphasis to the role the new socialist statelet was to play as an example to Asian neighbours.

Once the "vozhd" ["leader": the title often given to Stalin – on a par with the German "Fuehrer"] had ruled what was to happen, the Soviet government organs could also move. They did so quickly. Already on 12 June, a session of the Presidium of the Central Executive Committee (TsIK) of the USSR chaired by Abel Yenukidze[20] considered Khojibaev's report, which had been sent in by the Tajik government. They then issued a protocol for circulation to Stalin, as well as to the Central Executive Committee of the USSR, the Central Executive Committee of the Tajik ASSR, as well as Comrades Kirkizh, Khojibaev and Chutskaev (no further details) and the People's Commissar for Finance (Narkomfin) of the USSR. In this protocol the presidium considered it "timely to raise the question of the separation of Tajikistan from Uzbekistan and the advancement of the former to union republic status". The Congress of Soviets of Tajikistan, the Congress of Soviets of Uzbekistan and the Central Executive Committee of the USSR should discuss the matter. Meanwhile, a commission under the chairmanship of K.O. Kirkizh and including comrades Tajiev (no further details) and Chutskaev, as well as representatives of the TaASSR (later to be joined by Makeev of the Central Asian Economic Council[21] and Peters), should work out the procedure for the separation of the two states, which included the separation of their budgets.[22]

By 22 June 1929, the chairman of the Central Asia Office, Zelenskii, addressed the problems thrown up by the decision to separate the two republics in a top secret letter to Shubrikov, Makeev, Pismennyi and Boldyrev.[23] First, Zelenskii briefly ran through the decisions already taken with regard to transferring Tajik-dominated regions of UzSSR to Tajikistan. Khojand Okrug, including Nau, could be transferred. Samarkand and Bukhara could not. The regions of Surkhan-Darya, northeast of the Amu Darya, and the Babatag mountains, Termez town and Pata Gissar should be transferred. Part of the "Turkmen raion" should also be included, although the desirability of splitting the "raion" should be discussed. The frontier might run south via the Surkhan river. However, Zelenskii's thoughts on Surkhan-Darya clearly did not amount to a final decision since he recommended that the ethnic composition of the area be established, by comparing the data of the NTD (1924) with the national "Raionirovaniye" and the 1926 census. The dispute over Surkhan-Darya had clearly not yet been resolved.

Turning to the question of separating the two republics, Zelenskii, ever the true bureaucrat, sketched out the formalities which should be followed to give the impression that the initiative for the move had come from the Tajik masses: the plenary sessions of the Dushanbe and Ura Teppe Soviets should take the initiative by tabling motions, which should take the form of appeals to the government of the TaASSR. The Tajik Presidium could then discuss the appeals and call special sessions to do so. Finally a special (III) congress of the Soviets of the TaASSR should be called. In view of the hurry, Zelenskii reckoned they could dispense with "raion" and "viloyat" congresses and move straight to the All-Tajik Congress. A special commission under the chairmanship of Makeev would be established with one Uzbek and one Tajik member, to clarify frontier and other questions arising from the separation. Comrade Pismennyi would take on responsibility for agit and education, while Comrade Shubrikov would "renew the agit work".[24] A press campaign would have be launched, but under the strict control of the Party. The Agitprop department would have to work strictly within the "theses" of the Central Asia Office. Representatives of the War Commission for Water Supply (Voenvod) and the War Commission on the Economy (Voenkhoz) would be recruited for Makeev's commission. The whole operation was conceived to give the impression that the move had been initiated by "the toiling masses", while in fact both the original decision and the methods of implementation were carefully orchestrated from above.

Arrangements would also have to be made for the separation of the two regions' budgets and the credits that had been allotted to them. State organs like the State Trading Agency (Gostorg), Turkestan Silk Agency (Turksholk) and Aziabank would have to be split, and Tajik branches established. The consumer and agricultural and industrial cooperatives would have to be rationalised. Moreover, all of this would have to be carefully timed so as not to get out of sync with the different economic cycles and cause an interruption in the functioning of the various organisations.

Zelenskii had emphasised the need for speed. Those involved set to work without delay. By 6 July the Central Asia Office's Executive Committee held another meeting to push the process along and fix the date of the next plenum for 29 July. Meanwhile they also heard a complicated report from Shubrikov on the principles for dividing up the capital held by the various state agencies that existed in the UzSSR. His suggestion was that local state agencies like Uzbektorg (Uzbek Trading Agency), Uzavtopromtorg (Uzbek Automobile Industry Trade Agency), Uzselkhozbank (Uzbek Agricultural Bank), Uzgostorg (Uzbek State Trading Agency), Sredazselkhozsnab (Central Asian Agricultural Supply Agency) and so on, would be divided between the two republics. The Tajik SSR would receive the money originally allocated to the TaASSR, plus a proportion of that originally allocated to the UzSSR based on the proportion of the Uzbek population resident in the newly transferred territories, plus a further proportion of other shareholdings corresponding to the proportion of the Tajik population within the old frontiers of the UzSSR.[25]

As disputes arose over the marginal areas of the Khojand Olast' and over Surkhan-Darya, the Tajiks began to worry lest what had now become their principal objective i.e. the separation of their ASSR from Uzbekistan, might be held up. They wanted the question of Uzbekistan's cession of territory to be clarified, signed and sealed before the problems linked to separation could be addressed. Although the Central Executive Committee of the Congress of Soviets of the UzSSR had confirmed the "Act", handing over Khojand on 7 September 1929, there were various points which still worried the Tajiks. Nusratulla Maksum telegraphed to Enukidze on 19 September 1929 with a copy to Kirkizh, at that time Secretary of the Central Committee of the Uzbek Party, complaining that "the question of transferring the Tajik regions of Uzbekistan to Tajikistan is being held up. We consider it vital to unite the new regions prior to the Congress of Soviets and ask you to tell the Central Asian territorial commission to hurry up." Enukidze clearly asked the Uzbeks what was going on, as a telegram arrived from Samarkand (NB still the capital of

Uzbekistan) on 30 September (copied to Islamov, the Uzbek delegate) as follows:

> The Central Asian/Uzbek commission for investigating frontier questions has finished its work. The transfer of the Khojand Okrug to Tajikistan is formalised. The solution of some minor points has been deferred. We do not object to the definite formalisation of Tajikistan in accordance with your 01596.
> Signed Faizulla Khojaev and Ikramov.

Nusratullah Maksum came back on 8 October 29 attempting to raise the pressure still further:

> The presidium of the Central Executive Committee of Tajikistan protests against the Kirkizh commission's deferment of the resolution of our territorial disputes with Uzbekistan. We insist on a decision on the unification of the Tajik districts (okrugi) of Uzbekistan in the spirit of our written document before the re-constitution *** [illegible] as instructed by the Presidium of the USSR.

As the Tajik government had approved the Khojand "Act" on 2 October, it is probable that Maksum was by now concerned mainly with Surkhan-Darya. The beleaguered Enukidze replied with a telegram dated 10 October to Dushanbe:

> The resolution of the disputed question is postponed with the aim of ensuring the convocation of the congress of Soviets of Tajikistan at the appointed time. After the completion of the congress's work the disputed points will be quickly solved.[26]

So, in effect, a final decision on the thorniest issues (mainly Surkhan-Darya) was to be postponed until after the official declaration of Tajikistan's new status within the Union.

Despite the haste, the important part of the exercise had taken several months. However, by 8 October 1929, the Executive Bureau of the Tajik Party's Oblast' Committee (Obkom) was able to accept in principle Comrades Maksum's and Khojibaev's report on how the new SSR was to be announced at the forthcoming III All-Tajik Congress of Soviets. The final editing of the draft would be undertaken by a commission whose members would be Shohtimur, Glukhovskii, Vainer, Klok,[27] Maksumov and Sadullaev. At the same meeting, the prudent members proposed that the name of the capital city Dushanbe should be changed to Stalinabad. On 16 October 1929, the III Extraordinary All-Tajik Congress of Soviets issued an official declaration on the formation of the Tajik SSR. This was followed by a parallel declaration by the III Extraordinary Session of the Central Executive Committee of the UzSSR, while, in March 1930, the relevant decision of the II Session of the Central Executive Committee of the USSR concerning the Tajik SSR's acceptance into the Union was confirmed by the VI All-Union Congress of Soviets. With these elaborate rituals, the formal blessing of the Soviet government was given to the decisions taken earlier by the Party.

The Party's arrangements also had formally to be adjusted. On 25 November 1929, the Party's Oblast' Committee agreed to rename the local party the "Communist Party (Bolsheviks) of Tajikistan" and to rename itself the Central Committee of that party. This was announced on the same day by the Central Committee of the All-Russian Communist Party in Moscow.[28]

12

THE FINAL TERRITORIAL BATTLE – SURKHAN-DARYA

The relative delay attending the confirmation of Tajikistan's promotion by the All-Union Congress of Soviets in March 1930 reflected the long drawn-out nature of the battle for the Surkhan-Darya province – the last significant region of Uzbekistan the Tajiks' claim to which had not been resolved in 1929. During this dispute the Uzbeks again defended their retention of Surkhan-Darya by citing the 1926 census which gave them between 56% and 97% of the rural population throughout the province, and the majority of the urban population in all the towns except Baisun (it should be noted that at the time 95% of the population was rural). According to the Uzbek position, the only rural area where the Tajiks formed a solid mass of the population was Sari Asiyan, and even there they were only 37%. In all other districts the Tajiks formed "isolated islands in amongst the Uzbek areas of settlement and, anyway, between these areas with significant Tajik populations and the frontier of the Tajik SSR there was a zone inhabited exclusively by Uzbeks".

The study commissioned from I. Alkin of the Communist University of the Toilers of the East (see above) seems to support the Uzbek case in giving the Uzbeks 74% and the Tajiks 20% respectively.[1]

However, the study added that, before 1924, when EKOSA launched an expeditionary examination of the situation in Bukhara and Khorezm (still People's Soviet Republics at that time), nothing approaching an accurate population survey had been attempted. This had been too late for the NTD.

The argument about Surkhan-Darya came to the first of several critical junctures at the 26 July 1929 Session of the Commission for

Tajik questions chaired by Makeev and attended by Khojibaev (for Tajikistan) and Islamov (for Uzbekistan).[2] This was an extremely bad-tempered confrontation between the re-presentatives of the two sides, with Makeev vainly trying to keep the peace between them. Islamov annoyed Khojibaev at the outset by trying the diversionary tactic of claiming Kurgan Teppe, which had already been allotted to Tajikistan in 1924, on the grounds that the majority of the population there was Uzbek. Khojibaev's answer revealed that the Tajiks had learnt a thing or two since 1924, when they had been too modest to claim their rights. Whereas he admits that the 1926 and 1927 censuses gave the Uzbeks a considerable majority in Kurgan Teppe, now, thanks to the massive work being undertaken by the Party, the figures (not including resettled Tajiks) were: Tajik 30,604; Uzbek 20,000. The sceptical historian is bound to ask how, if Tajik internal immigration is excluded (which, incidentally, we know had already started), this turn-around was achieved. Islamov then tried a further diversionary tactic by venturing to reopen the question of areas surrounding Khojand, using economic, political and ethnic arguments wherever it suited him, without any regard for consistency. Kanibadam and Isfara (with Tajik majorities) should be part of Uzbekistan because of their economic links to Uzbek territory, and Nau (with its Uzbek majority) should also belong to Uzbekistan on ethnic grounds, although it depended economically on Tajik territory. The exchanges got ever more personal and crotchety. When Islamov referred to the 1926 census results, Khojibaev brushed them aside as "chuzh" (nonsense) and anyway challenged Islamov's authority to reopen any questions that had already been agreed. For his part, Islamov pointed out that Khojibaev himself signed the 1926 census statistics for Surkhan-Darya, which indicated that he must have agreed them. At some stage, Khojibaev threw in a charge that Uzbeks in Tajikistan were three times as well treated as Tajiks in Uzbekistan, adding for good measure that Uzbekistan had not yet returned the 500,000 gold roubles which Tajikistan handed over earlier (no further details are given about when and why this money was transferred).

Khojibaev adduced a number of historical arguments to support the Tajik case. Surkhan-Darya had been part of Eastern Bukhara. The Amir had had a summer residence in Dushanbe. The military-demographic census carried out by the Russian general staff had described Bukhara as a Persian not an Uzbek state. He too yielded to the temptation to reopen other claims. Samarkand was only 70 km from the Tajik frontier and it was nonsense to say they could not administer it. The Kyrgyz had been allotted Osh, which was miles from Frunze (Bishkek). Even Tamerlane in his diary, held in London, described Samarkand as a Tajik city.

In addition to the rural areas of Surkhan-Darya, the Tajik claim also included Termez. Both sides agreed that neither of them had a majority there, as the town was overwhelmingly populated by Russians. Nonetheless, it was an important centre for Tajikistan, being convenient for river transport to points upstream on the Pyandzh and Vakhsh rivers. Tajikistan was also planning a road to Jilikul, while the budget had been allocated for the railway to Dushanbe, which was to be finished by 1 September (despite efforts by the Uzbeks to delay it). A road was also planned to Kurgan Teppe.

In his final summing-up, Makeev reproached both Khojibaev and Islamov for behaving like representatives of their respective countries rather than members of the Communist Party. Khojibaev seemed even to have developed an appetite for new claims. History had been dragged in unnecessarily. Nobody needed Tamerlane. For his part, Islamov did not have a directive from the Party to resist on all points. So the dispute would have to go to arbitration.

Meeting again on 8 September, the commission heard a report on the ethnic make-up and economic situation in Surkhan-Darya produced by two specialists: Belov and Karpov. This report concluded that, albeit with only approximate accuracy, they could confirm a Tajik majority only in the volost' of Sari Asiyan and the uezd of Baisun. It therefore recommended the transfer to Tajikistan of Baisun, Sary Asiyan and also those parts of the Denau Raion that had a Tajik majority and adjoined the Tajik frontier. The transfer of Termez to the Tajik SSR for economic reasons was also recommended. Despite this, the figures were so close, and no doubt Makeev's patience so exhausted, that the commission not only rejected the Tajik claims but announced that its work was complete and that any further challenges would have to be addressed to the Central Executive Committee of the USSR itself. Makeev and Irismetov signed the document that certified this conclusion. The Tajik Muhieddinov and Afghan Nissor Muhammad refused to do so.[3]

The challenge was not long in coming. On 21 September, Muhieddinov asked the Central Asia Office for a review of this decision. The recommendations of the Belov/Karpov report should be rejected.[4] It was now the turn of the Central Executive Committee of the USSR in Moscow. Confronted with these labyrinthine arguments, they called for an assessment from the Central Statistical Directorate in Moscow. The Directorate's reply was signed by the director Yepatovskii and the director of the census department O. Kvitkin and dated 21 December 1929. Pointing out that, as the Okrug was only separated from Bukhara by the NTD of 1924, there were no reliable statistics on the ethnic composition of Surkhan-Darya before then, the assessment continued that:

> The censuses of 1897, 1917, 1920 and 1923 failed to cover this territory. The material produced by the Bukharan emirate in 1917 was never published but it is known that it did not contain information on the ethnic make-up of the region. Meanwhile, the statistical record of localities belonging to Bukhara which was compiled by the military authorities [in 1913?] has not been used anywhere in the ethnographical or statistical literature.

So a comparison with the data of the 1926 census could only be achieved on the basis of the local investigations carried out through questioning local leaders in 1924. This gave information on the permanent population linked in one way or another with the local economy, whereas the 1926 census covered the whole available population. This comparison permitted the conclusions that:

> 1. In all the uezds existing before the delimitation and in the territories corresponding to them which exist now, the Uzbeks form the dominant ethnic group. However, according to the data of 1924, before the delimitation, they made up a smaller proportion of the population than that registered in the 1926 census. According to this, the share of the Tajiks in these territories turned out in 1926 to be significantly less than it had been before the delimitation: in Baisun, for example, 37.9% as opposed to 43.9%; in Shirabad 6.8% instead of 18.5% and in Yorchi Uezd 22.4% against 35.9%.

> 2. A similar conclusion can be drawn regarding the weight of the Tajik element when looking at the number of households in

relation to nationalities. Only in the Baisun Uezd and its corresponding post-1926 okrug did the percentage of Tajik households remain almost the same: 38.6% against 38%. In other uezds they turned out to be many fewer: in Shirabad 7.3% against 16.3%; in Yorchi 24.4% against 36.3%.

3. Looking at the figures for volost's – an administrative term which existed only up to the delimitation – an absolute majority of Tajiks can be seen only in two: Sari Asiyan (60.9%) and Baisun (50.3%). In Bashkurd Volost' the Tajiks are a little behind the Uzbeks: making up 47.2% – whereas they used to be 58.4%, forming a comfortable majority. At that time the Jar Kurgan and Shirabad volost's were overwhelmingly Uzbek.[5]

The Central Statistical Directorate in Moscow seems, like virtually all other non-Central Asian observers, to have accepted that the 1926 census underestimated the Tajik population, although its report makes no attempt to explain how this came about.

Accordingly, the Central Executive Committee of the USSR decided to hold a meeting on 13 January 1930 to decide this thorniest of problems. The Uzbeks at once protested. Yuldash Akhunbabaev, the Chairman of the Uzbek government, fired off a telegram to Moscow "categorically protesting" and asking for the meeting to be postponed to allow the Uzbeks time to collect more materials including the conclusions of the "Central Asian organs" (by which he meant of course the Uzbek organs). These materials rehearsed the usual debate about census returns, but the Uzbeks had thought of additional arguments as well. Taking a couple of leaves out of the Tajik book, they drew attention to the relationship between the Uzbek tribes living in Surkhan-Darya province, mainly Kungrad and Qataqan, and those on the Afghan side of the Amu Darya. Given the uncertainty regarding the national question in Afghanistan, the Uzbeks argued that transferring the province to Tajikistan could not be regarded as a positive step. Moreover, like Tajikistan, Uzbekistan had its own plans for resettling peoples in areas of the country with a surplus of land, of which Surkhan-Darya was one. Already that year, the Uzbek paper claimed, some 5000 families would be moved there from the overcrowded Ferghana Valley as part of the national plan to boost the country's cotton production. The Uzbeks also disputed the

Tajik claim that the province was naturally connected with Tajikistan. It was in fact a self-contained unit whose traditional lines of communication ran westwards. Admittedly this argument could be used against the Uzbeks if the Tajiks were to gain their claim for Bukhara but the Uzbeks were confident that this claim would be rejected.

In spite of these arguments, the presidium of the TsIK of the USSR decided on the 3 February 1930 in favour of the Tajik claim, although they took care to make provision for the treatment of the non-Tajik population: "Bearing in mind that the development of the economic and cultural and social reconstruction amongst the indigenous population requires the simultaneous expansion and deepening of the provision for national minorities in both countries", the Surkhan-Darya Okrug, within its current frontiers, is to be transferred to the Tajik SSR within two months.[6]

The Uzbek reaction was swift. A note signed by Babeshko and Kleiner (no further details) protested that, in allocating Surkhan-Darya to the Tajik SSR, the Committee had

> not taken sufficient note of the data on the national composition and economic orientation of the Surkhan-Darya Okrug or the arguments for leaving it in the UzSSR ... In the name of the government of Uzbekistan, we request that the presidium reconsider its resolution on the Tajik SSR's claims.[7]

The protest was effective. On 13 February 1930 the Presidium of the USSR government revoked its earlier decision and decreed that Surkhan-Darya should remain in the UzSSR. The reasons for this last minute reversal remain a mystery. In his book *Istoriya Topornogo Razdeleniya*, the Tajik historian Rakhim Masov speculates that, had the Surkhan-Darya Okrug, along with Termez, been transferred to Tajikistan, Uzbekistan would have been deprived of its sole frontier with a country outside the USSR. Such an external frontier was, he claimed, a pre-requisite for union republic status.[8] If this was indeed the reason, one can only wonder why an organ as high as the Presidium of the TsIK of the USSR did not take it into account in its earlier deliberations or, if it comes to that, why the Uzbeks did not use it as ammunition for their earlier arguments.

CONCLUSIONS

With the National Territorial Delimitation in 1924, the Soviet Communist Party embarked on a project of unprecedented revolutionary daring. After the First World War, the fragmentation of the pre-war empires had presented the governments of the new political order with new challenges in the creation of national identities. Some, like Yugoslavia, had to create new unifying national doctrines. Others, such as Greece, felt the need to convert their newly acquired "other" (in this case Slav-speaking) minorities to their own (in this case Hellenic) national identity. The process of assimilation involved the erasure of previous identities and was often conducted brutally[1]. The Soviet project was much more complex and ambitious than this two-dimensional approach. The ultimate aim was to create an entirely new socialist identity in which it was believed that national self-awareness would in due course disappear.

In the pre-Soviet period, the Tajik element of the population of Central Asia possessed few if any of the characteristics regarded by modern historians and political analysts as necessary for the birth of nationalism or even the formation of an ethnic identity, let alone a nation or a nation-state. Certainly there was no sign of the industrialised society with its concomitant universally available education, which Ernest Gellner has regarded as vital for the formation of true nationalism. In a paraphrase of his analysis, the TaASSR was still in the agrarian phase, which might allow a select elite of initiates to enjoy the mysteries of Tajik identity, but did not have the means to spread the message sufficiently widely for true nationalism to develop.[2] However, as we have seen, in Tajikistan even the select elite could not so easily be found. Moreover the TaASSR fell far short of

Anthony Smith's definition of the requirements for ethnic identity: "a common proper name, myths of common ancestry, historical memories, an association with a given territory and one or more distinctive elements of culture." [3] Even a common name eluded most of those who in the early 20th century were invited to consider the question of their Tajik ethnic identity. As Sukhareva and Gabrielyan noted as late as the 1960s, Bukharan Tajik-speakers often described themselves as Uzbeks and, when called on to define those who called themselves Tajiks, simply replied "people from Tajikistan" (i.e. the mountains). Even the Tajiks of those mountains seem to have used the name only piecemeal. Speakers of Eastern Iranian languages called themselves "Tajiks" and Persian-speaking neighbours "Farsigu", whereas the "Farsigu" called them in return "Ghalcha". Although in the mediaeval period the term Tajik existed to describe non-Turkic people in the region, little is known about what the term meant to the Tajiks themselves and in any case this was long before the emergence of any sort of concept of the national state in the modern sense.

Nor were there many characteristics which set the Tajiks apart from their neighbours. In the Central Asian cities of the plains and their agricultural surroundings, Western (overwhelmingly Russian) observers could distinguish no difference in lifestyle, customs and beliefs between the Tajik speakers and their Turkic neighbours. They shared both their religion and their "national" myths. The famous poet Alisher Navo'i is revered in the post-Soviet nationalisms of Central Asia by both Uzbeks and Tajiks, who know him as Fani – the name under which he wrote much of his Persian poetry. Nor could outside observers see any difference in their physical appearance. The distinctive "European" look, which set the Tajiks apart from the "Asiatic" looking Turks, was confined to the Tajiks of the mountains.

The only distinguishing factor between the Tajiks of the plains and the Turks that surrounded them was language. Even here, in the "Sart" culture of the cities at least, bi-lingualism was extremely common and language was not necessarily perceived as a sure indication of ethnic or national identity. The Tajiks of Samarkand and Bukhara did not feel they had anything in common with the Persian-speaking Shi'i "Fars" and still less with the Jews, both of whom dwelt alongside them in the cities. As we have seen, these divisions stifled Tajik enthusiasm for the first Persian-language newspaper after the revolution, *Sho'leh e Enqelob*, which was produced mainly by the Shi'i immigrant Alizodeh. Even Sadruddin Ayni, the grand old man of Soviet Tajik literature, spoke both languages equally well and wrote poetry and songs in Uzbek as well as Tajik.

In such an atmosphere, in which the concept of national identity had not yet been developed, few if any Tajiks went so far as to consider whether or not they, whoever they might be, should be associated with a particular territory. By the early 20th century, the area over which their language was used for official purposes was administered by five different governments: the Emirate of Bukhara, the Tsarist Governorate-General of Turkestan, the Kingdom of Afghanistan, the Mamalek e Mahruseh of Iran, and, to some extent, British India. For as long as anyone could remember, the adjacent regions had always been a kaleidoscopic mosaic of empires, kingdoms and local khanates whose frontiers and rulers frequently changed and whose rulers usually spoke both Persian and Turkic. As for historic sites that might have been considered redolent of Tajik myth and legend, the two cities that best qualified for such a role had been presided over by Turkic-speaking khans since the 11th century. It was to take the organised identity-engineering of the post-Soviet state to remind the Tajiks that the Samanid rulers of Bukhara could qualify as their co-ethnic heroes of the distant past.

At the beginning of the 20th century, it had been Russian scholars who took up the cause of the Tajik nation. When in 1924, the Soviet government decided on the "National Territorial Delimitation", it was exclusively Russian "orientalists" who contributed to the exhaustive study of the Tajik nation that was to promote the realisation of the Tajik "ethnie". However, even these "orientalists" could not help noticing that the Tajiks of the cities of the plains, like Samarkand and Bukhara, were not only living "all mixed up" with the Uzbeks but were indistinguishable from them in appearance. It was the Tajiks of the high mountains where, if not always Persian, then at least Iranian languages were spoken, who struck them as different in manners, culture and appearance. But the Tajiks of the Soviet and post-Soviet periods saw their national territory not just in the mountains; they wanted the cities of the plains as much or even more.

There was one example of cultural exclusivity that played a certain role in the formation of the Tajik "ethnie" and was to be important in the first Soviet proposal for the creation of a Tajik Autonomous

Republic within the Uzbek SSR. In contrast to the Sunni Tajiks of the plains, a fair number of the high mountain Tajiks were Ismaili Sevener Shi'ites – followers of the Aga Khan. Political planners saw their Sovietisation as a possibly useful example to the other Ismailis in an India ruled by the hated British. This consideration seems to have been an important factor in the decision to elevate Tajikistan from the oblast' status originally proposed to the next administrative level up – Autonomous Soviet Socialist Republic –which would give a more solid base for the development of Tajik national consciousness and a better springboard for later promotion to union republic status. However, this Ismaili identity was confined to an influential but relatively small proportion of the Tajik population and could not be extended to embrace the Sunni majority who had more in common with their Uzbek co-sectarians.

Anyone reading the words of the project for the creation of a Tajik Autonomous Oblast' written in 1924 could be forgiven for wondering whether they might form the kernel of a Tajik persecution myth which could be used later to consolidate the Tajik sense of common identity. This formulation ran:

> The conquering Turkic peoples enslaved them. Part of them became totally Turkicised and adopted the language of their conquerors, while the rest, although they kept their language, took refuge in the mountainous and semi-mountainous regions of Samarkand Oblast' and Bukhara, and in the valleys of the mountain rivers and the basin of the Syr Darya and the Zeravshan where they were driven by their conquerors.

However, in the pre-Soviet period there appears to have been little or none of the national resentment so crucial for the birth of any sort of liberation movement. Probably the majority of Tajiks lived under the rule of the Amir of Bukhara – a rule which, though despotic, was sanctioned by Islam. Moreover, the official language of the Emirate was Persian and many if not most of the officials who ran this ramshackle state were entirely familiar with that language. Insofar as prejudice and persecution were levelled against any particular groups it was on religious grounds. Non-Muslims were disadvantaged – Jews barely tolerated as an inconvenient but occasionally useful historical presence, Christians and Twelver Shi'ites enslaved, and Sevener

Ismailis persecuted. To the extent that there was any movement against the despotic obscurantism of this state, it was articulated by the Jadids. But, so far from seeing themselves as Tajik nationalists, this group took its inspiration from the teachings of Ismail Gaspirali, the Tatar reformist for whom Muslim identity in the Russian empire was based on Turkic solidarity. The Persian language was, if anything, symbolic of the retrograde societies of the old Central Asian khanates. Those Central Asian intellectuals, such as Muhieddinov and Imomov, nearly all of whom were bi-lingual in Turkic and Persian, but who might have guided the spread of Tajik national consciousness in what Anthony Smith has described as the vertical type of "ethnie", had fallen under the spell of the pan-Turkic message of the Jadids. As members of the Jadid-inspired Young Bukhara movement, they hastened to identify themselves as Uzbeks. It was left to the Russian exponents of the Soviet message to offer the Tajiks their own autonomous state within the Uzbek SSR, a state in which they were to experience an ethnic discrimination unknown under the Amirs of Bukhara. In this new national state, the dominant "ethnie" were the Uzbeks, who were prepared to use political and economic weapons – the manipulated census and diversion of financial resources – to persuade the Tajiks to assimilate and adopt the prevailing ethnic culture, and to punish those who refused. In the years that followed the 1924 NTD, the Uzbek Party's neglect of its obligations towards the Tajik ASSR to whose development it was theoretically committed, proved a tactical error, as did its continued insistence on "Uzbekisation". Having been made aware of their group identity, Tajik leaders began to resent the injustice of Uzbek control. Some of those raised in the Turk-dominated Jadid tradition, like Abdulkadyr Muhieddinov, repented their earlier indifference to their Tajik identity. For other, younger, comrades such as Shohtimur and Ismailov, who had not been exposed to the same level of Jadid-dominated pan-Turkism, anger came more easily. As a tool to use against this worryingly nationalist and Turco-centric Uzbek urge for dominance, Moscow equipped the Tajiks with the arguments to fashion their own brand of Soviet nationalism, which was also to serve as a beacon for the oppressed Persian-speaking peoples of the region to the south of Central Asia.

As Rzehak has written, "the founding of Tajikistan was not the result of Tajik nationalism but the hour of its birth". Is the Soviet experience the exception to Ernest Gellner's contention that "it is

nationalism which engenders nations and not the other way round"?[4]
For it was Moscow's gift of ASSR status that brought the creation of
what Gellner has described as the congruence between (in this case the
Tajik) political and cultural entity, anger at the violation of which he
identifies with nationalism?[5] Once Moscow had given tangible and
territorial recognition to a Tajik political and cultural entity, however
small, people who until then had not bothered to identify themselves
as Tajik were invited to consider whether or not they might be part of
this newly identified "ethnie". True, not all Tajiks took advantage of
this opportunity, many preferring for various reasons to choose an
Uzbek identity. Nonetheless, within the 1924 frontiers of the
mountainous region forming the Tajik ASSR, the number of those
who were under Jadid influence was relatively smaller than in the
plains and large cities. In those remote hills, a state formation was
sanctioned by the new Soviet and Communist Party authority as a
focus for a national identity that had grasped the reasons for its
difference from the Uzbeks – a difference which was able to combine
linguistic particularity with a clear physical distinction and a mountain culture that was unlike that of the plains. Suddenly, those who,
like Imomov, had spurned the Tajiks of the mountains as "collectors
of snow and thorn bushes", could imagine that they belonged to the
very group they had earlier despised.

Furthermore, by becoming the official language of a Soviet state,
the Tajik language, as propagated in its new form by Ayni and *Ovozi
Tojik*, shed its brand-mark as the medium of the feudal and oppressive
rule of the khanates. Instead, it could become a unifying bond not
only for those who spoke it as their natural and only language, but
between them and others like Ayni who knew Chagatai Turkic as well
but preferred the Tajik idiom. It was startling how fast Tajik national
pride, even ardent nationalism, developed. In the language debates of
the late 1920s, voices such as that of the mysterious and anonymous
"Tojik" came across as being just as strident as anything the Uzbeks
or others were able to project.

Between 1924 and 1929, the relative success of the new statelet in
overcoming the threat of the Basmachi and the chaos left by their
insurrection encouraged such leaders to argue that it could also govern
large centres like Samarkand and Bukhara. The Uzbeks had, from the
creation of the Tajik ASSR onwards, rightly seen this construct as the
thin end of a destructive wedge that would split their regional

dominance. They fought hard to limit the damage. Initially, their obvious nationalism told against them in Moscow whose central government was guided by a new internationalist ideology. They were ordered to hand over Khojand and accept Tajikistan's promotion to union republic status. But why did Moscow shrink from transferring Samarkand and Bukhara, or Surkhan- Darya? The practical arguments – geographical separation from the Tajik heartland, an Uzbek-dominated countryside – were hardly persuasive. Had they been, Tashkent would have gone to Kazakhstan, and Osh and Khojand to Uzbekistan. As Dyakov himself admitted in the context of Ura Teppe, the decision was a political one. One can only speculate. Given the strength of the continuing "Young Bukharan" tradition in the government of the Uzbek SSR – where Faizulla Khojaev and Abdulrauf Fitrat were both prominent – the loss of that city in particular would have been an insupportable blow. As for making Samarkand the new capital of Tajikistan, for strategic reasons Moscow preferred a capital closer to the Tajik centre and of less consequence. The new statelet was perhaps too unstable and vulnerable. Russian memories of the Basmachestvo were too recent. Moscow was still worried about British machinations in the region. Should the Soviet grip on Tajikistan weaken, Dushanbe could be given up. The fate of Samarkand and Bukhara could not be viewed with the same equanimity. Although Moscow was prepared to "cut the Uzbeks down to size", she did not want to inflict too harsh a blow on what she rightly expected would remain the most important state in the region.

In 1924 the conditions were set for the birth of a Tajik identity. In 1929 the road was identified that was to lead the country first to the limited level of self-administration and identification offered by Soviet Union Republic status and then, with the collapse of the Soviet Union, to full independence. Under Soviet rule, tremendous technical progress was made. Railways and roads were built, hydro-electric dams raised, and agriculture, education and medical care developed to levels of which the pre-Soviet inhabitants of the country could not have dreamt. A sense of Tajik identity was also under construction, but what sort of identity? Moscow had originally aimed to create one that was "nationalist in form but socialist in content" which would in turn be replaced, not as in Greece or elsewhere outside the communist realm, by the identity of the ruling nation, but by a totally new Soviet one. In theory, this might well have been possible in a society which had until then not been aware of any particular national identity. It was not unimaginable that a society which conceived of itself entirely in religious and family terms i.e. in the case of the Tajiks, Islam and the family/clan, might substitute for these another set of ideological and family criteria i.e. Marxism and the collective. Surprisingly perhaps given the radical nature of this new programme, no attempt was made to achieve a total break with the past by imposing a new language. Uzbek would have been the natural choice. It had already been chosen by local intelligentsias as the vehicle of progress and revolution. But culturally it was too close to Tajik. Uzbek and Tajik societies were indistinguishable in the "Sart" world. A Tajik people speaking Uzbek would be just as "Central Asian" as one speaking Tajik, just as hard to reshape in the Soviet mould. To create a truly new nation, Moscow should surely have insisted on making the Tajiks literate in Russian, and only in Russian. However, both Lenin and Stalin were convinced that the best way to instil the new teaching in the minds of their non-Russian subjects was through their own languages. This seemed the only practical way of winning local converts to the cause.

In earlier times, there had of course been rulers who had succeeded in re-creating the self-identity of their subjects. The infamous Qin emperor of China had been an example. Stalin would later use methods which approached the barbarity of these earlier paradigms, but, in the early 1920s the Soviet state was too weak and embattled to afford such a draconian approach. By the time Stalin began to wield the scythe in the 1930s the damage was done. He might exterminate the original Jadid-aligned intelligentsia that had helped enshrine the new Soviet versions of Tajik and Uzbek. The new post-revolution generation of early Soviet writers might also go to the wall. The Communist Party might try to reshape the Tajik language and literature by drawing on those traditions which it regarded as politically and socially helpful and by discarding those that seemed damaging. But, once the concession to the native language had been made, it became clear that it was impossible completely to separate the old from the new. As Tajik writers reeled between the Scylla of Feudalism and Charybdis of the "proletkult", they could hardly escape the comfort of looking back at least to those classical works that did not smack too strongly of political feudalism. Untainted as they might be in this respect, they were still replete with pre-communist cultural and religious references. In the pre-Soviet "Sart" tradition, these references carried a cultural but not a national message, because there had been no national identity with which to associate them. Once the message of communism was tied to a "nation" as defined by language, the references infected the reformed language with nuances, which would in the end frustrate and distort the creation of a new Soviet identity.

Over the decades which followed the creation of the Tajik ASSR, its cultural leaders increasingly called on their imagined forebears to legitimise their special status in Central Asia. The first rivals from whom the new nation had to seek distance were the Turkic neighbours, especially the Uzbeks. The tragedy of the end of "Iranian" Samanid rule was conjured. The more recent tragedy of the Soviet allocation of the two great Tajik cities could also be invoked. Obscure Soghdian forms were used by inventive scholars to give a healthy explanation for what were obviously Turkic grammatical structures in the Persian dialects of Samarkand and Bukhara. Then it became necessary to define Tajik identity as different from Iranian and Afghan. Not only national but Marxist agendas could be satisfied by stigmatising the "feudal" or "aristocratic" characteristics of flowery Persian as practised in Iran in contrast to the pure and genuine language of the Tajik mountains. Anti-religious campaigns were marshalled to point up the backwardness of the Afghans, with whom earlier inhabitants of the region had seen no cultural or ethnic difference. A Tajik identity was constructed but one whose invocation of cultural memory had made it very different from other Soviet identities. Paradoxically, the one identity from which it sought to distance itself most was that to which it was the closest and with which it shared so much – the Uzbek.

The collapse of the Soviet Union might have been expected to offer the Tajiks the chance finally to define their common identity. Sadly, neither the historical roots first located by sympathetic Russian scholars, nor the Soviet Tajik patriotism inculcated by the Party provided the necessary glue. In the chaos and civil war that followed the collapse of the Union and its Soviet identity, all sides no doubt saw themselves as patriotic Tajiks. That is usually the case in civil wars. In Spain, both Phalangists and Republicans saw themselves as true Spaniards. In Greece, ELAS and the Monarchists likewise. However, issues were at stake that pushed aside the weak buttresses of the laboriously constructed Soviet Tajik nationality. While the Soviet solution had seemed to offer a form of national identity, Moscow had also, perhaps intentionally, built localised power structures that worked against national unity. These contradictions and fissures might have prevented manifestations of nationalism which were unwelcome to an imperial government. They were to prove disastrous in a country that was unprepared for the responsibilities of an independence that had been thrust upon it.

NOTES

All references to Russian archival materials are located in:

The Russian Centre for the Preservation of Documents of Recent History (RTsKhDNI)

and

The State Archive of the Russian Federation (GARF), both situated in Moscow.

Introduction

1   Baroat Abdurakhimovna Khodzhibaeva *"Abdurakhim Khodzhibaev. Stranitsy korotkoi zhizni "*. State Publishing House Rakhim Dzhalil, Khojand. 2000.

Khodzhibaev, Abdurakhim (Abdurahim Khojibaev), became Chairman of the Council of People's Commissars of Tajikistan. At the II Congress of the Tajik Communist Party on 7 January 1934 he was condemned with Maksum for bourgeois-nationalist tendencies, and of mistaken nationalist deviation and removed from his post. He was arrested with Maksum and seventy-six others in the wave of arrests of May 1934 and executed sometime between 1937 and 1938.

Note also that, in these notes, for Central Asian personal names of the Soviet period I shall use transcriptions of the Russian spellings, with, where helpful, the Western equivalent used in the text added in brackets. Otherwise, for example for place-names, I will use the most commonly used Latin transcription. So, e.g. Khodzhaev but Tajik.

Chapter 1. Central Asian Identities before 1917

1   RTsKhDNI Fond 62, Op 2, Delo 102, L 8, "Project for Organisation of the Tajik AutonomousOblast'".

2   V.V. Bartol'd, *Sochineniye,* Vol 2 (1), p. 449. *"Tadzhiki"*.

3   D. Sinor and S.G. Klyashtorny, *The Turk Empire,* UNESCO, Civilisations of Central Asia, Vol III, p. 345.

4   Professor Nicholas Sims-Williams, "New Documents in Ancient Bactrian", Newsletter of the International Institute for Asian Studies, March 2002.

5   Thomas Loy, *Jaghnob 1970.* Reichert, Wiesbaden. 2005.

6   Richard N. Frye, *The Golden Age of Persia.* Weidenfeld, London, 1975, p. 50.

7   N.V.Khanykov, *Opisanie Bukharskogo Khanstva,* St Peterburg, 1843.

8   Compare V.I. Masal'skii, *Turkestanskii Krai,* A.F. Devriena, St Peterburg, 1913, 2nd part (Population). Also Shishov, *Tadzhiki,* Tashkent, 1910.

9   Bartol'd, *Sochinenye,* p. 460, describes tensions between them during the period of the Khorezmshahs. At a time when there were both Turkish and Iranian commanders, in reply to a proposal from the Turkish commander that they cooperate, the Gurid commander is said to have replied "We are Gurids and you are Turks. We cannot live together." Likewise, when the (Turkic) Khorezmshah proposed an alliance with Mazanderan, his advisers warned "The paths are dark between Turk and Tajik" and "The Tajik will never trust a Turk."

10   A. Koichev, *"Natsionalnoe Territorial'noe Razmezhevaniye v Ferganskoi Doline",* Bishkek, 2001, pp. 4 and 5, Koichev describes how the author of the "Tarikh e Shahrukhi" lists the ethnic groups of the Kokand Khanate and includes Tajiks alongside Uzbeks, Kipchaks, Kazakhs, Kyrgyz, Karakalpaks, and "Turks". The Kyrgyz poet, Moldo Niyaz (1820–1896) describes the population of the Kokand Khanate in late 19th century as made up of Turks, Uzbeks, Tajiks, Kipchaks, Kyrgyz and Sarts. Again, in a letter to G.A. Kolpakovskii, Tsarist Governor General of the Steppe, the Kyrgyz leader Baitik Kanai-uulu wrote in 1863 that "in the Turkestan district a Tajik by the name of Mirza Davlet was in charge."

11   I am not aware of research that investigates the circumstances of this intermarriage. For example, did the Turkic new arrivals, as the victorious group, often take Tajik wives, while hesitating to give their daughters to the subordinate community? If so, was this because Tajik women were much admired for their beauty?

12   Bartol'd, *Sochineniye,* p. 461, discusses the origins of the word "Sart". He says it is a Hindi word which was applied by the Mongols to all Central Asians involved in trade. "Sartaktai" was the word Jingiz used to describe Arslan Khan Karluk, although the latter was of course a Turk. For his part, Plano Carpini, a Fransiscan monk, used the word "Sart" in describing Jingiz's campaign in Central Asia in 1246.

13   J. Klaproth. *"Asia Polyglotta",* 1823, pp 233 ff, quoted by O.A. Sukhareva, *Bukhara XIX – XX vekov.* Moskva, 1966, p. 119.

14 I.I. Zarubin, *Naseleniye Samarkandskoi Oblasti.* Leningrad. 1926. p. 14.

15 I.I. Zarubin, *Naseleniye*, p. 21.

16 I.I. Zarubin, *Naseleniye*, p. 14.

17 V.V. Bartol'd, "Sart", article for the *Encyclopaedia of Islam,* Brill, Leiden, 1997.

18 A.A. Semenov, *K Probleme Natsionalnogo Razmezhevaniya Srednei Azii,* Part IV, p. 12.

19 Alisher Ilkhamov, The Thorny Path of Civil Society in Uzbekistan, *Central Asian Survey*, Vol 23, (3/4), December 2004.

20 Obiya Chika, "When Faizulla Khojaev decided to be an Uzbek". in Stephane Dudoignon and Hisao Komatsu, *Islam in Politics in Russia and Central Asia (Early 18th to Late 19th Centuries),* Kegan Paul, London, 2001, p. 99.

21 L.J.Newby, *The Empire and the Khanate*, Brill, Leiden, 2005, p. 79, and p. 79, note 21.

22 Lutz Rzehak,*Vom Persischen zum Tadschikischen,* Reichert, Wiesbaden, 2001, p.19.

23 S.N. Andreev, "Po etnografyi Tadzhikov", in *Sbornik Statei* published by the Obshestvo dlya izucheniya Tadzhikskikh i Iranskikh Narodnostei za ego predelami. Tashkent, 1925, pp.150 ff.

24 India Office Library: L/PS/20/A100.

25 O.A. Sukhareva, *Bukhara XIX – nachala XX v: Pozdnefeodalnyi gorod i ego naseleniye,* Moskva 1966, p.113ff.

Chapter 2. The Turkic Ascendancy

1   By the late 19th century, the name "Sart" was used to describe the Turkic language spoken in Tashkent and the towns of the Ferghana Valley. The characteristics of this language were a lack of the vowel harmony usually found in other Turkic languages, and a strong admixture of Persian words and phrases. Like the use of the word as an ethnonym, the name "Sart" for the language also died out. Many pan-Turkic enthusiasts of the 19th century preferred the name "Chagatai", of which the modernised version became known as "Uzbek" after the Bolshevik revolution. More recently there has been a tendency to drop "Chagatai" and replace it with "Old Uzbek". Nonetheless, in the late 19th century, "Sart" was widely used for the language, as well as for the ethnic, or rather social, group, especially by Russians. V. Nalivkin, the Russian orientalist and briefly Governor-General of Turkestan under the Kerensky government, published a primer of the "Sart Language" in 1897, which was revised and reprinted in 1911.

2   Adeeb Khalid, Society and Politics in Bukhara, 1868–1920, *Central Asian Survey*, Vol 19 (3/4), September–December 2000, p.367–96.

3   Adeeb Khalid, *The Politics of Muslim Reform,* University of California Press, 1998, p. 208.

4   Guissou Jahangiri, The Premises for the Construction of a Tajik National Identity, 1920 – 1930, in Muhammad Reza Djalili, Frederic Grare and Shirin Akiner, *Tajikistan: The Trials of Independence*, Curzon, Richmond, UK, 1998, p. 19/20, quoting R. Masov, *Istoriya Topornogo Razdeleniya* (see note 6).

5   "Bektosh", alias of Nazrullo Haidari (1900–1938), was born in Bogh e Maidon near Samarkand. He compiled a teaching training course in the Paedagogic Institute in Samarkand and the Paedagogic Institute in Baku. From 1922 he was active as a teacher and literary figure. In 1930 he moved to Stalinabad (Dushanbe) where he taught history and the theory of Tajik literature at the Paedagogic Insitute. He became head of the Literary History in the Tajik Branch of the USSR Academy of Sciences. In the beginning of the 1930s he was declared an enemy of the people and was executed in 1938.

6   Article by Sh. Jabbarov in *Za Partiyu*, No 3–4, 1929. See R. Masov, *Istoriya Topornogo Razdeleniya,* Irfon, Dushanbe, 1991, p. 152.

7   Masov, *Istoriya*, p. 153.

8   Abdulkadyr Mukhitdinov (Muhieddinov) and his father led the opposition to the Emir of Bukhara and he became a revolutionary when young. 1924: Head of the Government of the TaASSR. 1934: Arrested in Tashkent. Although he gave all his possessions to the CP, he was vulnerable due to his social background as the son of Mukhitdin Mansurov a wealthy Bukhara merchant. According to Andrei Stanishevskii, former Cheka officer who saw him under arrest, Mukhitdinov blamed Faizulla Khojaev for his arrest. Shot.

9   RTsKhDNI.Fond 62, Op 2, Delo 100, L 3.

Here a brief explanation may be useful of the various Russian, Soviet and Central Asian administrative units whose names are mentioned in this narrative.

Pre-revolutionary Russian-administered territories were generally divided as follows in descending order:

Governorate-General/Oblast'/Uezd/Volost'.

In the same order, pre-1920 Bukhara was divided as follows:

Begstvo/Amlyakdarstvo.

Post-1923 these units were replaced in the Bukharan areas by:

Viloyat/Tuman/Kishlak or Kent.

and in the Turkestan ASSR by:

Viloyat, Volost and Selsovet. (but see Note 55 below).

and, after 1924, in the new Soviet republics, by:

Oblast'/Okrug/(in some areas) Jamagat.

In 1930, the Okrug was replaced by the Raion (except in the case of certain national Okrugy, but this exception was not found in Tajikistan at that time).

Throughout this paper, I shall refer to the different administrative units by the names used in the original languages. An approximate series of equivalents would be:

Oblast'/Viloyat = Province.

Okrug/Uezd/Tumen/Raion = District

Jamagat/Kishlak/Aul = Village/Nomad settlement.

10   Abdulrauf Fitrat was born in 1886, in Bukhara into a well-off merchant's family. He studied at the Mir e Arab madrasa. In 1909 the Tarbiya al Atfal society gave him a grant to study in Istanbul, where he remained from 1909 to 1914. There he was deeply influenced by the debates raging about the perceived decline of Islamic countries. In that period he wrote his first books (in Persian), of which two – *Debate between a Bukharan mudarris and a European* and *Tales of an Indian Traveller* – became very influential in Central Asia. He developed a simple classical style of Persian which, in Ayni's eyes, qualified him to be considered the founder of Tajik literature. He was certainly one of the leading writers (in both Persian and, increasingly as time went on, in Chagatai Turkic) in the Central Asian Jadid movement. After the revolution in Bukhara, where he became Minister for Education, he promoted the Chagatai language against Tajik (see text). In 1938 he was arrested, charged with nationalism, and shot.

11   Faizulla Khodzhaev (Khojaev) was born 1896, in Bukhara, the son of a rich merchant. He studied at a Bukharan madrasa and then at a private school in Moscow. He joined the Jadid movement and then the "Young Bukharans" of whose left wing he became leader in 1917. Formed an alliance with the communists to overthrow the Amir in 1920 and became Prime Minister of the Bukharan People's Soviet Republic. Joined the Communist Party in 1920. Member of the Central Asia Office (Sredazburo) from 1922. After the NTD, became the first Chairman of the Uzbek Revolutionary Committee (Revkom) and then Chairman of the Council of People's Commissars. In the 1930s he came into increasing conflict with Moscow's cultural and economic plans for Uzbekistan. Accused in a show

trial of Trotsky-ism and Right-ism, and executed on 13 March 1938 along with Akmal Ikramov, the first First Secretary of the Uzbek CP, and with Bukharin and Rykov.

Chapter 3. The Revolution and After

1   Turar Ryskulov, Kazakh, was born 1894 in Aule Ata. He joined the Communist Party in 1917. In 1919 he was elected president of the Turkestan ASSR's Party Executive Committee. In 1920 he led the motion that led to the change of the party's name to "Communist Party of the Turkic Peoples" and, unsuccessfully, of the republic's to the "Turkic Soviet Republic". From 1922–4 he was Chairman of the Council of People's Commissars of the Turkestan ASSR. In 1924 he was appointed to the Eastern Department of the Comintern and sent as representative to Mongolia. Executed in 1937. One of the leading Central Asian exponents of Sultan Galiev's doctrine of the need for Eastern peoples pass through a period of independent progressive development before achieving communism.

2   Alexander Park, *Bolshevism in Turkestan*, Columbia Press, New York, 1957, p. 301.

3   RTsKhDNI, Fond 17, Op 65, Delo 380, Page 2.

4   Georgyi Ivanovich Safarov (aka Vol'din) was born in St Petersburg 23 October 1891. He was educated in the Petersburg Polytechnic and at an electrotechnic institute in France, after he emigrated to Switzerland in 1910. Joined the RSDRP in 1908. In April 1917 he returned to Russia with Lenin in the sealed train and became a member of the St Petersburg committee of the RSDRP (b). Throughout the revolutionary period he filled various Party posts including in Ekaterinburg, where he played a role in the execution of imperial family. From 1920 onwards, he worked in Turkestan as a member of the Turkkommissiya, and by 1921 as chairman of the Turkestan Buro of the Central Committee of the RKP(b). After filling several Party posts, fell from favour and was expelled from the Party in December 1927. He was arrested in 1934, exiled in 1935 and then sentenced to 5 years imprisonment. Shot in 1942.

5   Yakov Khristoforovich Peters was born 21 November 1886 in Latvia into a "Batrak" family. 1904: Joined the CP. 1909: Member of the London Group of the Latvian Social Democratic Party (SDLK). Member of the British Socialist Party (sic). Representative of the SDLK at the TsK of the RSDRP(b). 1917: Member of the Petrograd VRK and a delegate of the 2nd All Russian Congress of Soviets. Participated in the uncovering of the Bruce Lockhart/Reilly Conspiracy. 1918: One of those directing the

liquidation of the Leftist SR revolt. 1920–2: Member of the Turkestan Bureau of the TsK RKP(b). Plenipotentiary Representative of the Cheka in Turkestan. From 1923: Member of the Collegium of the OGPU and member of the presidium of the TsKK. 1930–4: Chairman of the MKK of the VKP(b). At the 17th Congress elected member of the KPK VKP(b). Died 25 April 1938 (shot?).

6   Sh.Z. Urozaev, *V.I. Lenin i stroitelstvo sovetskoi gosudarstvennosti v Turkestane,* Tashkent. 1967, p. 225.

7   V.V. Bartol'd, *Sochineniye,* p 468.

8   Lutz Rzehak, *Vom Persischen zum Tadschikischen,* Reichert, Wiesbaden, 2001, p. 91ff.

9   Hoji Mu'in ibn Shukrullah Samarqandi had made a name for himself in the first decade of the 20th century as a reformist writer and teacher in the Jadid mould. He was the author of works of social criticism like "Juvanbozlik qurboni" (The victim of pederasty), "Eski Maktab – Yangi Maktab" (Old school – new school) and "Turkestan Maishatdan – Koknuri" (From Turkestan life – the opium smoker). He had for a while (1914–15) also been editor of the paper *Oyina* (*Mirror*) where Alizodeh had also worked. He wrote in both Turki and Persian cf Rzehak, *Vom Persischen,* p. 102.

10 Sadruddin Saidmurodzoda Ayni (1878–1954) took the name Ayni in 1896. Famous as the first Jadid teacher in the Persian language, Ayni became the leading exponent of the new Tajik language after the formation of the Tajik ASSR and the "grand old man of Tajik letters". Heavily criticised during the 1930s, he survived thanks to his pro-revolutionary novels and, as almost the sole survivor of the pogroms of the 1930s, died after the Second World War.

11 Rzehak, *Vom Persischen,* p. 109.

12 Rzehak, *Vom Persischen,* p. 76.

13 G. Safarov, *Kolonialnaya Revolutsiya – Opyt' Turkestan,* Moscow, 1921, p. 110.

14 Fitzroy Maclean, *Eastern Approaches,* Jonathan Cape, 1949, p 121.

15 Rzehak, *Vom Persischen,* p. 113.

16 Abdullo Rokhimboev (Abdullah Rahimbaev). (1896–1938) was born in Khojand in a "middle merchant" family; trained as a teacher in Tashkent 1917; joined the Communist Party in 1919; chairman of the Samarkand Obkom of the Turkestan CP; 1920 chairman of the TsIK of the Turkestan ASSR; member of the Collegium for nationalities of the RSFSR; 1923–4: 1st secretary of the TsK of the Bukharan CP; 1933–7 Chairman of the Council of Ministers of Tajikistan. In the show trials of the 1930s, was implicated in Ikramov's testimony. Accused of polygamy. Shot.

17 RTsKhDNI. Fond 62, Op 2, D 151, L 6. quoted by Masov, *Istoriya.* p. 32.

Chapter 4. The Road to Soviet Power

1　Compare Aleksandr Izraelovich Zevelev *et al. Basmachestvo: vozniknoveniye, sushchnost' krakh*, Izdatelstvo "Nauka", Moskva, 1981.

2　Dr Baymirza Hayit *"Basmatschi": Nationaler Kampf Turkestans in den Jahren 1917 bis 1934*, Dreisam, Köln, 1992.

3　Adeeb Khalid, *The Politics of Muslim Cultural Reform*, University of California, 1998.

4　*Izvestiya* of 18 August 1926 mentions a certain Abdulla Beg, a "Tajik chief", as a Basmachi commander

5　India Office Library: L/PS/10/950. P3961 of 20 May 1929.

6　Harold Nicholson. *Curzon: the Last Phase,* Constable and Co Ltd, London, 1934, p. 78, Footnote.

7　Members of the Ismaili or Sevener Shi'i sect are followers of the Aga Khan. For an exhaustive description of the sect, see Farhad Daftary, *The Ismailis, their History and Doctrines.* Cambridge University Press, 1992. The origins of the Ismaili community in the Pamirs remain rather obscure. However, its importance and indeed its survival, are in part due to the work and continuing influence of the great 11th century Ismaili poet/philosopher/ "da'i" Naser Khosrow, himself from the upper reaches of the Oxus, who died in Yumgan, Badakhshan, c. AD 1076.

8　RTsKhDNI Fond 62, Op 2, D 102, p. 8ff, Part II.

9　In 1932 the six "raions" in the Eastern Pamir Volost' (sic) were: Alichur, Rang Kul', Kyzyl Rabad, Murghab, Kara Kul' and Chash Tebe. Source: RTsKhDNI, Fond 495, Op 154, D 460a. pp.107–123. See also in Vostochnyi Sekretariat IKKI, 1926–35, *Ekonomicheskii Ocherk Vostochnogo Pamira.* Perversely we here have "raions" subordinated to a "volost'" (a pre-revolutionary term). At the same time (1932), these six "raions" were each linked to an "aul" with its own Soviet; see also RTsKhDNI Fond 532, Op 6, D 25, L 64. Aziz Niallo, *Ocherki istoricheskoi geografii Pamira.*

10　Described as "volost's" in the *Voenno-Geograficheskii Ocherk* of 1922. See Arkhiv GBAO Fond 25, Op 2, L 22.

11　N.A. Khalfin, *Rossiya i Bukharskii Emirat na Zapadnym Pamire.* Nauka, Moskva, 1975. p. 67.

12　Eduard Karlovich Kivekas, Finnish, was born 1866. First posted as junior officer to the Pamirs in 1887. Served for many years with the Pamir Frontier Detachment, being appointed its commander several times, the last being from January 1905 to October 1908. Served with the Russian army in the First World War, and retired with the rank of Major-General after the Bolshevik revolution in 1918. Joined the army of the new Finnish state in 1919. Died 1940 during the Russo-Finnish war.

13   A.V. Stanishevksii, *Shornik Dokumentov ob Ismailisme v Pamire*, Glavnoe
     Arkhivnoe Upravneniye pri Sovete Ministrov Uzbekskoi SSR, Moskva
     1984. Also Khalfin, *Rossiya*.

14   I.D. Yagello was an orientalist and former head of the 1914–17 Pamir
     Detachment. Appointed to the military-political expedition to the Pamirs
     in 1923 by Chicherin. Yagello was described in the *Who's Who in Central
     Asia* produced by the Indian General Staff in 1929 as Head of the
     Tashkent School of Languages in 1923. See India Office Library L/PS/20/
     A1222.

15   I.I. Zarubin was born 27 September 1887 in Crimea. Specialist in Iranian,
     especially Pamiri, languages. Professor in Leningrad University until
     1949. Died 3 February 1964.

16   Compare L.N. Kharyukov, *Anglo-Russkoye Sopernichestvo v Tsentral'noi Azii
     i Izmailism*. Moscow University, 1995. The sequence of events during this
     difficult period remains obscure. Stanishevskii's account dates Haidar Sho's
     appointment as "comrade chairman" after the February 1917 revolution.
     This is not in itself incompatible with a later re-appointment after the
     October revolution, but it is also possible that one of these two sources has
     got the date wrong.

17   Tarijan Dyakov studied in the Tomsk Polytechnic. Joined the CP(b) in
     1917. 1919, fought in the civil war in the Ukraine. 1919–20, member of
     the Special Department of the 10th Army. 1921, joined the special
     department of the Turkestan Front. 1921, Head of the Military-Political
     Expedition to the Pamirs. 1924, Head of OGPU for Tajikistan.
     Transferred to OGPU HQ in Moscow. Shot in 1937.

18   Shirinsho Shotimur was born in 1899 in Khosa to the poor peasant family
     of Shotimur Shomuzaffar. His mother Maisara was the daughter of
     Mamadnazarbek Zanjirbek from Tikhor, a neigbouring village. The group
     of villages was known by the name of Porkhenev in Shughnan volost'. His
     parents died when he was seven, and he went to a boarding school for
     locals in Khorog. Aged fourteen, he was taken by Staff-Captain Topornin
     to Tashkent, where he continued his studies with the teacher from his
     Khorog school who had also moved to Tashkent. From 1915–16 he
     supported himself with various jobs, notably as a tram-driver and then as
     a baggage-handler for the railway. By 1917 he had enrolled in a
     Paedagogic Institute to study to become a teacher but his plans were
     interrupted by the revolution. In 1920 he was sent to teach in Katta–
     Kurgan. Entered the CP in 1921 and was sent to work in Ferghana and
     Kokand with 500 "proletarian students". But in July 1921 was recalled
     to Tashkent by the Turkkomissiya and in 1922 appointed to the

Extraordinary Military-Political Tripartite Commission (Troika) in the Pamirs. October 1922 appointed Head of the Pamir Revolutionary Committee (Revkom). Married Husnibegum daughter of Alimadadshoh in spring 1923. From 1 October 23 to June 1924, worked in the Sovnarkom of the Turkestan ASSR and after that in the sub section for national minorities in the TsK CP Turkestan. At this time was reinstated in the CP after the rejection of Ostrovskii's accusations of bribe-taking. Divorced in the summer of 1924. 26 November 1924 member of the Revkom of the Tajik ASSR. 1924, married Olga Matvienko who died of TB in 1927. At same time was appointed plenipotentiary representative of the Central Control Commission of the CP Uzbekistan in Tajikistan and People's Commissar (Narkom) for Worker-Peasant Inspection. 1925, worked nine months in Kulyab in Commission for the Isolation of the Local Population from the Basmachestvo. June 1926, made Minister of Finance. Head of Extraordinary Government Commission to Yavan. 1926, Joint chairman of the first Constituent Congress of Soviets of Tajikistan. Appointed permanent representative of the Tajik ASSR in the Uzbek SSR. August 1927, enrolled at the Communist University for the Toilers of the East (KUTV) in Moscow. 12 March 1929 Head of the Executive Office (Ispolburo) of the Provincial Committee (Obkom) of the CP Tajikistan. Second secretary of the CP Central Committee (TsK KP) Tajikistan. 1932, sent to study in Moscow. Last visit to Pamirs (first since divorce from first wife) in 1936. Shot in 1937.

19 Aleksei Mikhailovich Dyakov was the elder brother of Tarijan. Qualified doctor from Moscow State University. He and Tarijan were sons of a nobleman from Tver governorate, who was also a doctor and member of the RSDRP. 1924, People's Commissar (Narkom) for Health in the Tajik ASSR. 1929, Director of the Printing Sector of the Central Asia Office (Sredazburo TsK VKP(b)). Chairman of the Organisation Office (Orgburo) of the Khojand Okrug. Removed 29 August 1929.

20 Khalfin, Rossiya p. 67.

21 Somewhat confusingly, at the same time, the TASSR presidium decreed that, until the "oblast'" status was confirmed, the Pamirs should be referred to as an "okrug".

Chapter 5. The National Territorial Delimitation

1 Edward Allworth, *Central Asia: A Century of Russian Rule,* Columbia University Press, New York and London, 1967, p.254–5, in Chapter 10 by Helene Carrere d'Encausse.

2 This office of the Central Committee of the CP with its HQ in Tashkent

had been created by Stalin in 1921 to manage Central Asia's development. It was dissolved in 1934.

3 The party, which eventually became known as the Communist Party of the Soviet Union (KPSS), changed its name several times after its foundation. At the first congress in 1898 it was given the name Russian Social Democratic Workers' Party (RSDRP). In 1917 the suffix (b) was added to signify the Bolshevik faction. In March 1918, at Lenin's instigation, the 7th Congress changed the name to the Russian Communist Party (Bolsheviks) (RKP(b)). In 1925, to take note of the formation of the USSR, the 14th Congress changed this once more to All-Union Communist Party (Bolsheviks) (VKP(b)). The title Communist Party of the Soviet Union (KPSS) was finally chosen in 1952.

4 B.A. Antonenko, *et al*, *Istoriya Tadzhikskogo Naroda*, Nauka, Moskva, 1964, Vol III, p. 153. See also R. Eisener, *The National Delimitation of Soviet Central Asia*, Islamistische Untersuchungen, Band 149. Bamberger Mittelasienstudien. Konferenzakten 15–16.6.90. Edited by B Fragner and B Hoffmann.

5 Article in the paper *Ak Jol* of 23 June 1924, based on an interview with Faizulla Khojaev who had just returned from Moscow.

6 Jan (Yan) Ernestovich Rudzutak was born 2 August 1887 in Latvia into a "batrak" family. Joined CP 1905. 1906, member of the Riga Committee of the RSDRP. 1909, sentenced to ten years' penal servitude. 1917, Member of Presidium of the VSNKh and chairman of the Moscow Sovnarkhoz. May 1921, Chairman of Turkkommissiya. 1922–24, Chairman of the Central Asia Office (Sredazburo). 1922, member of the Soviet delegation to the Geneva Conference. 1931, Chairman of the Central Control Commission (TsKK) of the VKP(b) and People's Commissar for RKI of the USSR. 1926–32, deputy premier and candidate member of the Politburo of the VKP(b). Arrested in 1937 (the first member of the Politburo to suffer this fate). Tortured and shot on 29 July 1938. His case may not have been helped by the fact that his nephew (or cousin) Ernst Pumpur, the People's Commissar for Foreign Affairs in the Pamir Raion in 1922, seems to have been involved with Afghan/British intrigues against the Soviet State. Pumpur eventually fled from the Soviet Union (L.N. Kharyukov, *Anglo-Russkoye Sopernichestvo v Tsentral'noi Azii i Izmailizm*, Moskovskogo Universiteta, 1995).

7 Chinor Imomov, (1898–1939) was born in Zebon, near Panjikent. 1918 CP member. 1911 Russian school in Samarkand. 1918 CP apparatchik in Ura Teppe, Jizzakh and Samarkand. 1924 Member of the Central Asia Office (Sredazburo). Had an important role in

publishing *Ovoz e Tojik*. Early 1930s, Tajik People's Commissar for Education and then Health.

8 Protocol of the Session of the Commission of the Central Asia Office (Sredazburo) of the Central Executive Committee (TsIK RKP(b)) on the National Territorial Delimitation (NTD) of Central Asia. The other members of the Uzbek sub committee were: Islamov, Ishanhojaev, Muhieddinov, and Pulatov. RTsKhDNI Fond 62, Op 2, D 100, L1, Note 7540.

9 GARF. Fond R 6892, Op 1, D 34, L 54. Session of the Commission for "Raionirovanie" of Turkestan. 17 October 1923 (but this date must be wrong – 1924?).

10 Benedict Anderson, *Imagined Communities,* Verso, London and New York, 1999, p. 164.

11 Annual Statistical Review for 1917–23, TES Tashkent, 1924.

12 Isaak Abramovich Zelenskii was born in 1890. He joined the CP in 1906 in Samara. Repeatedly arrested for subversive activity throughout period 1908–1915, twice escaping from captivity or exile. 1917, joined CP organisation in Moscow. 1918–20, in charge of supply work in Moscow. 1920, secretary of the Moscow Party organisation. 1924–31, Secretary of the Central Asia Office (Sredazburo). Appointed to the Plenum of the Provincial Committee (Obkom) of the Tajik CP. Elected to Central Committee (TsK) of the CP in 1931 and to the Central Executive Committee (TsIK) of the USSR. Implicated during their trials by Ikramov and Khojaev as a Trotskyite. Accused by Vyshinky of having mixed nails and glass in butter while he was responsible for supplies. Shot.

13 RTsKhDNI. FOND 62, Op 2, D 102, L 8.
"Project for the organisation of the Tajik AO."

14 Usmonkhon Ishonhojaev (Ishanhojaev, Usmankhan). 1922–24, People's Commissar for Education in the Turkestan ASSR. 1924–25, Editor of *Krasnyi Uzbekistan.* Head of the Agitpropo Dept of the Central Committee (TsK) CP Uzbekistan.

15 RTsKhDNI Fond 62, Op 2, D 130 c.

16 RTsKhDNI Fond 62, Op 2, D 88, L 3. Letter from Karklin to Stalin and Rudzutak, dated 7 August 1924, Tashkent.

17 Sa'id Ahrari (also known as Muhammad Sa'id Akhrarov) was an activist in the Young Bukhara movement; after the victory of the revolution in Bukhara he entered the Bukharan CP and was the first director of the Bukhara People's Soviet Republic (BNSR)'s state publishing house and also editor of the paper *Bukhoro Akhbori*. Also served as permanent

representative of the BNSR in Azerbaijan and subsequently worked in the office of the Council of People's Nazirs (Commissars), (note from F. Khodzhaev's Selected Works, V1, Tashkent 1920, p. 466).

18   Abbas Aliev. (1899–1958) was born in Bukhara. From 1918–20 he led the underground CP committee in Charjui. He was one of the founders of the BNSR and held several Party appointments there. From 1924–27 he was People's Commissar for Education of the Tajik ASSR. In 1933 he began studying history at the Tashkent Central Asian University and spent the rest of his life as an academic. Lutz Rzehak, *Vom Persischen zum Tadschikischen* , Reichert, Wiesbaden, 2001, p. 191.

19   RTsKhDNI Fond 52, Op 2, D 88.

20   S. Khudzhanov (Khojanov). 1924, member of the Central Committee (TsK) of the CP Turkestan and Deputy Director APPO (Agitprop) of the Central Asia Office (Sredazburo) , as well as being Chairman of the Central Executive Committee (TsIK) of Turkestan. Kazakh.

21   RTsKhDNI. Fond 62, Op 2, D 1744, L 14.

22   GARF, Fond 1235, OP 120, D 31, Part II, L 93.

The economic arguments also favoured allocation to Kyrgyzstan since Uch Kurgan functioned as a commercial and economic centre for the adjoining Kyrgyz raions of Ichkili and Isfairam [probably Isfara]. The Uzbek claim that Uch Kurgan served more as an economic centre for the Tajik town of Auval (which they therefore also claimed) could not be substantiated. The region was therefore allotted to Kyrgyzstan. Apropos the volost' of Sokh, the commission agreed to unite it with the Kyrgyz ASSR on the grounds that it adjoined Kyrgyz territory and was linked economically to the "raions" of Kuldin and Botkan-Buzhun with which it also shared an irrigation system. According to the Protocol of the Parity Commission of 24 January 1927 Uch Kurgan was allotted to the KaSSR (sic – presumably Kyrgyz ASSR), while on 25 January 1927 the Commission decided also to give Sokh to the Kyrgyz ASSR while leaving Isfara within the UzSSR. See also GARF, Fond 1235, Op 120, D 3/PART III, L 212.

23   RTsKhDNI. Fond 62, Op 2, D 1744, L14. Stenographic note of the Session of the Territorial Commission of 21 August 1924.

24   RTsKhDNI. Fond 121, Op 72 (43), L 48. 2 Aug 27. Dyakov's letter to the TsK VKP(b) about the Ura Teppe and Panjikent Vilkoms (Provincial Committees). "To be discussed at a closed session of the IspolBuro (Executive Buro)".

25   Rakhim Masov, *Ocherki po Istoryi Sovetskogo Badakhshana*. Irfon, Dushanbe, 1981, p. 20ff.

26 Sanjar Jafarovich Asfendiarov was born October 1889 in Tashkent, the son of a Major-General in the Russian army. He trained as an army doctor at the Naval Academy. Joined the CP in 1919 after being arrested, cashiered and imprisoned for political activity. 1917, member of the Bukhara and then the Tashkent Oblast' Soviet. 1918-1919, with the Red Army. 1921–4, member of the Central Committee of the CP TASSR. 1923–4, member of the Central Asia Office (Sredazburo). 1925–7, Secretary of the Council of Nationalities of the Central Executive Committee of the USSR. After holding increasingly responsible positions in Moscow and Kazakhstan, including that of People's Commissar for Health in Kazakhstan, was arrested in 1937 and shot in 1938.

Chapter 6. The New Tajik ASSR – Administrative Problems

1 Rakhim Masov. *Ocherki po Istoryi Sovetskogo Badakhshana*, Irfon, Dushanbe, 1981, p. 20ff.

2 Baymirza Hayit, *Basmatschi; Nationaler Kampf Turkestans in den Jahren 1917 bis 1934,* Dreisam, Köln 1992, p. 365.

3 Nusratullah Maksum (aka Lutfullaev) was born in 1891. Peasant background. Lower education. Member of CP from 1920. Party card no. 0841619. Volunteered for the RKKA (Red Army). Until revolution worked in agriculture and casual work. 1922, Chairman of Central Executive Committee (TsIK) of Eastern Bukhara. 1924: Chairman of the TsIK of Tajikistan. 5 December 1933, removed from his post by a decision of the Central Committee (TsK) of the CP of Tajikistan. Arrested during the wave of arrests that started in May 1934 and executed in 1937 or 1938.

4 Georgyi Vasilievich Chicherin was born 12 November 1872 into a noble family. Served 1897–1904 in the Tsarist MFA. Emigrated to Germany and joined the RSDRP. In 1917 was arrested in Britain but the Soviets obtained his release. Returned to become People's Commissar for Foreign Affairs, first of the RSFSR and then the USSR, until 1931. Died 7 July 1936.

5 I.K. Kalandarov: *Slavnyi Syn Tadzhikskogo Naroda*, Dushanbe, 1999, p. 19. Reference to Central Party Archive, Institute of Marxism/Leninism (TsPA IML), Fond 17, Op 3, D 468, p. 2.

6 Valerian Vladimirovich Kuibyshev was born in 1888 in Omsk into an officer's family. Joined the CP in 1905. Studied at the Military-Medical Academy in St Petersburg. Exiled to Siberia for student dissident activity. During the February 1917 revolution headed the CP in Samara. 1918–20, political commissar with the Red Army. 1919, with Kirov, took part in the defence of Astrakhan. Member of the Revolutionary War Soviet (RVS) of the 11th Army and took part in the campaign on the Turkestan Front. In

October 1919 was deputy chairman of the Turkkommissiya. From 1930 onwards was chairman of USSR Gosplan. Died (possibly murdered) in 1935.

7   Masov, *Ocherki*, p. 138. Article by, A.Ya Vishnevskii and, M.N. Nazarshoev *Istoriya Obrazovaniya i ideino-organizatsionnogo ukrepleniya Gorno-Badakhshanskoi Oblastnoi Partiinoi organizatsii.*

8   Lev Alekseevich Gotfrid. Russian. Studied electro-mechanics. March 1929, deputy head of the Executive Office (Ispolburo) of the Tajik Provinicial Committee (Obkom) of the CP Uzbekistan. Head of the Organisation Department (Orgotdel). Member of the Secretariat. With M. Gafiz, author of the book *Krasnyi Flag na Kryshe Mira*, Tadzh. Gos. Isd, Stalinabad, 1930.

9   Kuprian Osipovich Kirkizh was born in 1886 near Vitebsk. Joined CP in 1910. From 1927–9 Secretary of the Central Committee (TsK) of the CP Uzbekistan. Chairman of the commission for separating Tajikistan from Uzbekistan. Reached rank of member of Central Control Commission (TsKK) All-Russian CP (VKP(b)).

10   RTsKhDNI, Fond 62, Op 2, D 1272, L 3

11   RTsKhDNI, Fond 62, Op 2, D 1524, L 1. Report on the work of the Ispolburo (Executive Office) of the Tajik Provincial Committee (Obkom) of the CP of Uzbekistan, end of 1928.

12   RTsKhDNI, Fond 62, Op 1, D 545. L 224.

13   Boris Tolpygo. One of three chairman of the First Constituent Congress of Soviets of Tajikistan.

14   Rakhim Masov, *Istoriya Topornogo Razdeleniya*, Irfon, Dushanbe, 1991, p. 71, quoting RTsKhDNI Fond 62, Op 2, D 185, L 42.

15   Terry Martin, *The Affirmative Action Empire*. Cornell, Ithaca and London, 2001, p. 147.

16   The Koshchi (Uzbek: the "ploughman") was an organisation set up by the Soviets in 1922 to spread communist indoctrination and explain the aims of the Party to smallholders and the rural working class. It became very popular and many small peasants joined it. However, once the land reforms of 1925–7 got under way, the CP became nervous that it might become a source of opposition to the new system. The Koshchi was deprived of its official status in 1927 and finally ceased to exist in 1931. See G. Wheeler, *The Modern History of Central Asia*, Weidenfeld and Nicholson, London, 1964, p. 134.

17   OGPU (Ob'edinyonnoe Gosudarstvoennoye Politicheskoe Upravleniye = United State Political Directorate). Set up in 1922 to replace the VChK (Cheka) and the republican GPU offices and to "unite the revolutionary efforts of the union republics in the struggle against political and

economic counter-revolution, espionage and banditism". The OGPU functioned through its local plenipotentiary representatives in the republics' Councils of People's Commissars, as well as through the "special departments" of the army and was responsible for frontier protection. In 1934, the OGPU was absorbed into the structures of the People's Commissariat for Internal Affairs (NKVD), which, after a period as the Ministry of Internal Affairs (MVD), was re-formed as the Committee for State Security (KGB).

18   RTsKhDNI Fond 62, Op 2, D 1272, L 5.

19   RTsKhDNI Fond 62, Op 2, D 1391, L 1. OGPU report on the campaign for the emancipation of women in Khojand Okrug.

20   GARF Fond 3316, Op 22. D 127. Stenographic Record of the Commission for Examining disputes between the UzSSR and the TaSSR. Review of the TaSSR 1917/8, p. 5, paper on reform of the Jamsovety.

21   RTsKhDNI Fond 62, Op 2, D 1272, L 1. (Correspondence with the Sredazburo).

22   GARF, Fond 17, Op 27, Unit 14. Item 4 (Kirkizh's report on the Pamirs) and Protocol 75 for the Session of the IspolBuro of the TsK of the KP(b) Uzbekistan for 30 December 1928.

23   "Korenizatsiya", the policy of "indigenisation" adopted at certain times in the early Soviet period to promote regional languages and the appointment of local staff to government and party posts.

24   RTsKhDNI Fond 62, Op 3, D 459, L33. Resolution, Appendix to Protocol no. 20 of the Executive Committee (IsPolBuro) of the Uzbek CP's Tajik Provincial Committee (ObKom). 20–21 January 1929.

25   A.A. Znamenskii Plenipotentiary representative of the RSFSR in the BNSR. Arrived Tashkent 1924. Became concerned about pan-Turkic movement in Bukhara and called on other academics to defend the rights of the Tajiks. Chairman of the "Society for the Study of the Tajiks and other Iranian Nationalities Beyond their Frontiers", which produced the exhaustive study of Tajikistan in 1925 with I.L. Korzhenevskii as editor.

26   RTsKhDNI Fond 121, Op 2, D 172, L 97.

27   RTsKhDNI Fond 62, Op 3, D 369, L 1. Protocols of the Ura Teppe Provincial (Ura Tyubinskii Viloyatski) Conference of the KP(b) Uzbekistan, 15–18 December 1928.

28   RTsKhDNI Fond 62, Op 2, D 365, L 2. Session of the Executive Committee of the Tajik Provincial Committee of the Uzbekistan CP, 16 July 1928. Present: Kurbanov, Kozlov and Muhieddinov.

29   RTsKhDNI Fond 62, Op 2, D 1524, L 1. Report on the work of the Executive Committee of the Tajik Provincial Committee of the

Uzbekistan CP, late 1928. The 2nd Plenum of the Provincial Committee (Obkom).

30   Nissor Muhammad (1897–1937) born Peshawar in British India, from where he fled under sentence of death. Came in 1920 to Tashkent and took Soviet nationality. Head of the Department for Minorities in the Turkestan People's Commissariat for Education. Later head of the Tajik Educational Institute. From 1926 occupied leading positions in the Party and State Apparat of the Tajik ASSR, including Commissar for Education. In 1932 followed an academic career in the Moscow Institute for Oriental Studies. Shot during his interrogation. He had attacked the interrogator for insulting his wife.

31   T.V. Kashirina, *Narodnoe Obrazovaniye v Tadzhikistane 1924–32,* Donish, Dushanbe, 1986, p. 32.

32   Masov, *Ocherki*, p. 155. Article by A.Ya. Vishnevskii and M.N. Nazarshoev, *Istoriya obrazovaniya i ideino-organizatsionnogo ukrepleniya Gorno-Badakhshanskoi Oblastnoi Partiinoi Organizatsii.*

33   Kashirina, *Narodnoe Obrazovaniye,* p. 21.

Chapter 7. Purging the Party's Ranks

1   Grigoryi Anisimovich Sigin was born in 1898. Lower education. Mordvinian. According to the CP biography, he "Reads and writes Mordvinian". Member of the CP from 1917. Party card no. 0822663. Until 1917 worked as a typesetter in Kokand. Served in the Red Army (RKKA) from 1919 to 1920 and was not a member of any other party. Did not serve in the White Army. Chairman of the Party Collegium of the Provincial Control Commission (Oblast' KK). At time of the CP purge (1929) was People's Commissar (Narkom) for RDI (?).

2   RTsKhDNI Fond 121, Op 2, D 172. L 97. Protocol no. 2 for the Session of the "Troika" of the CP Central Committee (TsK VKP(b)) for purging and checking the senior membership of the Party Organisation of Tajikistan. Chairman, Manzhara. Members, Kul'kov, Islamov. For the full Control Commission report on the purge see Appendix E.

3   RTsKhDNI Fond 62, Op 2, D 1912, L 2. Agenda of local CP meetings in Khojand District (Okrug) in October 1929.

4   RTsKhDNI Fond 62, Op 2, D 1272, L 5.

5   Muminkhojaev (Muminhojaev), (fnu). Joint secretary of Tajik Provincial Committee (Obkom). Removed for incompetence in January 1929. See RTsKhDNI Fond 62, Op 2, D 1272, L 2 and L 3.

6   D.I.Manzhara was a member of Sredazburo. In 1929 was made chairman of the Troika set up to purge the Tajik party. At the 4th Congress of the

Uzbek Party on 2 March 1929, strongly criticised the leadership on behalf of the Central Control Commission (TsKK and RKI). See also RTsKhDNI Fond 121, Op 28, D 93, LL 21–8.

7   Aleksander Sergeevich Rossov. Party member from 1919. Party card no. 0439811. Social origin: service. Jew. Education, unfinished middle. 1929, member of the Provincial Executive Committee (Ispolburo, Obkom). Served in the Red Army (RKKA) 1918 to 1929. Worked in Party since demobilisation. 29 August 1929, dismissed from the Ispolburo. Participated in Trotskyite opposition in 1923 and, in 1928, in the internal army opposition. Described in the British *Who's Who in C. Asia* (Simla, 1929) as commissar of the 3rd Turkestan rifle division in November 1928.

8   Lutz Rzehak, *Vom Persischen zum Tadschikischen*, Reichert, Wiesbaden, 2001, p. 303.

9   Terry Martin, *The Affirmative Action Empire*, Cornell, Ithaca and London, 2001, passim.

10   Nikolai Mikhailovich Yanson was born in 1882 in St Petersburg into a working-class family. Joined the CP in 1905 and participated in the revolution of that year. The next year he emigrated to the USA. Returned to Tallin in time for the revolution in 1917 and became Secretary of the North Baltic Bureau of the RSDRP(b). In 1923 became secretary of the Central Control Commission (TsKK). In 1928 was People's Commissar for Justice. In 1931 deputy chairman of the USSR Council of People's Commissars. Died 20 June 1938.

11   RTsKhDNI Fond 121, Op 28, L 81.

12   RTsKhDNI Fond 62, Op 1, D 507, L 1 and 1a. Resolution of the Plenum of the Central Asia Office (Sredazburo) of the CP Central Committee (TsK VKP (b)) on the passing of a decision by the TsK VKP(b) on the basis of a document of the TsK of the Uzbekistan CP.

13   Work plan for the CP Executive Office (Ispolburo of the KP(b) of the Uzbek SSR) for the period September 1929 to February 1930.

14   RTsKhDNI. Fond 62, Op 2, D 1975, L 2. Letter from Mirsaidov of the CP Implant in the People's Commissariat for Education (Partchast' Narkomprosa) to the Central Asia Office (Sredazburo) for Comrade Khodzhanov, Deputy Director APPO (Agitprop) dated 11 March 1929, no. 2321.

15   RTsKhDNI Fond 62, Op 2, D 507, L 2.

16   GARF Fond 3316, Op 2, D 127.
     Proportions of minorities in the country and how their strengths are reflected in the Soviets:

TaSSR				
Whole population	National Minorities	Uzbeks	Kyrgyz	Turkmen
827,443	199,127	175,490	11,410	4147
	(24.1%)	(21.2%)	(1.4%)	(0.3%)
Members in Soviets	Members from National Minorities	Uzbek members	Kyrgyz members	Turkmen members
8,729	2466	2130	102	59
	(28.8%)	(24.5%)	(1.2%)	(0.7%)

17   RTsKhDNI. FOND 62, Op 2, D 1524, L 1.

Chapter 8. The Tajik Language

1   RTsKhDNI. Fond 62, Op 1, D 183. L 154. A review of the situation with regard to "korenizatsiya" in the Republics of Central Asia. Dated September 1926 and based on Sredazburo statistics. Here the literacy rates in the Uzbek SSR are given as follows:

Nation	Uzbek		Tajik		Kyrgyz	
Gender	M	F	M	F	M	F
Towns	19.9%	3.6%	12.1%	1.1%	55%	0
Villages	0.7%	0	3.1%	0.2%	3.1%	0
Nation	Kazakh		Russian			
Gender	M	F	M	F		
Towns	57.4%	0	75.1%	0 (sic)		
Villages	3.6%	0	56.1%	35.9%		

None of the many other tables in the paper refers to the Tajik presence as part of the "korenizatsiya" process. It is not entirely clear what language literacy refers to. It must also be remembered that more than 90% of the population lived outside the towns.

2   Lutz Rzehak, *Vom Persischen zum Tadschikischen*, Reichert, Wiesbaden, 2001, p. 149.

3   *Odina* was not the first novel written in the Persian language. This honour belongs to Haji Zain ul Abedin's *Siyahatnameh e Ibrahim Beg* or

San'atizadeh Kermani's *Damgustaran yo Enteghamkhwahan e Mazdak*, both written in the early years of the 20th century. Considering he was working in a relatively remote part of the Persian-speaking world, in a deeply unfavourable environment, and in considerable personal poverty, Ayni's achievement is truly remarkable.

4   See Jan Rypka, *History of Iranian Literature*. D. Reidel, 1968, p. 547 (essay by Jiri Becka on Tajik Literature from the 18th Century to the Present).

5   The main "internationalists" were: Alizodeh, Munzim, Zehni and Lakhuti. Some changed sides in the course of the debate.

6   Narzullah Bektosh (aka Haidari) (1900–1938) was born near Samarkand as the son of an artisan. After the revolution, he studied at the Teachers' Training Institute in Samarkand and then at the Paedagogic Institute in Baku. In 1930 he moved to Stalinabad where he taught History and the theory of Tajik literature. Head of the Literature Department of the Tajik branch of the USSR Academy of Sciences. In the 1930s was accused of a variety of crimes and shot.

7   Rzehak, *Vom Persischen*, p. 193, lists the following as supporters of this line: (from a literary point of view) Ayni, Zehni, Rahim Hoshim, as well as the Russians Semenov and Bertels; and (from a political ideological point of view) N. Yakovlev, Abbas Aliev and Bektosh. Rahim Hoshim was born in 1908 the son of a chemist in Samarkand. While studying at a Russian secondary school, he already started writing for the papers *Zarafshon*, *Maorif va Ugituvchi* and *Rahbari Donish*, often using the pen-name Mim. He became editor of the Tajik State Publishing House.

8   Aleksander Arnol'dovich Frejman (1879–1968) was born in Warsaw, studied Iranian linguistics in Russia and German linguistics in Germany. From 1934 onwards he taught at the Leningrad Oriental Institute.

9   RTsKhDNI, Fond 62, Op 3, D 459. L 111. Appendix to Protocol 10 of the Provincial Committee (Obkom) session of 18 March 1929.

10 RTsKhDNI, Fond 62, Op 3, D 459. L 13. Protocol 19 of a session of the Ispolkom of the Tajik Obkom. 28 January 1929. Present: Shirvani, Klok, Muhieddinov, Gotfrid, Khojibaev, Polyaev, Anvarov, Belyanov, Kys'michev.

11 M. Tursunzade, *Ocherk istorii Tadzhikskoi Sovetskoi Literatury*, Stalinabad, 1955, p. 14ff.

12 Badruddin Azizi (1894–1944) was born in Ura Teppe, the son of the poet Hazmi. He studied in madrasas, first in Ura Teppe and then in Bukhara. After the October revolution he attended a two-year teacher-training course in Tashkent after which he returned to work as a teacher in his birthplace. Having begun his literary work in both Persian and Turki under the pen-name Azmi while studying in Bukhara, he went on to write

in Tajik in the 1920s under the pen-names Tarsonchak and Tarsaki. Became well-known for his literary and language critical contributions to the satirical weekly *Mullo Mushfiqi*.

13   Mirza Abdulvohid Burhonzoda (aka Munzim) was born between 1872 and 1877 into a Bukharan official family. His father Abduljalil Misrikhon, who had the title Qaravolbegi at the Amir's court, died when he was young. He then grew up in the house of the enlightened judge Sadri Ziyo, where Ayni was working as a servant. At that time he worked for the development of Jadid schools in Bukhara. Began writing around 1900 and continued after the revolution. From 1922–24 he led a youth group sent for training in Germany. In 1927 was deputy head of the Tajik Latinisation Committee. 1930–3 worked on *Tojikistani Surkh*. Died after an illness in 1934.

14   Pairav Sulaimoni (1899–1933) was born in Bukhara into a merchant family, attended a madrasa and then a Persian elementary school in Merv. He learnt Russian and became attracted to Russian literature. In 1916 he entered the Kagan Realnoe Uchilische for which he was persecuted by the conservative establishment. His early work was seen as having "Nepmannish" tendencies (sic). In 1928 he wrote his first truly Soviet work *"Qalam"*.

15   Muhammadjan Rahimi was born in 1901 in Faiq, near Bukhara, the son of a poor musician. Worked as a cobbler before joining the Red Army to fight the Basmachi. Began publishing in 1924. His works include: Hast Leninism, Ittihod, Sufiyo, Murshid, Gul dar kenari hasti, Pamiri Surkh etc).

16   Muhieddin Aminzadeh was born in 1904. He studied music and teaching in Samarkand until 1930 and began writing in the 1920s.

Chapter 9. Economic Reconstruction

1   RTsKHDNI Fond 62, Op 3, D 459. Protocol 19 of a session of the Executive Committee (Ispolkom) of the Tajik Provincial Committee (Obkom), 28 January 1929. Item V. L 13.

2   RTsKhDNI Fond 62, Op 2, D 1272/3. Letter from Gotfrid to Zelenskii and Gikalo and copied to Kirkizh. Dated 26 June 1928.

3   RTsKhDNI Fond 62, Op 3, D 459, L 111.

Chapter 10. Tajikistan's Foreign Relations

1   In 1917, after its defeat at the hands of the Bukharan army, the Tashkent Soviet had recognised the Emirate as a separate political entity in the Treaty of Kyzyl Teppe.

2   India Office Library, L/PS/12/2274, p. 7089.

3   Farhad Daftary, *The Ismailis,* Cambridge University Press, 1990, p. 544.

4   RTsKhDNI Fond 62, Op 1, D 184. L 62. Protocols nos. 26 and 27 of the meetings of the Special Frontier Commission of the Central Asia Office (Sredazburo) of 20 November 1925 and 30 October 1926 respectively. Chaired by Znamenskii.

5   Zakat. The tax on property, whether possessions, livestock, commerce or the product of mining, levied on all Muslims.

6   Rakhim Masov, *Ocherki po Istoriyi Sovetskogo Badakhshana, Irfon, Dushanbe, 1981,* chapter by M. Shergaziev and S.A. Radzhabov, p. 110.

7   A.V. Stanishevskii. *"Ismailizm na Pamire: 1902–31",* Ts. Arkhiv Uzbek SSR, 1964, Fond 2464, p. 40.

8   L.N. Kharyukov, *Anglo-Russkoye Sopernichestvo v Tsentral'noi Azii i Ismailizm,* Moskovskii Universitet, 1995.

9   C.H. Ellis, *Transcaspian Episode,* Hutchinson, London, 1963.

10   F.M.Bailey, *Mission to Tashkent,* Jonathan Cape, London, 1946, p. 238.

11   India Office Library L/PS/10/950 p. 248.

12   India Office Library L/PS/10/950 p. 8926 (20).

13   India Office Library L/PS/10/950 p. 8926 (20) 1 June 1923.

14   India Office Library L/PS/10/1132 p. 3131.

15   RTsKhDNI, Fond 495, Op 154, D 460a. Vostochnyi Sekretariat IKKI, 1926–35.

16   Stanishevskii, *Ismailizm.*

17   Nasir Khosrow (1004–c1078). Poet and outstanding Ismaili philosopher. Born in Kubadadhyan in present-day Tajikistan. After much travelling, including to Mecca and to Fatimid Cairo, Nasir Khosrow was obliged to seek refuge from Sunni persecution and flee to Yumgan in Badakhshan, where he wrote many of his philosophical works. The leading Ismaili philosopher of the Fatimid period and, because of his origins and his sojourn in Badakhshan, especially revered by the Ismailis of that region.

18   RTsKhDNI Fond 62, Op 2, D 1744, L 14. Stenographic note of the Session of the Territorial Commission of 21 August 1924.

Chapter 11. The Creation of the Tajik SSR

1   RTsKhDNI Fond 62, Op 2, D 1744, L 14. Stenographic note of the Session of the Territorial Commission of 21 August 24.

2   Alimdzhan Akchurin. Leftist in the Bukharan Communist Party. His fraction was dissolved in 1922 but he remained in the CP. Posted to the Tajik Revolutionary Committee (Revkom).

3   RTsKhDNI FOND 62, OP 2, D 102.

4   RTsKhDNI. Fond 62, Op 2, D 1744, L 2.

5   Rakhim Masov, *Istoriya Topornogo Razdeleniya*, Irfon, Dushanbe, 1991, p. 70. Citing RTsKhDNI Fond 62, Op 2, D 827, L 63,64,71,72. Contents of letter of 9 June 1927 from the Tajik Delegation in Moscow to the Soviet of Peoples' Commissars of the Tajik ASSR complaining about Uzbek behaviour.

6   Lutz Rzehak, *Vom Persischen zum Tadschikischen*, Reichert, Wiesbaden, 2001, p. 152.

7   Ibrohim Ismailov was born in 1901 in Badakhshan, where he attended the Russian school. Joined the CP in 1921. 1923–24 Chairman of the Ishkeshim Revkom and Deputy Chairman of the Badakhshan Revkom.

8   W. Kolarz, *Russia and her Colonies*, Macmillan, London, 1952, p. 238.

9   RTsKhDNI Fond 62, Op 2, D 1744, L 6. See also Appendix C for the twenty-seven names.

10 RTsKhDNI Fond 62, Op 3, D 417, L 1a. Session of the Secretariat of the CP Uzbekistan with members Gikalo and Yusupov, date 10 April 29; also Fond 17 Op 27 D 17 L 98, for Protocol no. 7 of the Session of the Uzbek CP Executive Committee (IspolBuro TsK KP(b) Uzb) of 31 March 29, point 2 "To set up an Orgburo to deal with all the problems connected with this transfer with the following membership: Chairman, Tyurabekov; Deputy Chairman, Dyakov; Members, Abdinov; Epaneshnikov; Grachev; as well as of representatives of the Khojand and Ura Teppe OKRIK".

11 GARF. Fond 3316, Op 22. D 127. LL 148–50, Review of the Tajik ASSR 1927/28.

12 M.N. Gurevich and Sh.Z. Salianov, *KPSS i Sovetskoe pravitelstvo v Uzbekistane*, Tashkent, p. 31.

13 I.K. Kalandarov, *Slavnyi Syn Tadzhikskogo Naroda*, Dushanbe, 1999, p 39.

14 Nikolai Petrovich Ostroumov. 1846–1930. Russian orientalist. Studied with Nikolai Il'minskii in the Kazan Spiritual Seminary, specialising in Turkic languages and Arabic. Came to Tashkent in 1877 as inspector of schools. Editor of *Turkistan Viloyatining Gazeti* from 1883 to 1917.

15 RTsKhDNI Fond 62, Op 1, D 552.

16 RTsKhDNI Fond 62, Op 3, D 417, L 1b and GARF Fond 3316, Op 22. D 127, L 181.

17 RTsKhDNI Fond 62, Op 2, D 1744, L 4.

18 Khodzhibaeva, Baroat Abdurakhimovna. *"Abdurakhim Khodzhibaev. Stranitsy korotkoi zhizni"*. State Publishing House Rakhim Dzhalil, Khojand, 2000. P. 63. Footnote 1. Also Sh. Jalilov and A. Kadyrov, "Chairman of the Seventh Republic", *Kommunist Tajikistana*, 7 August 1991.

19 Kalandarov, *Slavnyi Syn*, p. 39.

20 Abel Yenukidze, was a Georgian Bolshevik and early associate of Stalin and his wife Nadya, whose god-father he had been. Hedonist with a

penchant for teen-age ballerinas (see Simon Sebag-Montefiore's masterly description in *The Court of the Red Tsar,* Phoenix, London, 2003). In charge of the Kremlin in 1932. Denounced by Yagoda (NKVD head) in 1937 for plotting with Marshal Tukhachevskii to overthrow Stalin. Shot on 20 December of that year.

21   Makeev (first name unknown). Chairman of Central Asian EKOSA and member of the Commission for separating Tajikistan from Uzbekistan (summer 1929).

22   GARF, Fond 3316, Op 22, D 102–4, p. 38a. Extract from Protocol no. 2 for the Session of the Presidium of the TsIK USSR for 12 June 1929.

23   RTsKhDNI, Fond 62, Op 1, D 560, L 65.

24   RTsKhDNI, Fond 62, Op 1, D 521. Point 2 of Protocol 13 of the 22 June 1929 of the Session of Executive Committee (Ispolkom) the Central Asia Office (Sredazburo).

25   RTsKhDNI Fond 62, Op 1, D 560, L 4. Protocol no. 15, for the Ispolkom of the Sredazburo meeting of 6 July 1929.

26   GARF, FOND 3316, Op 22, D 127, L 77ff.

27   Samuil Isaakovich Klok was born in 1885. Social background: service. Lower education. In various jobs before 1917. From 1903–17 he was a member of the "Bund" party. He was arrested in Warsaw for this and put in prison in the Novo-Georgeevskii Fortress. On remand was sent to Tsarynskii Krai. Member of the CP from 1919. CP card no. 08345. Did not serve in the Tsar's army. Served in the Red Army (RKKA) from 1920–26. Active in Soviet work from 1926 onwards. 1929, Head of the Tajik Central Executive Committee's Organisation Department (Orgotdel, TsIK).

28   RTsKhDNI Fond 17, Op 28, D 18, p. 111. Protocol No.58 for Session of Tajik CP Provincial Committee (KP ObKom).

Chapter 12. The Final Territorial Battle – Surkhan Darya

1   Alkin's study gave the following data:

For the urban and rural population of the Surkhan Darya Oblast' (source: 1924 Expeditionary Project):

(Percentages. 95% of the population is rural).

	Russian	Uzbek	Tajik	Kazakh/Kyrgyz
Urban	9	12.3	68.4	0.4
Rural	0	64.9	30.4	0.1

	Arab	Jew	Lokay
Urban	2.1	0.5	2.7
Rural	0	4.5	0

According to the same 1924 assessment, the ethnic composition of the rural population by viloyats (the old administrative unit) was as follows:

	Uzbek	Tajik	Kazakh/ Kyrgyz	Lokay
Baisun	58.5	41.5	0	0
Sari–Assiya	66.9	30.3	0.3	2.3
Shirabad	75.6	14.9	0	9.5

The 1928 figures are very similar:

Baisun	Uzbek 19064 (53%)	Tajik 16864 (46.9%)	Kazakh	Kyrgyz
Total 35970	Turkmen	Arab 6	Jew 36	Other
Sari Assiya	Uzbek 55844 (66.7%)	Tajik 26977 (32.3%)	Kazakh 80 (0.1%)	Kyrgyz 185 (0.2%)
Total 83629	Turkmen 165 (0.2%)	Arab 150 (0.2%)	Jew	Other 228 (0.3%)
Shirabad	Uzbek 44542 (78.8%)	Tajik 6783 (12%)	Kazakh 24	Kyrgyz
Total 56542	Turkmen 4165 (7.4%)	Arab 132 (0.2%)	Jew	Other 896 (1.6%)

Source: Raionirovaniye of Central Asia 1928. Book 1, Part 1, Tashkent.

According to Alkin's study, in the materials connected with the "Raionirovaniye" of Uzbekistan (issue no. 1, Samarkand 1926) the following data are given for the ethnic composition of the whole Surkhan Darya Okrug:

Uzbeks 74.5%; Tajiks 20.2%; Turkmen 3.8%.

[Interesting that, in summarising, the "raionirovaniye" listed Turkmen but no Kyrgyz].

2   RTsKhDNI Fond 62, Op 2, D 1744, L 10.
3   RTsKhDNI Fond 62, Op 2. D 1744, L 15. The commission's session of 8 September 1929 was attended by Makeev as chairman, Nissor Muhammad and Muhieddinov for the Tajiks and Irismetov for the Uzbeks.
4   RTsKhDNI Fond 62, Op 2, D 1744, L 16.
5   GARF Fond 3316, Op 22, D 127, L 148.
6   GARF Fond 3316, Op 12, D 13, LL 113–4.
7   GARF Fond 3316, Op 12, D 13, L 306.
8   Rakhim Masov, *Istoriya Topornogo Razdeleniya*, Irfon, Dushanbe,1991, p. 100.

Conclusion

1   Anastasia N. Karakasidou, Fields of Wheat, Hills of Blood, University of Chicago, 1997.
2   Ernst Gellner, Nations and Nationalism, Blackwell, Oxford, 2002, passim.
3   A.D. Smith, The Ethnic Origins of Nations, Blackwell, Oxford, 1986, pp. 29–31.
4   Gellner, Nations, p. 55.
5   Gellner, Nations, p. 134ff.

APPENDIX A

Source: RTsKhDNI: FOND 62, OP 2, D 102.

The frontiers of the Tajik Autonomous Oblast' (AO) as defined in the working paper commissioned in 1924 by the Commission for the National Territorial Delimitation (NTD):

TABLE1. By agreement between the Uzbek and the Tajik commissions, the following frontiers are to be defined for the Tajik AO:

NORTH FRONTIER: Beginning somewhat east of the Alla Isman pass along the Turkestan range, running east across the Guradash pass, via Chandyi, Shahrestan, Dana-Agby, Yakhrut, Ak-Chukur, Daili-Mazar, Kyrk-Bulaq, to the Matcha pass.

From the Matcha pass, via the range forming the watershed between the Sokh and Kyzyl-Su basins, crossing the Tuteh pass, via Karagush-Khana, Hoja-Tai, Archa, Yangi-Daran pass, Bok-Bash pass, hitting the Kyzyl-Su a little west of its confluence with the Katta Karmyk.

EAST FRONTIER. From the Kyzyl-Su crossing via the watersheds of the left-hand tributaries of the Kyzyl-Su and Muk-Su which it crosses where the Kush-Tan feature is situated, across the Muz Tilga and Sandal, south to the Garm peak. Thence to the former Kamal-Ayaz and Tanimas. Thence turning sharply east to the Aral glacier, via the Tanimas river, at a height of 11,700 (?) the Ko-Jar and Ail-Utek passes, Southwest to the Tuz-Bel pass, Southeast to the mouth of the Boz-Baital, south to the Kara-Bulak pass; a little east of the Kara-Bulak spring west via the Murghab river to the ravine of Kara-Korum Sai, south across the passes to the Suidi feature and the Marjan pass, turing west via

Rushan range to the Vikhraij pass, across the Gunt, to Varkhidz. South to the Duzazhdara pass, between Balyk-Kul and Turuntai-Kul across the Gurum pass and Koh Bai pass, via the Pamir range to the Yul Bazan pass, via Khargush and Kumdy, to the Zorkul lake.

SOUTH FRONTIER: Following the Oxus to the Ovrazhnogo post.

WEST FRONTIER: Coincides with the current western frontiers of Falgar and Iskanderov volost's to the intersection with the present frontier separating the Bukharan republic from the Turkestan ASSR. Going south from the Yanchik river's upper reaches to Karatai-Dary river, via this to Sari-Kul river, Southwest to Urta Buz village, via Hoji Sher, Chittak to a point some versts north of Rogar. Southwest to the village of Dayna to Ishkabad-Tugai; West via the existing frontier between Sari Asyan and Kurgan Tyube [Teppe] vilayets to Baba-Taq, via the Baba-Taq range to south of the pass of Hozrat Baba via the heights 5531, 1547, 2219, south to the Amu Darya just east of the Ovrazhnogo post.

The TAO will cover an area of 76,100 square versts with a population of 399,714.

POPULATION

The 1924 vilayets' population breaks down as follows:

1.	KurganTyube	33,687
2.	Part of Sari Asyan and Rogara-Karataq	22,500
3.	Dushanbe	126,500
4.	Kulyab	177,500
5.	Garm	191,939
6.	E.Samarkand	23,756
7.	W. Pamir (Shughnan, Roshan, Ishkeshim and Lyangan)	18,388
8.	SeresniRaion	1,033
9.	Part of Vakhan volost', east of the former Bukharan frontier	nil

Total   599,714

The Oroshov Volost' which is currently part of Rushan, also includes pastures used by Tajik Vakhanis whose territory stretches to the western end of the Zorkul lake.

The information on population in Bukhara is taken from the Bukharan government's count, reduced by 40–5% from the Emirate's figures of 1913, assuming that many of the population died. The mountain regions of Zeravshan and Pamir are based on the 1917 census.

Given that, according to the same Bukharan count, the Tajik AO population is c. 600,000 it breaks down into ethnic groups as follows:

EAST BUKHARA	Total	Tajik	Uzbek	Kyrgyz
Pamir, Garm	168850	145805	11545	11500
		86.4%	6.8%	6.8%
Darvaz	23089	23089		
		100%		
Sari Asyan/Karataq	15000	5000	10000	
		33%	66.7%	
Regar	7500	1500	6000	
		20%	80%	
Dushanbe Vilayet	126500	87500	39000	
		69.2%	30.8%	
Kulyab Vilayet	177180	79540	97640	
		44%	55.1%	
Kurgan Teppe Vilayet	33686	1684	30318	1684
		5%	90%	5%
TOTAL for East Bukhara	551805	344118	194503	13184
		62.4%	35.2%	2.4%

It is proposed that the following parts of the Samarkand Oblast' and Pamirs be added to the TAO. The following statistics apply:

SAMARKAND OBLAST'	Tajik	Uzbek	Kyrgyz	Total
Iskander	6337			6337
	100%			
Falgar	10856			10856
	100%			
Matchin	10557			10557
	100%			
TOTAL	27750			27750
	100%			
PAMIRS				
West Pamirs	19396		25	19421
	99.9%		0.1%	
TOTAL for projected Tajik AO	392264	194503	13209	599976
	65.4%	32.4%	2.2%	

Because of the discrepancies between the various censuses, and because some of the figures have clearly been rounded up (or down), these statistics can only be regarded as approximations. Despite this, they do seem to offer a fair picture of the ethnic distribution at the time of the 1924 NTD. It should remembered that the original plan for the Tajik AO did not include Mountainous Badakhshan (later to become the GBAO).

APPENDIX B

Source: GARF: FOND R6892, OP 1, D 34, L 54.

Session of the Commission for "Raionirovanie" of Turkestan, 17 October 1923.

Krasnovski's presentation.

TAJIKISTAN

The TaASSR's "raionirovanie" is a special case. The republic was formed from parts of the former Bukharan People's Republic; Samarkand Oblast'; the Pamir raion of the Ferghana Oblast'.

From Bukhara, Tajikistan received:

Tyubinksii vilayet.
1 Tuman from the Sari Asiyan vilayet.
(these lie on the middle and lower reaches of the Karernigon [sic: presumably Kafarnikhon is meant] and Vakhsh rivers. This region is mountainous and inhabited entirely by Tajiks.

From the Turkestan ASSR Tajikistan received:

Panjikent Raion (including Panjikent, Matchin, Falgar, Mashano-Forab, Kshtut, Avtobruin, and Iskandarov volosti).
Ura Teppe Raion (including: Bosmandin, Ura Tyube, Shakhristan, Dalyan and Ganjin volosti).

Those territories received from Bukhara were called: vilayeti, tumani and kenti.

Those received from Turkestan were called vilayeti (sic – i.e. raiony), volosti and selsoviety.

To start with Tajikistan was divided into eight vilayeti as follows:

Gornyi-Badakhshan - six volosti.
Kulyab - four tumani.
Pendzhikent - six volosti.
Ura Teppe - six volosti.
Kurgan-Teppe - four tumani.
Sari Asiyan - two tumani.
Dushanbe - five tumani.
Garm - six tumani.

Later Sari Asiyan was divided – part going to Dushanbe, and part (Sari Asiyanskii Tuman) going to the Surkhan-Darya oblast of the UzSSR.

Later, too, the Gornyi-Badakhshan Vilayet was re-formed as the Gornyi-Badakhshan Autonomous Oblast'. Kenti were abolished and replaced by Jamagat Soviety.

APPENDIX C

This statement (evidential note) is signed by the following members of the Tajik Obkom of the KP(b) Uzbekistan (spellings transliterated from the Russian except where stated):

Nusratulla Maksum
Muhieddinov (in Arabic script)
Safaev
Shirvani
Ismailov
Ismailzadeh
Gotfrid
Klok
Khojibaev
Abdujabbarov
Solntsev
Dzhabbari
Khakberdiev
Nisarmukhamedov
Polyakov
Fedin
Kariev
Sigin
Dadabaev
Yakubov
Gudenko
Abdinov
Musava
El'chibekov
Stren'lnikov
Madakhov
Sadullaev

APPENDIX D

Source GARF, FOND 3316, OP22, D127, L91.

"ACT"

We, the undersigned, the commission of the TsIK of Soviets the UzSSR presided over by Abidova [NB a woman] with members from the UzSSR Abdurakhmanov and Portnov, and, from the TaASSR, Nissar-Mukhamedov [sic], Schastiev, and from the Khojand Okrug, Mirsaidov, appointed by the Presidium of the USSR resolution dated 31 August, have composed this Act as follows:

1. In implementation of the resolution of the 3rd Kurultai of Soviets of the UzSSR held from 29 April to 10 May 29, the representatives of Uzbekistan gave, and those of Tajikistan accepted the Khojand Okrug within its administrative frontiers of today's date, consisting of five raions, fifty-seven selsoviets, and a population of 250,723. A list of raions and selsoviets is attached [not in fact attached].

2. All institutions of the Khojand Okrug are considered transferred to the TaASSR as of today's date, bearing in mind that the implementation of both the state and local budgets will be carried out on the basis of an agreement between the Uzbek and Tajik responsible organs by the end of the 1929/30 budgetary year.

3. The TaASSR takes upon itself the formulation of the Khojand state and local budget in accordance with the resolutions and directives appertaining.

4. All industrial commercial state and cooperative institutions in the Okrug are, as of today, considered subordinate to the government of Tajikistan and its responsible organs - always remembering that the formalisation of this point will be settled by a special resolution of the UzSSR and TaASSR governments.

5. The question of capital belonging to the state, cooperatives, and other institutions is to be transferred as per para. 4 above by special governmental acts.

APPENDIX E

Protocol no: 2 for the Session of the Troika of the TsK VKP(b) for purging and checking the senior membership of the Party Organisation of Tajikistan. Chairman: Manzhara. Members: Kul'kov, Islamov [probably 1928]. The most senior of those checked included:

MEMBERS OF THE OBLAST CONTROL COMMITTEE

1 Sigin, Grigoryi Anisimovich. Chairman of the Party Collegium of the Ob KK. Member of the CP since 15 ? 1917. Party card no. 0822663. Born: 1898. Lower education. Mordvinian. Reads and writes Mordvinian. At time of check is Narkom for RDI. Served in the RKKA from 1919 to 1920 and was not a member of any other party. Did not serve in the White Army. Until 1917 worked as a typesetter in Kokand. Has worked with the Party line since 1924. Passed.

2 Bal'nykh, Sergei Ivanovich. Member of CP since 1 Oct 1917. Party card no. 0822663. Born 1898. Social origin: worker. Lower/intermediate education. Currently deputy secretary of of the Party Collegium of the ObKK. Served in the RKKA from 1920 to 1926. No other party membership. Did not serve in the White army. Has worked in the Soviets and Party since 1926. Passed.

3 Emuranov, Georgii Matveevich. Party member since 1919. Party card no. 0471156. Born 1903. Social origins: service. At time of check was working as senior inspector of RDI. Served voluntarily in RKKA from 1918 to 1920. Did not serve in the old army. No other Party membership. Until 1917 was a student telegrapher. Has received penalty for infringing party ethics. A note has been made. Has worked in the Soviets since 1920. Passed.

4. Dyachkov, Pavel Fedorovich. Party member since 1919. Card no. 1841577. Born 1896. Social origin: service. Middle education. Currently Deputy

Minister of Justice. Served two years in the old army on being called up. Volunteered for the RKKA from 1918–20. No other party membership. Has done Soviet work since demobilisation from the RKK. Passed. Propose that he studies political theory on his own and takes steps to study a range of basic points in the policy of the Party, especially in revolutionary justice and the work of the RDI on the basis of Lenin's articles.

MEMBERS AND CANDIDATE MEMBERS OF THE ISPOLBURO

5 Rossov, Aleksander Sergeevich. Member of the Ispolburo Obkom. Party member since 1919. Party card no. 0439811. Social origin: service. Education: unfinished middle. Now working as Head of the Obkom Orgotom. Served in RKKA 1918 to 1929. No other party membership. Working in Party since demobilisation. In the past manifested doubts over ideology. Participated in Trotskyite opposition in 1923. In 1928 in the internal army opposition. Has confessed his errors. Passed.

6. Nusratulla Maksum. Member of Obkom Ispolkom. Member of Party since 1920. Party card no. 0841619. Born 1891. Peasant background. Lower education. Currently chairman of the TsK. Vounteered for the RKKA. No other party membership. Until revolution worked in agriculture and casual work. Chairman of the TsK since 1924.

7 Sluchak, Vladimir Efremovich. Member of the
Ispolkom. Member of the party since 1919. Party card no. 57785. Born 1898. Social background: service. Currently deputy chairman of the Social NarKom of the TASSR. Served with the old army about a year after call-up. Volunteered for the RKKA from 1917–18. Until 1917 was in the circle of Zionist Youth. Has been working in Soviet professional line since 1918. At the 8th congress of professional unions at the Fraktsiya congress voted against the TsEK proposal to induct one of the TsEK secretaries into the congress presidium. To recognise his action and that of his comrades as a mistake. Passed.

8 Belyaninov, Petr Stepanovich. Member of the Party since 25 Nov 1919. Party card no. 0829158. Born 1895. Social background: service. Middle education. Served as a private on being drafted into the Tsarist army from 1915 to 1917. Volunteered for the RKKA from 1919–22. No other party membership. In Trade Union work since 1926. Passed. Despite weak theoretical and political knowledge has taken no steps to improve. Should correct this.

9 Anvarov, Said Ahmad. Candidate member of the Ispolkom. Party member since 1919. Card no. 0841570. Born 1894. Social background: worker. Middle

education. Currently Narkomzem (People's Commissar for Agriculture). Not in RKKA. No other party membership. In Soviet work since 1918. Passed.

10 Davydov, Mitrofan Mikhailovich. Candidate for the IspolBuro. Party Card no. 0945285. Social background: service. Education higher/middle. Head of Vodkhoz (Water Supplies) TASSR. Volunteered for RKKA from 1917–21. In 1917 was for about 5 months member of the Socialist Revolutionary Internationalists party. Until 1917 studied in Leningrad Middle Technical College. In Vodkhoz work since 1921. Passed.

11 Makhsudova, Zyuleikha Akhmedova. Candidate member of Ispolburo. Party member since 1925. Party card no. 0839116. Born 1901. Social background: service. Lower education. Now head of women's dept of the ObKom. No other party membership. Not in RKKA. Until 1917 was a housewife. Has worked in the women's organisation since 1924. Passed. To work in collective work to attract Tajik and European women to be activists, especially Tajik-speakers. IspolKom should pay attention to the work of the Zhenotdel.

MEMBERS OF THE OBKOM OF THE UZBEK KP(b)

12 Klok, Samuil Isaakovich. Member of the Party since 1919. Party card no. 08345. Born 1885. Social background: service. Now head of the Orgotdel of TsIK. Lower education. Not in Tsar's army. In RKKA on mobilisation from 1920–26. In various jobs before 1917. From 1903–17 was a member of the "Bund" party and was arrested in Warsaw and put in prison in the Novo-Georgeevskii Fortress. On remand was sent to Tsarynskii Krai. In Soviet work since 1926.

13 Kostylev, Ilya Sergeevich. Member of Party since August 1927. Party card no. 0841756. Born 1902. Social background: worker. Lower education. Currently a people's judge on Labour Matters in the 23rd Sector. No other party membership. In RKKA from 1918–25. Appointed a judge in 1929 after working as an electro-monteur. Passed. Should strive fully to understand the job he's in. Should turn for help to the higher party organs if he feels he's out of his depth.

14 Kurbanov, Mirzo Ali Babajan. Member of Party since 1929. Party card no. 0841876. Born 1905. Social background: worker. Lower education. Now Department Secretary of the Tajik Obkom Komsomol. Not in the RKKA. A "batrak" until 1917. In Komsomol work since 1928. Passed.

15 Khasanov Husain Najar. Member of the Party Obkom since 1927. Born 1904. Social background: worker. Lower education. Not in the RKKA. At school until 1917. In his job as a typesetter since 1924. Passed.

16 Nazarov, Saiddzhan. Party member since 1928. Party card no. 0841762. Born 1902. Social background worker. Now deputy representative of the Sovprof TaASSR. A "batrak" until 1917. No other party membership. Volunteered for the RKKA and fought against the Basmachi. Passed.

MEMBER OF THE REVISIONARY COMMITTEE

17. Konradi, Irmgaard Aleksandrovna. Party member since 1920. Party card no. 0833054. Born 1891. Social background: service. Now Temporary Head of the Obl. Zhenotdel. Was a book–keeper before 1917. Served in the RKKA 1920–5. No other party membership. Passed.

OTHERS

Polyayev, Konstantin Sergeevich. Member of the Ispolkom of the Obkom. Member of the Party since 1925. Party card no. 0841585. Born 1894. Social background: worker. Lower/middle education. Head of the Tajik department of the OGPU. Drafted into the Tsar's army 1914–7. Volunteered for the RKKA 1918–20. Has worked in the OGPU since 1921. No other party membership. Passed.

BIBLIOGRAPHY

Alekseenkov, P., *Kokandskaya Avtonomiya*, Uzgosizdat, Tashkent, 1931a , Istpart Sredazburo TsK VKP(b).

Alekseenkov, P., *Khivinskoe vosstaniye 1916 goda*, Uzgosizdat, Tashkent, 1931b, Sredneaziiatskii Nauchnyi-Issledovatel'skii Institut Istorii Revolutsii (SANIIR).

Allworth, E., *Central Asia: A Century of Russian Rule*, Columbia University Press, New York and London, 1967.

Anderson, Benedict, *Imagined Communities*, Verso, London, 1999.

Andreev, S.N., "Po etnografyi Tadzhikov" in *Shornik Statei* published by the Obshestvo dlya izucheniya Tadzhikskikh i Iranskikh Narodnostei za ego Predelami, Tashkent, 1925.

Antonenko, B.A.. (chief editor), *Istoriya Tadzhikskogo Naroda*, "Nauka", Moskva, 1964.

Asimov, M.S. (ed.), *Ocherki po Istorii Sovetskogo Badakhshana*, Irfon, Dushanbe,1981.

Babaev, Yu., *Mas'alhoi Adabiyoti Muosiri Tojik*, Irfon, Dushanbe, 1970.

Bailey, F.M. *Mission to Tashkent*, Jonathan Cape, London, 1946.

Bartol'd, V.V. *Turkestanskiye Druziya*, Tashkent, 1927.

Bartol'd, V.V. *Sochineniye*, Vol 2 (1), Vostochnoi Literatury, Moskva, 1963.

Becker, Seymour, *'Russia's Protectorates in Central Asia'*, MA thesis, Cambridge, 1968.

Betger, Evgenyi K.. *Obshchestvo dlya izucheniya Tadzhikistana*, Instituti Tarikhi bo nomi A. Donesh, Trudy, Izdatelstvo Akademii Nauk Tadzhikistana, Stalinabad, 1953.

Chugunov, A.I., *Bor'ba c Basmachestvom v Srednei Azii 1931–33,* Istoriya SSSR, 1972.

Conquest, Robert, *The Great Terror*, Macmillan, London, 1968.

Daftary, Farhad, *The Ismailis*, Cambridge University Press, 1990.

Djalili, Muhammad Reza, Grare, Frederic and Akiner, Shirin. *Tajikistan: The Trials of Independence*, Curzon, Richmond, UK, 1998.

Dudoignon, S.A.., and Komatsu, Hisao (eds), *Islam in Politics in Russia and Central Asia, (Early 18th to late 19th Centuries)*, Kegan Paul, London, 2001.

Ellis, C.H. *Transcaspian Episode*, Hutchinson, London, 1963.

Frye, Richard, Article in *Ex Oriente*, publication in honour of Jiri Becka, Czech Academy of Sciences, Oriental Institute, Prague, 1995.

Gavrilyuk, Aleksandr and Yaroshenko, Viktor, *Pamir*, Planeta, Moskva, 1987.

Gellner, E., *Nations and Nationalism*, Blackwell, Oxford, 2002.

Gotfrid, A. and Gafiz, M., *Krasnyi Flag na Kryshe Mira*, Tadzhikskoe Gosudarstvennoe Izdatelstvo, Stalinabad, 1930.

Gurevich, M.N. and Salianov, Sh.Z., *KPSS i Sovetskoe pravitelsto v Uzbekistane*, Tashkent, 1972.

Hayit, Baymirza, *"Basmatschi": der Nationaler Kampf Turkestans in den Jahren 1917 bis 1934,*, Dreisam, Köln 1992.

Iskandarov, V.P., *Vostochnaya Bukhara i Pamir v period prisoedineniya k Rossii*, Tadzhikskee Gosizdatelstvo, Dushanbe, 1960.

Kalandarov, I.K., *Slavnyi Syn Tadzhikskogo Naroda*, Dushanbe, 1999.

Karakasidou, Anastasia N., *Fields of Wheat, Hills of Blood*, University of Chicago Press, 1997.

Karmysheva, V.Kh., *Ocherki etnicheskoi istorii yuzhnikh raionov Tadzhikistana i Uzbekistana*, Nauka, Moskva, 1976.

Kashirina, T.V., *Shornik Statei po Istorii Sovetskogo Tadzhikistana*, Donesh, Dushanbe, 1978.

Khaidarov, G.Kh., *Ocherki iz Istorii severnikh raionov Tadzhikistana*, Gos. Pedagogicheskii Institut, Leninabad, 1967.

Khalfin, N.A., *Rossiya i Bukharskii Emirat na Zapadnym Pamire*, Nauka, Moskva, 1975.

Khalid, Adeeb, *The Politics of Muslim Reform*, University of California Press, Berkeley, 1998.

Khanykov, N.V., *Opisanie Bukharskogo Khanstva,* St Petersburg, 1843.

Kharyukov, L.N., *Anglo-Russkoye Sopernichestvo v Tsentral'noi Azii i Ismailizm*, Izd. Moskovskogo Universiteta, 1995.

Khodzhaev, Faizulla, *Izbrannye Trudy,* (3 vols), "Fan", Tashkent, 1970.

Khodzhibaeva, Baroat Abdurakhimovna, *Abdurakhim Khodzhibaev. Stranitsy korotkoi zhizni.* State Publishing House Rakhim Dzhalil, Khojand, 2000.

Koichiev, Arslan, *Natsional'noe Territorialnoe Razmezhevaniye v Ferganskoi Doline*, Kyrgyz State National University, Bishkek, 2001.

Kolarz, W. *Russia and her Colonies*, Macmillan, London, 1952.

Korzhenevskii, N.L. (ed.), *Tadschikskii Shornik Statei*, Obshchestvo dlya izucheniya Tadzhikistana i Iranskikh Narodnostei, Tashkent, 1975.

Loy, Thomas, *Jaghnob 1970*, Reichert, Wiesbaden, 2005.

Maclean, Fitzroy, *Eastern Approaches*, Jonathan Cape, London, 1949.

Martin, Terry. *The Affirmative Action Empire*, Cornell University Press, Ithaca, 2001.

Masal'skii, V.I., *Turkestanskii Krai*, A.F. Devriena, Sankt Peterburg, 1913.

Masov, Rakhim, *Ocherki po Istoryi Sovetskogo Badakhshana*, Irfon, Dushanbe, 1985.

Masov, Rakhim, *Istoriya Topornogo Razdeleniya*, Irfon, Dushanbe, 1991.

Masov, Rakhim, *Tadzhiki, Istoriya pod Grifom "Sovershenno Sekretno"*, Tsentr Izdaniya Kul'turnogo Naslediya, Dushanbe. 1995.

Mukhammadyarov, S.F., *K Istorii provedeniya Natsional'ngo Razmezhevaniya v Srednei Azii.* Sovetskoe Vostokovedeniye, Moskva, 1955.

Nicholson, Harold, *Curzon: the Last Phase*, Constable and Co Ltd, London, 1934.

Park, Alexander, *Bolshevism in Turkestan*, Columbia Press, New York, 1957.

Pervaya Vseobschaya Perepis' Naseleniya Rossiiskoi Imperii, Sankt Peterburg, 1897.

Postnikov, A.V., *Skhvatka na Kryshe Mira*, Pamyatniki Istoricheskoi Mysli, Moskva, 2001.

Prokhorov, A.M.(ed.), *Bol'shaya Sovetskaya Entsiklopaedia*, 3rd edition, Sovetskaya Entsiklopedia, Moskva, 1969–81.

Radzhabov, Z.Sh., *O Druzhbe Tadzhikskogo i Uzbekskogo Narodov*, Donish, Dushanbe, 1968.

Rypka, Jan. *History of Iranian Literature.* D. Reidel, 1968.

Rzehak, Lutz, *Vom Persischen zum Tadschikischen*, Reichert, Wiesbaden, 2001.

Sabol, Stephen, "The Creation of Central Asia", *Central Asian Survey*, Vol 14 (3), 1995.

Safarov, G., *Kolonialnaya Revolutsiya – Opyt' Turkestan*, Moskva, 1921. Reprint in edition of Central Asian Society, 1985.

Shcherbakov, N.M., *Takim bylo Nachalo – Vospminaniya o Boevom Pokhode Amudarinskoi Gruppy Voisk v 1919–20 gg*, *"Uzbekistan"*, Tashkent, 1969.

Sebag-Montefiore, Simon, *The Court of the Red Tsar*, Phoenix, London, 2003.

Sel'skoe Naseleniye Ferganskoi oblasti.(1917), *Materialy Vserossiysikh Perepisei*, Tashkent, 1924.

Semenov. A.A. *Materialy po istorii Tadzhikov i Uzbekov Srednei Azii, (Vol 1)*, Akademiya Nauk Tadzhikistana, Stalinabad, 1954.

Sengupta, Anita. "Imperatives of the National Delimitation", *Central Asian Survey*, Vol19 (3/4), 2000.

Shamsuddinov, R.T., "Sovety i obrazovaniye Natsion-al'nykh Respublik Srednei Azii", *Voprosy Istorii*, 1986.

Sheehy, Anne, "The Khorezm Communist Party", *Central Asian Review*, 1968.

Shishov, A.., "Tadzhiki, Etnograficheskoe i Antropologicheskoe Issledovanie", *Srednyaya Azyia,* Tashkent, 1910.

Sims-Williams, Professor Nicholas, "New Documents in Ancient Bactrian", *Newsletter of the International Institute for Asian Studies*, March 2002.

Sinor, D. and Klyashtorny, S.G., *The Turk Empire*, UNESCO, Civilisations of Central Asia, Vol III, 1996.

Smith, Antony D., *The Ethnic Origins of Nations*, Blackwell, Oxford, 1986.

Smith, Anthony D., *National Identity*. University of Nevada Press, Reno, 1993.

Stanishevskii A.V., *"Ismailizm na Pamire: 1902–31"*, Ts. Arkhiv Uzbek SSR, 1964

Stanishevksii, A.V., *Sbornik Dokumentov ob Ismailizme v Pamire*, Glavnoe Arkhivnoe Upravneniye pri Sovete Ministrov Uzbekskoi SSR, Moskva, 1984.

Sukhareva, O.A., *Bukhara XIX do nachala XX veka, Pozdnefeodalnyi gorod i ego naseleniye.* "Nauka", Moskva, 1966.

Terent'ev, M. *Materialy dlya statistiki Turkestankogo Kraya*, 1873.

Tursunov, Kh.T. "Natsional'noe Razmezhevaniye Srednei Azii i Obrazovaniye Uzbekistana", *Voprosy Istorii*, 1954.

Tursunov, Kh.T. *"Natsionalnaya Politika KP v Turkestane".* "Uzbekistan", Tashkent, 1971.

Tursunzade, M. *Ocherk Istorii Tadzhikskoi Sovetskoi Literatury*, Izd. Akademyi Nauk Tadschikistana, Stalinabad, 1955.

Urozaev, Sh.Z. *V.I. Lenin i stroitelstvo sovetskoi gosudarstvennosti v Turkestane*, "Fan", Tashkent, 1967

Vakhabov, M., *Formirovanie Uzbekskoi sotsialisticheskoi natsii*, Gosizdat UzSSR, Tashkent, 1965.

Vinnikov, V., *Sovremennoe rasselenie narodov i etnograficheskikh grupp v Ferganskoi doline.* Sredneaziatskii etnograficheskii sbornik. Vypusk 2, Moskva, 1959.

Wheeler, Geoffrey, *The Modern History of Central Asia.* Weidenfeld and Nicholson, London, 1964.

Willfort, Fritz, *Turkestanisches Tagebuch. 6 Jahre im Russischen Zentralasien.* Braumueller, Wien and Leipzig, 1930.

Zarubin I.I., *Spisok natsionalnostei Turkestanskogo Kraya*, Leningrad, Rossiiskaya Akademiya Nauk, 1925.

Zarubin, I.I., *Naseleniye Samarkandskoi Oblasti*, Leningrad, 1926.

Zarubin. I.I., *Spisok Natsional'nostei SSSR*, Trudy kommissii po izucheniyu plemennogo sostava naseleniya SSSR i sopredelnikh stran, Leningrad, 1927.

Zevelev, Aleksandr Izraelovich, Polyakov, Y.A., Chugunov, A.I., Mints, I.I., *Basmachestvo: vozniknoveniye, sushchnost' krakh,* "Nauka", Moskva, 1981.

Zyadullaev, S. K. (chief editor), *Tashkent Entsiklopediya*, Glavnaya Redaktsiya Uzbekskoi Sovetskoi Entsiklopedii, Tashkent, 1984.

INDEX

Vologda governorate 70
volost'/volosti (administrative unit/s)
    ix, 33, 36–7, 44, 52, 138–9(n9),
    142(n9–10), 165–6
Vom Persischen zum Tadschikischen
    (Rzehak, 2001), xi, 141(n9),
    154(n7)
Voroshilov, K.E. (1881–1969) 113
Vyshinsky, A. (1883–1954) 146(n12)

wages 87
Wakhan 10, 31, 33, 48
Walidi, A.Z. 96
War Commission on Economy
    (Voenkhoz) 115
War Commission for Water Supply
    (Voenvod) 115
Warsaw 154(n8), 158(n27), 171
water 49, 52, 171
    "cause of inter-community
    disputes" 43
Wheeler, G. 149(n16), 176
Who's Who in Central Asia (1929)
    143(n14), 152(n7)
wines 88
women 17, 48, 60, 62, 65, 74, 75,
    82, 150(n19), 151(n30), 153(n1),
    171
    Tajik 136(n11)
workers 50, 67, 110, 112, 169–72
    rural 149(n16)
    Uzbek, Kyrgyz (Kazakh), Turkmen
    41
    Uzbek proletariat lacking 59
Workers' Faculties (Rabfaks) 63
World War I (and aftermath) 19, 25,
    30, 125, 142(n12)
World War II 27

Yagello, I.D. 35, 143(n14)
Yaghnob River 5
Yaghnobis 5, 11
Yagoda, H. 158(n20)
Yakhsu, River xii, xiv
Yakovlev, N.F. 80
    "linguo-technologist" 80
    new Tajik language 80, 154(n7)
Yakubov (fnu) 167

Yanson, M.Y. (1882–1938) 71,
    152(n10)
Yarkand (Xinjiang, China) 90, 93, 94
Yavan [toponym] 144(n18)
Yenukidze, A. 114, 157–8(n20)
Yepatovskii (fnu) 122
Yorchi Uezd 122, 123
Young Bukharans 19, 26, 39, 40,
    129, 131, 139(n11), 146(n17)
Young Khivans 26, 39
Yugoslavia 125
Yumgan (Badakhshan) 142(n7),
    156(n17)
Yunye Lenintsy (journal, "Young
    Leninists") 51
yurts 36
Yusupov (fnu) 157(n10)

Za Partiyu (journal) 18
Zaamin (Uzbekistan) 8
Zain ul Abedin, Haji 153–4(n3)
zakat 34, 93, 94, 97, **98–9**
    accounting methods 98
    definition 156(n4)
Zanjirbek, M. 143(n18)
Zarafshan mountains 11
Zarafshon (newspaper) 154(n7)
Zarubin, I.I. (1887–1964) 7–8, 8–9,
    35, 137(n14–16), 176
    biography 143(n15)
Zebak (Afghanistan) 94
    location xiii
Zebon (near Panjikent) 145(n7)
Zehni (fnu)
    "internationalist" 154(n5)
    new Tajik language 154(n7)
Zelenskii, I.A. (1890–1938) 45, 52, 58,
    61, 70, 78, 106, 107, 114, 116
    biography **146(n12)**
    "true bureaucrat" 115
Zeravshan Oblast' 53
Zeravshan Okrug 44
Zeravshan River 3, 4, 5, 53, 128, 163
    location xii, xiv
    "Tajik-inhabited area" 110
    upper reaches 11, 46
Zevelev, A.I., *et al.* (1981) 142(n1),
    176